Gatekeeping Th

Gatekeeping is one of the media's central roles in public life: People rely on mediators to transform information about billions of events into a manageable number of media messages. This process determines not only which information is selected, but also what the content and nature of messages, such as news, will be. *Gatekeeping Theory* describes the powerful process through which events are covered by the mass media, explaining how and why certain information either passes through gates or is closed off from media attention. This book is essential for understanding how even single, seemingly trivial gatekeeping decisions can come together to shape an audience's view of the world, and illustrates what is at stake in the process.

Pamela J. Shoemaker is John Ben Snow Professor at the S.I. Newhouse School of Public Communications at Syracuse University. She is author of *News Around the World* (with Akiba Cohen), *How to Build Social Science Theories* (with James Tankard and Dominic Lasorsa), and *Mediating the Message* (with Stephen Reese).

Tim P. Vos is Assistant Professor of Journalism Studies at the University of Missouri.

Gatekeeping Theory

Pamela J. Shoemaker
Tim P. Vos

Routledge
Taylor & Francis Group

NEW YORK AND LONDON

First published 2009
by Routledge
270 Madison Ave, New York, NY 10016

Simultaneously published in the UK
by Routledge
2 Park Square, Milton Park, Abingdon, Oxon OX14 4RN

Routledge is an imprint of the Taylor & Francis Group, an informa business

© 2009 Taylor & Francis

Typeset in Charter and Folio by Keyword Group Ltd
Printed and bound in the United States of America on acid-free paper by
Walsworth Publishing Company, Marceline, MO

Library of Congress Cataloging in Publication Data
A catalog record has been requested for this book

ISBN10: 0-415-98138-7 (hbk)
ISBN 10: 0-415-98139-5 (pbk)
ISBN10: 0-203-93165-3 (ebk)

ISBN13: 978-0-415-98138-5 (hbk)
ISBN 13: 978-0-415-98139-2 (pbk)
ISBN13: 978-0-203-93165-3 (ebk)

Contents

Acknowledgments

Many individuals contributed to this project, but four deserve special mention. This project ranged over several years and generations of graduate assistants. While a Masters student at Syracuse University, Rebecca Reynolds, now director of research at World Wide Workshop Foundation, originally helped to update the literature, past the 1991 edition of *Gatekeeping* in Sage's Communication Concepts series. The task was taken on by Kevin Gang Han, now an assistant professor of journalism at Iowa State University. Bringing the book to publication were Syracuse's John Ben Snow, research assistants Hyunjin Seo and Philip Johnson. They once again updated the book's literature and responded to thousands of requests from us.

Thanks also to colleagues Amy Nyberg at Seton Hall University, Bryan Greenberg at Elizabethtown College, and Patrick Plaisance at Colorado State University, who have shared their thoughts and encouragement. A special thanks to Suzette Vos for her support and encouragement throughout this project.

Introduction
The Significance of Gatekeeping

Gatekeeping is the process of culling and crafting countless bits of information into the limited number of messages that reach people each day, and it is the center of the media's role in modern public life. People rely on mediators to transform information about billions of events into a manageable subset of media messages. On the face of it, narrowing so many potential messages to so few seems to be impossible, but there is a lengthy and long-established process that makes it happen day in and day out. This process determines not only which information is selected, but also what the content and nature of messages, such as news, will be. Explaining such a powerful process is the purpose of this book, and a look at recent history demonstrates what is at stake.

When the United States invaded Iraq in 2003, few journalists from the mainstream American news media questioned their country's actions. Those who did were reprimanded as unpatriotic by the government, as well as by audience members, and some lost their jobs. With few exceptions, the news organizations fell into line and conveyed the news from reporters "embedded" with troops in the field (Boehlert, 2006).

When the Bush administration's case for the preemptive attack began falling apart in 2003 and 2004, some journalists retraced their steps to see what, if anything, they had done wrong. The *Columbia Journalism Review* asked whether reporters and editorial page writers should have been more aggressive watchdogs when examining the administration's case for war (Mooney, 2004). But such questions apparently had limits. When the so-called Downing Street memo was discovered, suggesting that American officials intended to fix the evidence to support the war, the mainstream U.S. news media initially gave the story little coverage (Bicket & Wall, 2007). How did information about the memo travel to and through channels of communication? What gates did it pass through and what gates closed? How did the mainstream American media come to the decision to give little attention to the memo? Gatekeeping scholarship helps us arrive at answers to such questions.

The theoretical underpinnings of American media law and policy assume that more media outlets are better than few. More news media create more messages that cover multiple aspects of an event and that vary in the information they contain. Thus a larger and more diversified menu of information makes it to the public, and the truth about an event is more likely to be revealed. Truth is supposed to be hard to hide when a marketplace of ideas is fostered through competition among many media outlets (Carter, Franklin, & Wright, 2005).

As it turns out, such a theory was supported by the story of the Downing Street memo, because reporting by the alternative U.S. news media ultimately forced the mainstream press to look at the memo and the war more closely. The fact remains, however, that initially the mainstream news outlets underplayed information that questioned the government's legitimacy. They sent essentially the same messages to the public. This does not support the assumption that having more media organizations results in a more diverse and rich information environment. Rather it suggests that most media organizations transmit news that is essentially alike, and the Downing Street memo is not a unique example. What can explain how so many media organizations can produce such similar output?

On the other hand, sometimes there are important differences in how news organizations cover an event—different information is selected and different messages are produced. The history of the American media is replete with such examples, including coverage of the civil rights and women's rights movements in the middle of the last century, and in the 1970s the *Washington Post* broke a series of news reports that ultimately forced an American president to resign (Streitmatter, 1997). Instances of some news media breaking important and controversial stories also require explanation. Such news organizations dramatically depart from the usual consensus of what the world is like, but there are also differences in how even routine events are covered on a daily basis. Modern American journalism rests on an ideological notion that the media will produce accurate, factual accounts that correspond to an objective reality (Schudson, 1978). So, how can the media, facing essentially the same material reality, produce different versions of it?

These contradictory questions deserve to be answered. For the above examples, we could point to another assumption in U.S. journalism, that news and editorial messages have different purposes—news to give factual coverage of the day's events and editorials or opinions to carry a point of view, a conclusion. Hence, similarities in news coverage could be explained by the fact that journalists begin with information about the same social system, whether it is as small as a city or as large as the world, and end with messages that have much in common. Differences in opinion messages could be explained by people's varying points of view yielding multiple conclusions about the social system. News content is alike and editorial (opinion) output is varied because that is the way it is supposed to be.

But reality is not so neat and orderly. News coverage of the civil rights movement, not just editorials about it, produced very different pictures of reality. American editorials about a case for war in Iraq, not just news stories, had much in common (Mooney, 2004). Straightforward explanations are apparent—that the source of variation in civil rights reporting was surely geographical and cultural. News organizations in the South viewed the civil rights movement differently than did ones elsewhere in America.

While considering ad hoc explanations based on particular events is worthwhile, it is not as useful as building theory that can predict the media's role in future events. We believe that the job of media scholars should be to build theory that will synthesize explanations for both discrepancies and commonalities into a systematic whole. *Theories* are sets of statements—assumptions, propositions, and hypotheses—that are interrelated and logically consistent (Shoemaker, Tankard, & Lasorsa, 2004). They describe, explain and predict some portion of reality. Gatekeeping Theory describes the process through which events are covered by the mass media, explains this process by considering concepts on five levels of analysis, and shows just how difficult it is to predict anything involving people.

THINKING ABOUT GATEKEEPING

Constructing a theory of gatekeeping is vitally important. Gatekeepers determine what becomes a person's social reality, a particular view of the world. Although a single gatekeeping decision may itself seem trivial, both varied messages and common messages emerge every day, making the gatekeeping process complicated and highly significant.

Theories of both social change and stability need to account for gatekeeping, the ideas about which have been a concern for the likes of Jefferson and Marx, Gramsci and Bourdieu. As Bagdikian (1983) has put it: "The power to control the flow of information is a major lever in the control of society. Giving citizens a choice in ideas and information is as important as giving them a choice in politics" (p. 226). Hardt (1979) writes: "Control over the media of dissemination may suggest control over the mind of society" (p. 22). The gatekeeping process determines the way in which we define our lives and the world around us, and therefore gatekeeping ultimately affects the social reality of every person. We use the term *social reality* to reflect the obvious fact that we do not all see the world in the same way. Although an objective reality may in theory exist, describing it is beyond the scope of this book.

The most obvious effect of gatekeeping on the audience is cognitive—shaping the audience's thoughts about what the world is like—what some have called "cognitive maps" (Ranney, 1983). Information that gets through all gates can become part of people's social reality, whereas information that stops at a gate generally does not. But news decisions also include an evaluative dimension and have the potential to influence attitudes and opinions (J. C. Alexander, 1981). For example, as agenda-setting research points out (McCombs & Shaw, 1976), issues that get through the gates are accorded the most importance by the audience and affect public opinion on that issue. But we also recognize that the gatekeeping process can affect audience attitudes and opinions directly to the extent that supporting or conflicting messages pass through the gates. For example, the U.S. military's ability to control access to information about the 1991 Persian Gulf war did not reduce the huge volume of news stories about U.S. involvement in the war, but the military may be responsible for the fact that few stories were negative. Not only was the war at the top of the news and public agendas, but President George H. W. Bush's approval rating reached unprecedented levels in opinion polls following the conclusion of the war.

Media influence on public opinion is at its height when their versions of reality agree. Noelle-Neumann (1980) refers to this as a *consonant* version of reality. Consonance results from the media's presentation of an event in roughly the same manner, and the result is that the audience has a limited range of information from which to form opinions. We know from research, however, that media depictions of the world are not always consonant; the vast number of decisions made by gatekeepers does not *necessarily* result in similar images of social reality. For example, in Luttbeg's (1983a) content analysis of more than 100 newspapers in the early 1980s, front pages were found to be dissimilar. The author suggests that such differences—which might be the result of gatekeeping or a random process—result in views of the world that vary significantly from city to city. Miller, Goldenberg, and Erbring (1979) found that differences in the public's confidence in their cities' governments correlated with the number of critical news stories that appeared in local newspapers. Network television news seems to vary less. Bantz (1990b) suggests that media organizations such as ABC, NBC, and CBS often produce very similar views of the world because they operate within the same news environment, are influenced by what other media do (see Chapter 6), and have a tendency to replicate what they have done before. Although we assume that the internet makes diverse sources of information available, we can observe that the pictures of the world created by news portal sites are made primarily from mainstream news organizations.

Such discussions of similarities and differences in how an event is covered are primarily on the operational level, that is, they look at the manifest content, in which every story is in fact different from others to one extent or another. Such differences can be trivial or vitally important. When the *nature* and newsworthiness of stories are taken into account at a theoretical level, however, we are better able to explain why events are covered in both similar and different ways. Shoemaker (1996) has proposed that human brains are "hard-wired" to prefer information about oddities, threats, and change. These forms of deviance are found in the news media of countries around the world (Shoemaker & Cohen, 2006). Additionally, a country's culture can define how deviance is defined and the social significance of events, both dimensions of newsworthiness.

Yet perhaps the most important aspect of gatekeeping is that issues and events that are not covered are absent from the worldviews of most audience members. People cannot know about what the media fail to tell them, unless the people have personal experience of the event. The existence of a large publicity industry in the United States and other countries is based on an assumption that media coverage is vital, that it lends prestige, power, and opportunities to those people and organizations that find their way into media content. Even countries conduct public relations campaigns within other countries. The United States requires other countries to register these activities with the U.S. government, perhaps to ensure that it knows that it is being persuaded. Countries may assume that if Americans do not think well of foreigners, they will spend less money in their countries. Other advantages of a favorable foreign image include cooperation in military and economic alliances (Wang, Shoemaker, Han, & Storm, 2008).

Although public relations efforts serve primarily those who already possess power, they can also promote new ideas: The mass media provide a conduit through which new ideas and the groups who introduce them can reach the larger public. Media exposure is a contingent condition for acceptance of new ideas, and groups fight for access to the media and, therefore, to the audience (Hart, 1994). Whereas media coverage does not ensure acceptance of new ideas—particularly if the ideas are deviant and, therefore, treated as not legitimate (Shoemaker, 1984)—a lack of coverage almost certainly dooms them to failure.

UNDERSTANDING GATEKEEPING

This book presents a Gatekeeping Theory in three parts. First, we explore how gatekeeping has been theoretically defined. Here we connect gatekeeping to what is sometimes called media sociology, the study of factors that influence how media messages come to turn out the way they do (Schudson, 2003). Second, we catalog the explanatory factors that have emerged from the media literature over several decades. These factors are arranged into a typology of five levels of analysis. Third, we offer a gatekeeping model and explore how the five levels relate to each other. In other words, we sketch a systematic whole, i.e., a model of our Gatekeeping Theory.

In developing a theory, specificity of language is important. When a concept is called by several terms, confusion can arise. Therefore, we have decided that the stuff being moved about in the gatekeeping process is to be called *information*. Occasionally we refer to *units*, *bits*, or even *items* of information, but our purpose is to describe the flow of information in general terms. The information is generally about *events*. When the mass media aggregate information for presentation to the audience, we call these *messages*. Messages can include news, opinion, features, video, and more. Messages that actually become news are called *news items*.

We use the term *mass media* to describe organizations that transmit information to many people, such as those that create web pages, news portals or blogs on the internet, newspapers, television and radio companies, as well as magazines. When we differentiate between *mainstream* and *alternative* media, we refer both to whether the thoughts expressed therein lie within the usual scope of debate in modern American culture and to something about their audience sizes. Although mainstream media at the national level tend to have larger audiences than the national alternative media, such a relationship between centrality of ideas and circulation or reach is not inevitable.

Although we are trained in journalism and are most likely to think of news examples and use news terminology, our theory is intended to address other types of content as well. Therefore we do not refer to the *press*, which connotes not only news but also news on paper. Films, music, books, and plays are also mass media, and, although they are less likely to be found in the gatekeeping literature, we believe that the ideas in Gatekeeping Theory can be useful for scholarship involving them and encourage creative thought.

Although at the time of writing there is a tendency for some authors to capitalize the term *internet*, we do not, just as we do not capitalize *newspaper* or *television*. In the case of the internet, capitalization may have reflected the oddity of what was once called the *new media*, a term that we also reject. The internet has been around for decades, coming into regular use for functions such as email in government and universities in the 1980s and as a serious news medium in the 1990s. The new media are now well established. And finally, although we adopt the usual term *online* to refer to information received by the audience through the internet, we are just old enough to dislike the rest of life being referred to as *offline*. This traps us, however, into occasionally using the unfortunate term *traditional* for referring to mass media that are not online.

Our job became even more complicated as, toward the end of the 20th century, the internet became a viable news medium, validated by playing its new role in the 2000 U.S. presidential election. Not only did many "traditional" news organizations create their own web sites,[1] but news organizations unique to the internet were created. News *portals* were created to capture news items from among internet news sites and use computer code (i.e., Lewin's set of rules) to determine which stories (from other news organizations) are included. The algorithms also determine the order of stories, how quickly they appear, under which category (e.g., world news), links to other news organizations, and so on. The algorithms generate probabilities that measure how newsworthy news items are and follow rules for manipulating them.

Compared to other mass media, the internet provides much more opportunity for audience members to interact with news makers, news creators, and each other. This high level of interactivity turns audience members into gatekeepers. Readers may personalize *Google News*' front page by asking for more or less of a category and may reorder categories on the page, thus acting as their own gatekeepers. At the *New York Times* online, readers can as easily email an article to many people as to one. The *Times* own algorithms continuously gather this information and present it on the newspaper's front page as the rank-ordered "most emailed articles."

---

1 The terms *internet* and *world wide web* are often used synonymously to refer to the technology (computers and the networks among them), software (programs that move information across networked computers), and the specific locations of, for example, the *New York Times* online. Although it has come into fashion, we consider the term *offline* an inelegant way to differentiate between the *online* world of the internet and the real world. But we cannot think of an adequate substitute.

Audience members have become active in a secondary gatekeeping process, one that begins when the usual mass media process stops. Just as Mr. Gates showed a personal preference for one topic over another, so do readers. And now the *New York Times* staff can "look over the reader's shoulder" at what people read and at what they think others should read. It must be a marketing department's dream: Hard data about what sorts of articles are most popular, no longer relying on unreliable self-report from surveys and incomplete participation in focus groups.

As for the editorial departments, hard data about what readers want to read butts up against the social responsibility canon to give readers what they need to read. We don't know whether journalists pay any attention to the most emailed list or use it to make gatekeeping decisions. But we do know that the dotted line representing a weak audience feedback loop in mass communication models can now be made solid. And we know that neither the diffusion nor the gatekeeping processes end with the mass media. The audience is a force to be recognized when we study the flow of information.

The sophistication of these gatekeeping rules is shown by the ability of readers to tailor the content to their own interests, for example by asking for more world news and less sports information. These "more or less" rules and placement of categories on the web page turn into algorithms created by individual readers and are remembered by the news portal's servers, so that when the reader enters the site again, the *cookies* (audience-defined sets of information and rules) left behind by the web site on the person's computer allow the server to recognize the person and his preferences.

The internet was a significant force in the election of 2004 and a crucial part of the 2008 election for candidates, news organizations, and voters in both fund raising and communication directly from the candidates' staffs to the audience. This caused some people to say that the internet represents the death of Gatekeeping Theory, arguing that there is no gatekeeping on the internet. We disagree. Information units are not spontaneously and entirely created at the moment a blog entry is posted, and the information often is neither original nor different from that in any other blog or news site. Information from blogs is highly redundant and includes information that bloggers could not have experienced first hand. Information diffuses through mass media and interpersonal channels to the bloggers and their staffs, and they combine it with their own understanding of the world. The result may be idiosyncratic, but it is based on information that has traveled through many gates.

Part I Understanding Gatekeeping

Writer and social reformer Upton Sinclair despaired in the early 20th century that mainstream press barons held a tight grip on what made it into the newspapers. Sinclair had achieved fame as a muckraker when he published *The Jungle* (1906), a book that chronicled the health and safety hazards posed by the American meat-packing industry. In 1920 he examined the problems of American journalism in the *Brass Check*. Sinclair concluded that the modern newspaper was "an enormous and complex institution" (p. 223) that did not tell the whole truth. Some messages were passed on to readers, but some very important ones were not. His book sought an explanation. He argued that "the majority of newspaper reporters were decent men" (p. 417) whose work was manipulated by powerful publishers working in a capitalist system. The system had its way with the press. Sinclair concluded that "journalism is one of the devices whereby industrial autocracy keeps its control over political democracy" (p. 222).

This study of newspapers from the last century may lack methodological sophistication by modern social scientific standards, but Sinclair's themes and conclusions are similar to those offered by Bagdikian (2004) or McChesney (1997). Indeed, some of his themes also foreshadow the seminal works of White (1950), Tuchman (1978) and Gans (1979a). Writing in the same time period, Walter Lippmann (1922) argued that the press's ability to select what to report is its most important feature. "Every newspaper when it reaches the reader is the result of a whole series of selections as to what items shall be printed, in what position they shall be printed, how much space each shall occupy, what emphasis each shall have" (Lippmann, 1922, p. 63). Lippmann urged readers to look to newspaper conventions and newspaper audiences, not to the tastes or judgments of editors, to understand how news turned out the way it did. Lippmann's emphasis on the routine practices of the news process is reflected in Gieber's (1964) critique of the seminal gatekeeping study by White (1950), which centered more around the gatekeeper's personal choices.

Observers and practitioners of journalism—Sinclair and Lippmann were both— have seldom been short on conclusions about why the news media tell some stories and not others. So what makes today's gatekeeping scholarship substantially different from the observations that came before it? We believe that recent scholarship's value is its theoretical lens for studying how media messages come to turn out the way they do. To begin creating that lens, we distinguish between the gatekeeping concept and gatekeeping as a process.

1 Understanding the Concept

Regrettably, theorizing about gatekeeping has not been in large supply, a problem we explore in a later chapter. The selectivity inherent in the communication process lacked a theoretical focus until Kurt Lewin (1947a) provided the metaphor of the gatekeeper and David Manning White (1950) gave the gatekeeper life under the pseudonym of Mr. Gates. The gatekeeper metaphor offered early communication scholars a framework for evaluating how selection occurs and why some items are selected and others rejected. It also provided a structure for the study of processes other than selection, such as how content is shaped, structured, positioned, and timed.

KURT LEWIN'S "THEORY OF CHANNELS AND GATE KEEPERS"

The first pairing of the terms gatekeeping and communication apparently came in the posthumous publication in 1947 of Kurt Lewin's unfinished manuscript "Frontiers in Group Dynamics II: Channels of Group Life; Social Planning and Action Research" in the journal *Human Relations*. At the time of his death, Lewin was director of the Research Center for Group Dynamics for the Massachusetts Institute of Technology, but he had earlier held appointments at other U.S. universities, including the University of Iowa (Marrow, 1969).

A second version of the "frontiers" manuscript appeared as part of the chapter "Psychological Ecology" in the 1951 book *Field Theory in Social Science*, an edited and synthesized collection of Lewin's work.[2] Field theory refers to one segment of German psychology at about the time of the First World War, with the concept of

---

2 Lewin had previously written about gatekeeping and "channel theory" in a 1943 government research report, "Forces behind Food Habits and Methods of Change," for the National Research Council, but the report did not generalize the gatekeeping process to communication items, as did his 1947 manuscript.

field having been borrowed from physics (Bavelas, 1948). One group of psychologists wanted to reduce the person and the environment into isolated elements that could be causally connected. Lewin, trained as a physicist, was more aligned with the group that "attempted to explain behavior as a function of groups of factors constituting a dynamic whole—the psychological field" (Bavelas, 1948, p. 16). The *field* consists of both the person and the surrounding environment. Field theorists look at a problem in terms of the dynamic interplay between interconnected factors rather than as relationships between isolated elements. Lewin was working on a way to express psychological forces mathematically, using "geometry for the expression of the positional relationships between parts of the life space, and vectors for the expression of strength, direction, and point of application of psychological forces" (Bavelas, 1948, p. 16). Lewin argues that psychologists can mathematically define the forces shaping people's behaviors, in much the same way that forces such as gravity are defined by physicists.

Lewin wrote primarily about changing a population's food habits, but his purpose more generally was to understand how psychologists can effect widespread social changes (1947a, p. 146). In his analysis of food eating, he began with the assumption that not all members of the population are equally important in determining what is eaten. Therefore, social change can best be accomplished by concentrating on those people with the most control over food selection for the home. Lewin thought of food as reaching the family table through *channels*. One channel is the grocery store, where food is purchased, but other channels also carry food, such as the family garden. Figure 1.1 illustrates how channels may be subdivided into *sections*, and the beginning of each section represents an action point. In the grocery channel, for example, the first three sections include discovering the food at the grocery store, buying it, and transporting it home. Food traveling along the garden channel begins with buying seeds or plants from a garden store and planting them. As the fruits and vegetables grow, some are weeded out, some are eaten in the garden by insects or children, and others fail from lack of fertilizer or water. Of the fruits and vegetables available to the household, only some are harvested; others languish on the vine or branch.

At this point, the grocery and garden channels combine into the kitchen channel. Storage decisions must be made (*in the refrigerator or pantry?*) for each food unit. As a consequence, some foods are "lost" in the deep recesses of the refrigerator, and others are wasted because they were incorrectly stored (*does an opened jar of jelly have to be refrigerated?*). Next, the cook decides whether (and how) to cook the food or to pass it through raw to the next section, preparation for the table. Finally, the cook places and stages the food on the table, ready for the family to eat (Lewin, 1947a, p. 144). At each section, food can be rejected or accepted, but even more importantly the process of moving down the channel changes the food. Vegetables are cut up, steak is prepared rare or well done, potatoes are fried or baked. We conclude, therefore, that gatekeeping involves not only the selection or rejection of items, but also the process of changing them in ways to make them more appealing

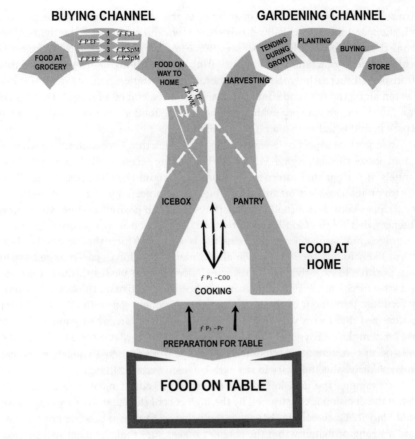

Figure 1.1 Lewin's gatekeeping model shows how food items pass through two channels on their way to the family table. Channels are divided into sections, and at the front of each is a gate that regulates movement through the channel. Forces on both sides of the gate can either constrain or facilitate the movement of items through channels.
Source: Lewin (1947a, p. 144).

to the final consumer. If we think of the final decision point as whether the food is eaten, we can see that even the colors of food items and how they are placed on the platter can affect whether they are eaten. Even their environmental context is important. A nice tablecloth, candles and low lighting create a context in which food may be more appreciated.

The entrance to a channel and to each section is a *gate*, and movement within the channel is controlled by one or more *gatekeepers* or by *a set of impartial rules* (Lewin, 1951, p. 186). For example, some food never gets into the grocery channel

→ Definitions

because of the buying decisions or policies of the store manager/gatekeeper, and each shopper/gatekeeper walks down some rows and so misses some items. From among those items that the shopper sees, some items are bought and others rejected, perhaps because of a family rule about eating meat. Although most purchased food is transported successfully to the household (transportation section), part of it may be eaten along the way and some perishables may be ruined in transit. Once in the home, the cook/gatekeeper evaluates whether the food should be cooked, how to prepare it, and whether to offer it to the family.

An important aspect of Lewin's theory is his idea that *forces* determine whether an item passes through a gate. With gates controlling access to all sections within all channels, it is clear that forces are at work throughout the channels. These forces work for or against selection and also influence the processing of items. When a grocery shopper considers a food item for purchase, both positive and negative forces influence whether the food is put in the cart. Attractiveness is a positive force that encourages purchase, whereas high expense is a negative force that makes the shopper less likely to buy the item. Lewin also contends that forces can change polarity (from positive to negative or the reverse) once an item passes through the gate. A negative force on one side of the gate can become positive on the other and actually facilitate movement of the item through subsequent gates. In addition, Lewin hypothesized that forces vary in strength, with stronger forces being more likely to move an item through a gate. Therefore the concept of *force* is central to the theory: Forces occur throughout the channel, they range from positive to negative and can change polarity, plus they vary in strength between and within items.

For example, the decision to buy an expensive cut of meat may be difficult, because the decision is constrained by the high cost of the meat—*It's very expensive; should I buy it?* Once bought, however, the negative force can become positive and create a strong probability that the shopper makes sure that the meat will successfully pass through the remaining gates and reach the table—*It's so expensive; I must take extra care to transport, store, cook, prepare, and serve it carefully and well.* Because the forces before and following a gate differ in strength and polarity, whether an item passes through the channel depends on the forces on both sides of each gate.

In Figure 1.1, arrows show how forces act to facilitate or constrain the passage of items either within a channel section or on both sides of a gate. Forces are designated in italics; for example, $fP\ EF^1$ represents the force associated with the attractiveness of the food within the buying section, and it helps the food move through the next gate into the transporting-to-home section. Other forces are also present within the buying section, however, such as the force $fP\ EF^2$, which represents the expense of the food item. As Figure 1.1 shows, the high-expense force yields to a countervailing force of equal strength against spending money, fP,S_pM, and thus it is unlikely that the food item will pass through to the next section. Foods that do get into the "on way to home" section leave it with a force against wasting money, $fP\ WM$, which helps ensure that the food passes into the appropriate icebox or pantry section.

Lewin believed that this theoretical framework could be applied generally:[3] "This situation holds not only for food channels but also for the traveling of a news item through certain communication channels in a group, for movement of goods, and the social locomotion of individuals in many organizations" (Lewin, 1951, p. 187). This was the inspiration for studying the flow of information using the gatekeeping model.

Although the terms *channel*, *section*, and *gate* imply physical structures, it is clear that they are not objects at all but represent a process that describes why and how some items pass on their way, step by step, from discovery to use. Sections correspond to things that occur in the channel, such as the copy-editing process. Gates are decision or action points. Gatekeepers determine both which units get into the channel and which pass from section to section, exercising their own preferences and/or acting as representatives to carry out a set of pre-established policies. They also decide whether to make changes in the item.

DAVID MANNING WHITE AND "MR. GATES"

The first communication scholar to translate Lewin's theory of channels and gatekeepers into a research project was David Manning White, who learned about Lewin's work while serving as his research assistant at the University of Iowa. White persuaded a wire editor on a small-city newspaper—whom he called "Mr. Gates"—to keep all of the wire copy that came into his office from the Associated Press, United Press, and International News Service during one week in February 1949. Mr. Gates also agreed to provide written explanations of why each of the rejected items was not used—and about 90 percent of the wire copy received was not used. This allowed White to compare the items actually used with the aggregate of stories that the wire services transmitted during the week.

The selection decisions, according to White, were "highly subjective" (1950, p. 386). About a third of the time, Mr. Gates rejected stories based on his personal evaluation of the merits of the item's content, especially whether he believed it to be true. The other two thirds of items were rejected because there wasn't enough space for them or because other similar ones were already running.

Figure 1.2 is a visualization of White's gatekeeper model (McQuail & Windahl, 1981, pp. 100–101). News sources (N) send news items to the media gatekeeper, who turns some away (e.g., N_1 and N_4) and sends others (N_2^1 and N_3^1—the superior numerals indicating that the news items are changed as they pass through the gate)

3 Legend has it that Lewin and Wilbur Schramm shared a backyard fence when both were at the University of Iowa, and that they hoed weeds and talked about theory by the hour. Perhaps these conversations were the inspiration for Lewin's suggestion that gatekeeping could be applied to the study of communication.

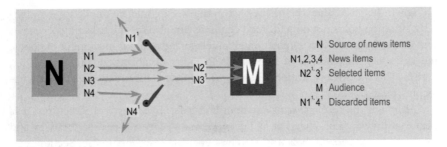

Figure 1.2 David Manning White's vision of gatekeeping.
Source: McQuail and Windahl (1981, pp. 100–101).

on to the audience (M). We can interpret Figure 1.2 as having either one gatekeeper or a set of gatekeepers acting in concert. The model is limited in that it does not recognize that multiple gatekeepers may each have their own role conceptions or positions in gathering, shaping, and transmitting news items.

A 1966 replication of White's study by Paul Snider, with the original Mr. Gates, yielded much the same result. Although Mr. Gates was 17 years older and could choose only from one wire service, his story selections were still based on what he liked and on what he thought his readers wanted. He used fewer human-interest stories in 1966 but more international war stories, either showing more of an interest in hard news or reflecting the increasing amount of news about the Vietnam War. Mr. Gates defined *news* as "the day by day report of events and personalities and comes in variety which should be presented as much as possible in variety for a balanced diet" (Snider, 1967, p. 426).

OTHER GATEKEEPING MODELS

White's study encouraged many scholars to use the metaphor of gatekeeping, if not the full theoretical model. In 1965 Webb and Salancik said that the gatekeeping metaphor was used in many journalism research studies, and that it was an example of how "journalism research has moved appreciably toward a more rigorous approach to data" (p. 595). In one of these studies, Gieber (1956) looked at 16 newspaper telegraph editors' selections of wire copy, and his conclusion was quite different than White's. Whereas White concluded that the gatekeeper's personal values were an important determinant of selection, Gieber described the editor as being "caught in a strait jacket of mechanical details" (1956, p. 432) that keep personal values from having a major influence on the selection of stories. Gieber proposed that personal subjectivity was less important in gatekeeping than structural considerations, including "the number of news items available, their size and the pressures of time and mechanical production" (1964, p. 175). The wire editor, he said (1956), is essentially

↱ The Wire editor

passive, and the selection process is mechanical. He concluded that the organization and its routines were more important than the individual worker's characteristics.

A year later Westley and MacLean (1957) proposed what became a popular model of mass communication. They combined the idea of gatekeeping as an organizational activity with Newcomb's (1953) psychological model of interpersonal communication, termed *coorientation*. For Newcomb, every communicative act involved transmitting information about an object; the simplest model involved person A sending information about object X to person B. Westley had been Newcomb's student and saw that the ABX model could be modified to study mass communication.

Westley and MacLean expanded the model by adding C to designate a mass media channel (the organization as gatekeeper). In their model, X indicated a message, and f designated feedback (Westley & MacLean, 1957, p. 35). Arrows in Figure 1.3 show the flow of information (whether news items or feedback) from one actor to another. It can flow between A and B through C, or it can skip the mass media channel entirely. The model also shows that some information is rejected and some changed by media gatekeepers. Westley (1953) saw news judgment as the essential explanation of gatekeeping decisions.

As in the model describing White's study, not all information bits are successful in passing through the media channel to the audience. B receives a subset of the messages available to C and may provide feedback both to C and to A about the messages. In this extension of Newcomb's model, Westley and MacLean point out that at any given point in time there are multiple As, Bs, and Cs communicating. Whereas White's study focused on the decisions of one person, Gieber's study and Westley and MacLean's model treat the media organization as monolithic, with individual workers collectively acting as one gatekeeper, presumably by following a set of rules. For example, Gieber's (1956) study of 16 wire editors emphasized that it was not the

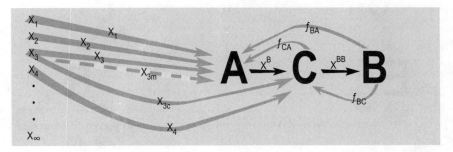

Figure 1.3 Information (X) moves to the audience in one of three ways: from senders (A) through the mass media channel (C), to receivers in the audience (B), from senders to the audience personally, or through the audience's direct experience with it. Feedback (f) can be sent from the audience to senders and to the media, as well as from the media to senders.
Source: Westley and MacLean (1957, p. 35).

individuals' attributes or attitudes that were important, but the organizational constraints imposed on the individual. The organizational channel in Westley and MacLean's (1957) model is another example.

In these later approaches, individual communication workers are unimportant: Individuals are passive and have no important distinguishing features; they are interchangeable cogs in the media machine. On the other hand, White understood gatekeeping as a process performed by people, not organizations. He saw individual decisions being influenced both by the individual's characteristics and values and by organizational constraints, such as deadlines.

Later studies pick up this idea of individuals acting as gatekeepers. McNelly (1959) proposed a model that showed how international news items pass through multiple individual gatekeepers on their way from the source to the audience. As Figure 1.4 shows, a story (S) is written about an event (E). The story passes from one gatekeeper (C) to another, each of whom may cut, reorganize, or merge it with another story before it ultimately reaches the receiver (R). Gatekeepers include foreign correspondents, editors, news service editors, copy editors, and radio or television news editors. For information about an event to reach audiences in other countries requires it to "run an obstacle course of reportorial error or bias, editorial selection and processing, translation, transmission difficulties, and possible suppression or censorship" (1959, p. 23). Another innovation of the McNelly model is

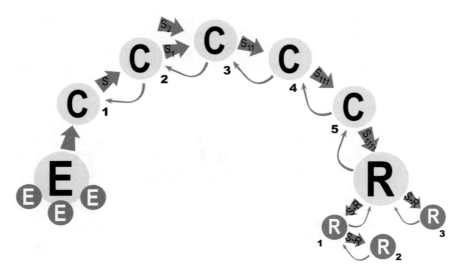

Figure 1.4 This model of international news flow shows that items must pass multiple individual gatekeepers on their way from the source to the audience. When later items pass through a gate, they can either integrate with existing items or replace them.
Source: McNelly (1959, p. 23).

Figure 1.5 Two types of individuals are most important in the gatekeeping process—news gatherers and news processors.
Source: Bass (1969, p. 72).

showing how new items may enter subsequent gates (e.g., item S2 in Figure 1.4), either to displace existing items or to be integrated with them. Curved arrows represent feedback, which McNelly says is infrequent.

Bass (1969) also looked at individuals as gatekeepers, but in his approach the individual's job within the organization is of interest—not the person. The individual represents the organization in doing things necessary to the flow of news messages. Bass argued that all news gatekeepers do the same sorts of things, and he produced yet another model (Figure 1.5) to show the two primary functions that result in "double-action internal news flow" (Bass, 1969, p. 72). News *gatherers*, according to Bass, take the information that comes to them from various channels and turn it into news copy. In newspapers, they have job titles such as writers, bureau chiefs, reporters, or city editors. A second type of gatekeeper—the news *processor*—modifies and integrates the copy into a finished product that can be transmitted to the audience. News processors include editors, copyreaders, and translators. Thus Bass broadened the study of individual gatekeepers from White's study of one news processor to the study of multiple gatekeepers of two distinct types.

In a similar argument a year later, Halloran, Elliott, and Murdock wrote that gatekeeping begins not in the office (with the news processors) but with the "reporter on the street" (the news gatherer) and that the extent to which editorial staff act as gatekeepers varies among newspapers (1970, p. 131). Chibnall (1977) disliked the terms gatherer and processor because they imply that news exists independently of the media: "The reporter does not go out gathering news, picking up stories as if they were fallen apples, he creates news stories by selecting fragments of information from the mass of raw data he receives and organizing them in a conventional journalistic format" (1977, p. 6). News is constructed from a variety of raw materials, the most important of which is information from sources; reporters rarely use their own direct experience in covering an event. Chibnall argues that the journalist/source nexus is the most important arena of gatekeeping. By the time the message gets to an editor, the most important gatekeeping decisions have already been made: "Events have occurred, they have been experienced, accounts of experiences have been constructed for particular audiences, accounts of those accounts have been fashioned and these have either been stored away or transformed into full-fledged news stories. At every stage selection and processing has taken place" (Chibnall, 1977, p. 7).

In some cases, however, the materials that come to the journalist are not so raw. As Gandy (1982) points out, one role of the public relations industry is to provide "information subsidies" that are in a form attractive to and easily used by the media. In such cases, much of the gathering and processing has occurred before the item comes to the attention of the journalist/gatekeeper. This substantially increases the likelihood that the item will be selected to pass a media gate, and so news gatekeepers are now understood not only to include news gatherers, sources, and news processors but also public relations practitioners and other representatives of interest groups who want to shape mass media content.

GATEKEEPING AND THE GENERAL COMMUNICATION PROCESS

The concept of gatekeeping has been popular with mass communication scholars, particularly in the study of news selection. Gatekeeping has clear applicability to programming entertainment content (Cantor, 1980), but it has less often been used by those who study interpersonal communication. According to Hirsch, this may reflect the

> larger role and institutional function of journalism in a democratic society more than it signals differences between constant categories at the production level, for a discovery that news editors' selection criteria are subject to personal bias and political pressure suggests more significant implications for public policy. (1977, p. 21)

There are, however, instances in which the gatekeeping metaphor has been applied to interpersonal communication. For example, in their study of communication among members of small groups, Bales, Strodtbeck, Mills, and Roseborough (1951) used the term *channel of communication* to refer to interaction between any two members of a group or between any member and the group as a whole. Their interest was not in the selection of items to be communicated but in what the distribution of communication among channels revealed about the relative power of group members.

In his study of formal channels and power within an organization, Hickey (1966, 1968) identified three types of organizational information control: through a *communication handler*, who controls the passage of messages within an organization; a *channel mediator*, who controls the nature of the channels or networks through which information can pass; and a *content manipulator*, who performs both of the other two roles and shapes the nature of the content. Of these roles, the content manipulator has the most power. In Hickey's (1966) network analyses, combinations of five people were asked to solve a problem. One person was in the center of the network, acting as a gatekeeper for the four people around the periphery. Hickey showed that the person with the most centrality—seen in terms of the control of information, for example, by a gatekeeper—was accorded the highest status in the group and was perceived as being the most powerful. Hickey criticized Lewin (1947a) and White (1950) as viewing gatekeeping from the vantage point of the gate, dwelling on whether the gate was open or closed. A more productive interpretation might include perceptions of the gatekeeper by others in the field and the gatekeeper's own reactions toward the status of the job.

Another interpersonal approach to the study of gatekeeping includes theories of *cognitive heuristics* (e.g., Kahneman, Slovic, & Tversky, 1982; Nisbett & Ross, 1980). The *representativeness heuristic*—a person's automatic assignment of an item to a category based on its similarity to other items in the category—can be applied to the gatekeeper's assessment of whether a message should be selected or rejected. For example, Tuchman (1974) showed that journalists assign events to several categories, such as hard or soft news, to organize an otherwise uncontrollable job— handling the flood of information that is presented to them each day. If a story is deemed representative of the hard news category, it is treated quite differently than if it is determined to be soft news. We return to the topic of cognitive heuristics in more detail in Chapter 3.

The gatekeeping metaphor has also been compared with that of *boundary role persons* in the organizational communication literature (e.g., J. S. Adams, 1980). Boundary role persons interact with other organizations and outside people, controlling the messages that both come into and leave the organization. This aspect of gatekeeping is covered in Chapter 5 on the organizational level of analysis.

In addition, research on the diffusion of information is applicable to gatekeeping: Gatekeepers can facilitate or constrain the diffusion of information as they decide which messages to allow past the gates and which to stop, making them important actors in the diffusion process. As Chaffee (1975) points out, the factors that constrain and facilitate diffusion are the most interesting to study because they result in diffusion patterns that deviate from the standard S-shaped (cumulative normal) curve found in many studies. If gatekeepers constrain the flow of information, then it may not completely diffuse throughout the social system, whereas if they facilitate information flow, news of the event may diffuse more quickly. Because information may diffuse both through interpersonal and mass media channels, any audience member may be a gatekeeper for others. But not all individual gatekeepers are equally powerful; those who represent the mass media control the diffusion of information for millions of people, a fact that gives them extraordinary political and social power.

2 The Gatekeeping Process

The basic premise of gatekeeping scholarship is that messages are created from information about events that has passed through a series of gates and has been changed in the process. Some information ends up on a newspaper's front page, some in the middle of a newscast or web page, and some never makes it into the news at all. Similarly, an event may appear in some news media but not others. Or information may be given the most prominent placement in one medium but buried inside another. As noted at the outset of this book, the Downing Street memo was the basis for many news reports in Europe but relatively few in the mainstream American media. In this chapter, we explore how information items enter a channel, the characteristics of those items, and the nature of forces in front of and behind the gates.

ENTRANCE OF ITEMS INTO THE CHANNEL

The FIRST gate →

Gatekeeping begins when a communication worker forms information about an event into a message. This is the first gate for that event.[4] Where does the pool of items/messages come from? Some come knocking (public relations) and others have to be dragged kicking and screaming (investigative journalism) through the gate. Information comes to communication organizations through a variety of channels. Sigal (1973) categorizes these as routine, informal, and enterprise: *Routine* channels include public records and information about non-spontaneous events, such as speeches or events held specifically to get media attention. The public relations industry has a media relations arm dedicated to this task. *Informal* channels include background briefings, those who talk off the record, other journalists, and other mass media. *Enterprise* channels include spontaneous events created by the journalist by talking to people or by thinking critically about a problem.

Routine and informal channels bring information to the communication organization from the outside, where a communication boundary role person (J. S. Adams, 1980) makes the first in/out decision. Many sources—for example, government

---

4 Most news items begin with an event, but some are about people generally or about issues.

officials or public relations practitioners—create their own messages and work to ensure that they will enter media channels and pass through all gates. They create messages that are particularly attractive to the journalist. Such messages carry a strongly positive force in front of the first news gates, and this can facilitate the message's movement through the channels. As is often the case, however, both positive and negative forces can exist at the same time. Journalists sometimes disdain public relations products, a negative force in front of early gates that makes publication less likely. In contrast, journalists in smaller communities may use public relations messages as the basis for their editorial (non-advertising) content; in this situation, the force would be strongly positive. Some news releases trigger ideas about how to cover an event, with the message about it being largely the product of a journalist's own work. In this case, the news release would have a positive force, if bringing information to the journalist's attention moved even some of the information in the news release through early gates.

Information coming through enterprise channels is either initiated and developed by the communication worker (e.g., reporter-initiated interviews) or a result of the communication worker being in the right place at the right time when an event (e.g., a fire) occurs naturally in the environment. In the former case, sources may alert the mass media of some events or journalists may experience them firsthand. A journalist who deems the event sufficiently newsworthy allows it past the first gate by creating or directing the creation of a message that begins its way through the media organization. Sometimes journalists are on hand when an event occurs, thus bringing the event to the first gate themselves. This was the case with the attacks of September 11, 2001, when many national journalists looked out of their windows to see the World Trade Center towers burn and fall or to watch a fireball emerge from the Pentagon. Other enterprise reporting involves investigative journalists developing their own stories by tying disparate ideas and events together into a logical whole, cajoling reluctant sources and uncovering a story that might not have come to light on its own (Ettema, 1988). The classic example is Woodward and Bernstein's (1974) investigation of the Watergate scandals, which led U.S. President Richard M. Nixon to resign.

In Sigal's study of the *New York Times* and the *Washington Post*, most information came through routine channels, with about half of the items from the U.S. government, indicating the influence that officials—particularly those from government—have in composing the queue of news items at the first news gate. Berkowitz (1987) found a similar reliance on routine sources in national and local television newscasts.

Limitations of the human senses exert another constraint on the entry of messages into a media channel. Some events are invisible to most of us, such as the movement of subatomic particles, and others may occur without human witnesses, such as the proverbial tree falling in a forest empty of people. Even when there are witnesses, firsthand accounts and interpretations of what they have seen often differ widely. In addition, when considering the same event, one person may interpret it as

↳ *due to our perception of the event*

trivial and usual, whereas another may consider it important and newsworthy. Only the latter decision brings the event to the attention of the first media gatekeeper.

We also know that decisions can be influenced by the actions of earlier gatekeepers and by those who transmitted messages earlier. For example, Whitney and Becker (1982) suggest that newspaper editors tend to select news items in roughly the same proportion as they were received from news services. Hirsch's (1977) and McCombs and Shaw's (1976) reinterpretations of White's (1950) study suggest that Mr. Gates' selections were influenced more by what the news services sent him than by his own opinions. This might mean that many gatekeepers' work is not very important—if an editor merely follows someone else's lead in deciding how many messages should be created within topic categories, then that editor can make selection decisions within each topic, but not between topics. We return to this idea in Chapter 5 on the organizational level of analysis.

Other gates may be "low" or "easy" to pass, as Judd found in his study of a newspaper that tried to include "something for everyone" (1961, p. 40). For example, other things being equal, an event is more likely to be covered by a newspaper in a community where fewer events occur than in a big city. The small-town newspaper has a smaller pool of events from which to choose in writing news items, making its gates easier to pass. In addition, gates tend to be easier to pass on some days of the week: Most governmental and business organizations' offices are closed on the weekend, resulting in some items being selected on the weekend (low gate) that would be rejected on another day. Gates may also vary in size (Shoemaker & Cohen, 2006): Traditional newspapers and web sites cover events that do not make their way into most television and radio news programs. Newspapers represent big gates, and so can transmit many more news items than most television and radio programs. Internet news media sites are not quite infinite in size, but they may hold an enormous amount of information. The *New York Times* web archives date back to the 1880s.

CHARACTERISTICS OF NEWS ITEMS

The term *news item* refers to the content actually published and transmitted by a mass medium, the end of the traditional gatekeeping process. At the beginning of the process, however, are *events*, and it is clear that some events are more likely than others to make it to the first gate. Billions of events happen every day and very few are covered by the news media. What distinguishes ignored events from events that are covered in news items?

The ignored events may be trivial for the society at large and judged by all sources as not worth reporting, for example your child's school report card or your most recent doctor's visit. Such events don't make the news because they represent normal conditions, the way the world happens if all is going well. When the world is operating the way our laws and norms say it is supposed to, such events are rarely news, but if you kill your child because she failed math this probably will make the news. And if you are President of the United States, the outcome of your annual physical will be covered by some news organizations.

A primary characteristic of newsworthy events is whether the event, the people, or the issues are deviant. Laws and norms define the boundaries of the civilized world. Inside the boundaries is civilization, society as it is supposed to exist. The outside is deviance, a world full of norm and rule breaking, some minor and some fully evil. Events happening outside of the boundaries are more likely to become news items (Shoemaker, Chang, & Brendlinger, 1987; Shoemaker & Cohen, 2006). For example, the normal efficient and ethical work of government officials gets little media coverage, whereas a questionable or inefficient action can generate protracted public debate and many news items. This appears to be true the world over (Shoemaker & Cohen, 2006).

There is also a tendency for news items to be predominantly about celebrities and other prominent people. In the context of most people's lives, the lives of celebrities are deviant and therefore interesting to gatekeepers. Whereas information about your neighbor's cancer surgery may be important to you, it is probably not important to news gatekeepers. If people are prominent enough, however, even routine activities can leap tall gates and result in an astonishing number of news items. This accounts for the endless parade of celebrity news and gossip columns, which over the past few decades has made inroads into news programming. The line between entertainment and news about the world is so blurred as to be non-existent in some media.

Even having personal experience with an event does not ensure that journalists will send it through the first gate. If a journalist concludes that nothing important happened at the planning commission meeting, a message is unlikely to be prepared and the meeting will not be related in a news item. Journalists, like all people, make judgments about how newsworthy they think events are. What kinds of events do people think are most newsworthy? There are many lists of news attributes, but they generally include some or all of the following: timeliness; proximity; importance, impact, or consequence; interest; conflict or controversy; sensationalism; prominence; and novelty, oddity, or the unusual (Eberhard, 1982; Evensen, 1997; Hough, 1995; Itule & Anderson, 2007). Some of these relate to the deviance of an event, and others to its level of social significance, of which four dimensions have been identified—political, economic, cultural, and public welfare (Shoemaker & Cohen, 2006). Because of these factors, a highly prominent television news item is not necessarily more newsworthy than a less prominent one.

Newsworthiness is a cognitive construct that only partially predicts which events make it into the news media and how those events are covered (Shoemaker, 2006). It is important to recognize that events are not inherently newsworthy; only people can decide whether an event is newsworthy. Events such as the assassination of a political leader relate to people's social realities in many, intense ways. People recognize the event as having political and economic significance, as well as statistical, normative, and social change deviance (Shoemaker & Cohen, 2006). This results in evaluating the event as newsworthy, regardless of a person's station in life—whether a banker, baker, or journalist. Once the cognition is formed, bankers and bakers may talk about the event with others, but journalists are responsible for transmitting information about the event. They create messages that carry information about the event to people locally or around the globe. Thus journalists survey the environment and act as institutional surrogates for the rest of us. Journalists create social artifacts, the words and images that convey information.

It is not correct, however, to assume that the day's set of news items is composed of the events that are thought to be most newsworthy. Newsworthiness is only one variable on the *routine practices* level of analysis in the hierarchical model (Shoemaker & Reese, 1996). Whether newly created news items are ultimately transmitted as news depends on many factors across many levels of analysis, which we discuss in the next five chapters. We know only that people (including gatekeepers) continually evaluate information about events and judge how newsworthy each is.

Newsworthiness is not the only judgment that gatekeepers make about events. In Nisbett and Ross's (1980) cognitive approach to the study of message attractiveness, they assert that humans are more likely to store and remember vivid rather than pallid information, implying that vivid events and issues are more likely to enter a channel. Vivid information grabs hold of the imagination and is exciting, whereas pallid information is dry and unappealing. Information is most vivid if it is "(a) emotionally interesting, (b) concrete and imagery-provoking, and (c) proximate in a sensory, temporal, or spatial way" (Nisbett & Ross, 1980, p. 45). This means that a homeless family's efforts to celebrate Christmas for its 4-year-old child should be more likely to enter a channel (and to pass by individual gates) than a dry, statistical account of the plight of the homeless during the holidays. If the message can provoke more images—*the little girl with long, dark hair who has always wanted a doll who looks just like her*—then its chances of moving through the channel are even better. If the girl and her family are seen by the source living in a local park, then their plight is still more likely to become a news item.

In addition, information about people we know is more interesting to us than facts about strangers, and people for whom we have strong feelings are considered more interesting than those about whom we are neutral. Concrete details about individual people, their actions, or their situations make the information more "imaginable," thus prompting the production of cognitive images. Information obtained firsthand is more vivid than that obtained secondhand. Anecdotes and case histories may be more likely to enter a channel than data summaries (Nisbett & Ross, 1980). This may account for journalists' use of anecdotes in many news items and for readers' tendency to email such news items to others (Shoemaker, Seo, & Johnson, 2008).

Vivid information is more likely to be remembered because concreteness and our ability to imagine promote both recognition and recall. Possibly for this reason, pictures—which are concrete and both supply and elicit images from memory, whether in print or streaming video—are remembered better than verbalizations. Vivid information may also recruit memory schemas that suggest whether it is appropriate for information to enter a channel (Nisbett & Ross, 1980).

Messages of high quality or attractiveness have positive forces and should be more likely to pass the gate, whereas items that are similar to those that have already passed a gate have neutral or negative force and therefore are less likely to get through. Items of doubtful truthfulness should be less likely to pass the gate—at least in the form received; a process of second-guessing (Hewes & Graham, 1989) may result in the message being reinterpreted. In addition, items that attack the gatekeeper's beliefs are thought to cause cognitive stress (Festinger, 1957), and this may either slow the decision process or cause errors in judgment, such as whether to categorize a message as hard or soft news (Greenberg & Tannenbaum, 1962).

Narrative theory provides another approach to looking at the characteristics of events that become news items. White (1950) and others sometimes conflate the terms *item* or *information* with news *story*. To become news items, information is sometimes narrated in the form of a story. Stories are mental configurations that have closure, that have beginnings, middles and ends. They are not, Carr argues, primarily the constructs of a narrator (1986, p. 49). But while "departure and return" and "problem and solution" may be appropriate for some experiences, we should not expect that they work for all. Hence, narrative structures, such as news stories, can be misapplied to describe experiences.

Gans argues that narrative structures play a role in the selection and construction of news—"news which does not fit the story format, such as stories 'which do not make a point' or which lack an ending, can fall by the wayside" (1979a, p. 162). This happens when gatekeepers take on the storyteller's point of view and are captivated by those elements of experience that display the formal characteristics of stories. Items that lend themselves to storytelling are more likely to make it past the gate. Epstein cites a memo from a network news executive that instructed reporters on how to construct news—"every story should have structure and conflict, problem and denouement, rising action and falling action, a beginning, a middle and an end" (1973, p. 153). Bennett concludes that events often become news only when they have reached dramatic proportions, which are then depicted in news stories as "classic dramatic fare, with rising action, falling action, sharply drawn characters, and of course, plot resolutions" (1988, p. 24). Information and items that can be cast in familiar plots and themes stand a better chance of getting in the news.

THE FORCES IN FRONT OF AND BEHIND GATES

As discussed earlier, one of Lewin's (1951) central ideas is that of "forces" in front of and behind each gate and that forces can change polarity (change from positive to negative and vice versa) as an item passes through the gate. For example, an event may be difficult to cover if it occurs far away in a location where a news organization has few reporters or stringers. This negative force (remote location) works against the passage of the event into the first news gate. If, however, executives deem that the event is important enough to devote the large resources required to move people and equipment to the remote location—in other words, to make a commitment to move information about the event through the gate—then the previously negative force becomes positive: Cost becomes value. As the network spends more and more money getting coverage of the event, journalists are more likely to pass information about the event through subsequent gates and to give it prominent play in that day's or week's news.

Gandy's (1982) concept *information subsidy* shows how sources can give an event a positive force. Information subsidies are messages prepared outside the mass media—for example, by a public relations firm—in a format that the media can easily use. The subsidized message may be attractive to a television network (a positive force) if it is of high quality and requires little or none of the network's resources to use, leading us to predict that the message has a higher probability of passing through the first gate. Once in the news organization, however, the positive force might turn negative: *This comes from a public relations firm; should we use it? Can we trust it?*

The issue of forces is far from fully elaborated, however. There are at least four issues involving forces that Lewin (1951) did not address. The first is that forces may retain their polarity (e.g., remain positive) after passing through a gate. For example, the more newsworthy an event is (positive force), the more likely it is to pass through the first news gate. Once inside the organization, newsworthiness facilitates movement through subsequent gates—at least until it becomes "old" news. Our point is that the polarity of forces before and behind the gate is not constant, and there is no general rule governing direction and no guarantee that change will occur.

The second issue is that forces may vary in strength, some conflicting with others. Strong forces should, by definition, have more of an effect on the movement of items past gates and through channels than weak forces. For example, news items that are more vivid (such as more striking or lifelike) generate more extreme attitudes than pallid items, perhaps because they remain in memory longer. The strength of a news item's force should be positively related to how vivid the message is: A vivid message (such as an account of a murder) should exert a stronger positive force than a pallid message (such as murder rate statistics) and help it move through the channel and past the gate. Why? Because vivid items get more attention and interest than pallid ones, and the fact that they tend to be thought about more may reflexively lead the gatekeeper to conclude that a vivid item is more important: *If it weren't important, why would I be thinking about it so much?* (Nisbett & Ross, 1980).

A third issue is that forces may have a bidirectional influence through a gate, with forces behind a gate influencing those before the gate. The number of items in front of or behind the gate may affect the strength of forces that act on them. For example, if in front of the gate there are three messages about one event and only

↓ helps move Through a Channel + past a gate

one message about another, this may increase the collective strength of the three-item event and improve the likelihood that one of the three items will be selected to pass the gate. Conversely, if three messages about an event have already passed through the gate, this may weaken the strength of the force acting on a fourth message that is still in front of the gate. If these suppositions are true—and there is support for them in White's (1950) original study—then the passage of items through gates may not simply be unidirectional, with the forces in front of the gate affecting those behind it but not the reverse. This raises the question of under which circumstances forces behind a gate affect the forces in front of it. There is, however, no theoretical principle to address this point.

Fourth, we should consider how differing forces and polarities affect the entire gatekeeping process, not just selection. Donohue, Tichenor, and Olien (1972) define gatekeeping as also including the shaping, display, timing, withholding, or repetition of messages. By conceptualizing gatekeeping as a broader process—not simply selection—they go beyond Lewin's (1951) theory, and we can readily see how the forces around a gate influence these broader gatekeeping processes. Not only should items with a positive force be more likely to be selected (pass through the gate), but they should also be shaped in an attractive or attention-getting fashion, get more coverage, be timed to attract the largest audiences, and be repeated. Items with negative forces are less likely to be selected, and many are purposely withheld or censored. If messages with negative forces are selected, then they will be given unfavorable display, shaping, and/or timing, and will be unlikely to be repeated. Thus the nature of the forces—their number, strength, and polarity—helps determine what happens to a message once it enters a communication organization.

Part II
Gatekeeping—
Levels of Analysis

Gatekeeping Theory applies to many aspects of the lives of communicators and their messages. We address some of these approaches in the next five chapters, in which we divide the world of mass communication into five theoretical levels of analysis. These order the world into a hierarchy that can help us study communication and build theory. Levels of analysis are created by dividing up a continuum ranging from looking at the micro world of single people or social artifacts (e.g., blog entries) to looking at the macro world of countries and continents, and of course everything in between.

There are no hard and fast rules about breaking the continuum into levels; scholars use as many levels as they think will help build theory, and they define those levels for their own research. In this book, we will apply five levels of analysis to the study of gatekeeping: the individual communication workers (for example, their political attitudes), the routines or practices of communication work (such as deadlines or the inverted pyramid), the organizational level (looking at variables such as media ownership patterns), the social institutional level of analysis (including influence from government, advertising, and interest groups), and the social system level (looking at variables such as ideology and culture) (Shoemaker & Mayfield, 1987; Shoemaker & Reese, 1996).

In Chapter 3 we begin with the individual level of analysis, which generally involves studying the characteristics of people—their demographic profiles, their life experiences, their personal values and attitudes, and their work experiences. However, when we study characteristics of social artifacts—units of communication content—these may also be considered on the individual level of analysis. Examples include news stories, blog posts, web pages, and emails. Their characteristics could include, for example, volume or quantity (square centimeters, seconds, words), prestige of the medium they are from, topic, and author.

Routines of communication work form the next level of analysis, because these are practices by people who cross communication organizations, practices that are emblematic of the field, rather than of a person or an organization. One example is the application of routine news values, such as timeliness, proximity, interest, or oddity. We can evaluate the number of news web sites that use each of them, the average characteristics of writers who emphasize them, or the relative amount of space or time devoted to each.

The organizational level of analysis is the study of characteristics that differentiate among communication organizations. For example, is the organization small (such as one or two workers) or large (such as a national newspaper)? In addition to size, organizations vary in their decision-making structure, their ownership, and the characteristics of their markets. Although media organizations are themselves important actors in society, studying them apart from, for example, corporations that provide advertising revenue allows us to study each, controlling for the other.

When we look at social institutions' gatekeeping roles, we concentrate on forces outside of media organizations, such as advertisers and their audiences, governments, and interest groups. The interrelationships among social institutions—of which the mass media are a part—reveal a web of cooperation that surface differences belie.

At the social system level of analysis, we look at the extent to which a country's political or economic system controls the gatekeeping process, as well as influences from the culture's ideology.

We divide the world into these levels because they help us show the gatekeeping process in more complexity. Within each level of analysis, we can derive hundreds of research questions and hypotheses using thousands of variables, all of which are relevant in some way to gatekeeping. Looking at relationships within one level facilitates a detailed analysis but may obscure the connections between the levels, such as interlocking directorates among media and other corporations.

3 The Individual Level of Analysis

Because Mr. Gates was the focus of the first communication gatekeeping study (White, 1950), it is natural for people to think of gatekeeping as a process heavily influenced by individuals. Although Mr. Gates followed professional news values and his employer's likes and dislikes, he also made decisions based on his own preferences. For example, he didn't like the Catholic Pope and he didn't like stories with too many figures and statistics. That individuals influence gatekeeping decisions is obvious. We pass along some information to those around us and change it in both unconscious and deliberate ways. When we write for scholarly journals, we make hundreds of decisions about which references to include, how much space to give them, and how to integrate them into our own ideas. Bloggers decide what they write about and in what way. We are all gatekeepers.

In this chapter we consider how the characteristics, knowledge, attitudes, and behaviors of individual people affect the gatekeeping process. We begin with theories of thinking, that is, how gatekeepers evaluate and interpret messages, then move on to theories of decision making, and finally to the characteristics of the individual gatekeeper's personality, background, values, and professional role conceptions.

MODELS OF THINKING

Decisions require thinking. Before a gatekeeper can decide whether a news item should pass through a gate, the gatekeeper must think about the item, considering both its individual characteristics and the environment in which the item resides. Snodgrass, Levy-Berger, and Hayden (1985) outline three theories about the mechanisms of thought: associationism, gestaltism, and information processing.

Associationism is the oldest of the three approaches, essentially representing the stimulus-response school of behavioral psychology. Thought processes are conceptualized as being linear, with one idea recalling related ideas or connecting with other ideas, either remembered or imagined. A stimulus in a person's environment evokes an associated mental response. Therefore, the focus of associationism is to examine "how events or ideas can become associated with one another in mind" (Sternberg, 1999, p. 69) and how this affects learning. Many studies in psychology discuss its concepts or validity (Carlston & Skowronski, 2005; Carlston & Smith, 1996; S. Koch & Leary, 1992; L. L. Martin & Davies, 1998; Palmer & Donahue, 1992).

Associationism leads us to understand gatekeeping as a series of linked relationships between one item and others like it. When confronted with new information, the gatekeeper connects it with any that may already be in memory. This connection improves the likelihood that the new event also passes the gate. The gatekeeper can also add other information, such as the frequency of such stories and the type of event: *We have already run many stories about this type of event, so we don't need this one*.

As in most stimulus-response models, if an association is positively reinforced, it is strengthened; negative reinforcements weaken associations. The stronger the association between new and past events, the more likely the new event is to pass the gate. Because stimuli in the environment are routinely categorized with little conscious awareness, when an association is made and that association is positively or negatively reinforced, then all associated stimuli are reinforced. This is important because of the gatekeepers' (and all humans') tendency to categorize new stimuli. Gatekeepers who are confronted with many new events must use this categorization process to do their jobs; every new event cannot be interpreted as unique without experiencing information overload. When gatekeepers use categories to evaluate whether new information ought to be accepted or rejected, the associative approach can exert a powerful influence on decision making. A weakness of this somewhat mechanical theory is its inability to explain innovative thinking, leaps of intuition, or the "hunch" that a big story is about to break.

[Gestalt theory] conceives of the thinking process holistically, proposing that thoughts are not merely the sum of individual thinking activities, as associationism implies. Therefore, gestalt psychology opposes the idea of breaking down psychological phenomena into parts, arguing that they can be best understood when viewed as "organized, structured wholes" (Sternberg, 1999, p. 74). In the same vein, gestalt psychologists say we can see a form as a square regardless of how the sides are constructed, and all that matters is "a certain relationship among the features" (Haber, 1992, p. 263). The gestalt approach's emphasis on the structure of the entire thinking process rather than specific cognitive activities has identified two types of structures: *reproductive thinking*, which taps old information and applies it, and *productive thinking*, which includes imagination and new uses of information. Instead of focusing on categories and chains of associations, gestalt thinking is continuous, with insights about the complete task. Indeed, some gatekeepers may understand their jobs as creating a worldview for presentation to the audience, rather than as a series of in/out decisions. Context—understanding the whole rather than just the parts—is the frame of reference when making a decision. *What overall impression have I given about the war so far? What element is missing? What would help people understand what's really happening?*

The gestalt approach underlies Lewin's (1933) work in field theory, which emphasized dynamic connections between the person and the environment. A strong gestalt approach was not favored by Lewin, however, because he felt that the parts would totally lose their independence and exist only in relationship to the whole. He favored a theory that would include individually oriented decision making.

The *information processing* approach conceives of problem solving as a series of logical steps, with linearity like associationism but lacking the assumption that associations or relationships between stimuli would be positively or negatively reinforced. Information processing reduces thinking tasks to the minimum cognitive processing functions necessary, such as computer simulations of human thinking. This emphasis on the quantity of thinking leads naturally to the concept of *channel capacity*—the number of unrelated items humans can process in short-term memory. One way to increase the number of items to cognitively process is to group them into meaningful chunks. This is consistent with Tuchman's (1974, 1978) suggestion that journalists group events into categories as a way of coping with an essentially unmanageable task—selecting from among the vast number of potential news items those few that actually make it past all gates. If, however, the amount of information to process increases quickly, then the information processing approach indicates that the quality of processing degrades. This suggests that gatekeeping decisions made during breaking news events may differ from those made on slower news days.

SECOND GUESSING

Second guessing is a theoretical approach that explains how people evaluate and interpret messages according to their need for truthful information (Hewes & Graham, 1989). When second guessing, a person tries to "correct" or "debias" information by using prior knowledge to reinterpret the original message's manifest content. Figure 3.1 shows that Hewes and Graham's (1989) model of the second-guessing process consists of four general phases. The first phase is acquiring content, which begins when the gatekeeper receives information from a source. The message is initially interpreted at face value. However, because it conflicts with information already in memory or because aspects of the message seem false, the gatekeeper doubts the information's truthfulness. If the gatekeeper has little reason to think that the information is untruthful, then it is accepted at face value and there is no second guessing. In the extreme opposite condition, the gatekeeper is fairly sure that the information is untruthful, but there is little need to know that the information is accurate. As with the first condition, there is no second guessing, and the message is rejected.

Second guessing occurs when the gatekeeper thinks the information received may be false, and high accuracy is needed. In this condition the gatekeeper may engage in a type of second guessing called *reinterpretation*. Because the gatekeeper doubts the veracity of the information, he or she may add alternative interpretations of the information that could make it more accurate than the message taken at

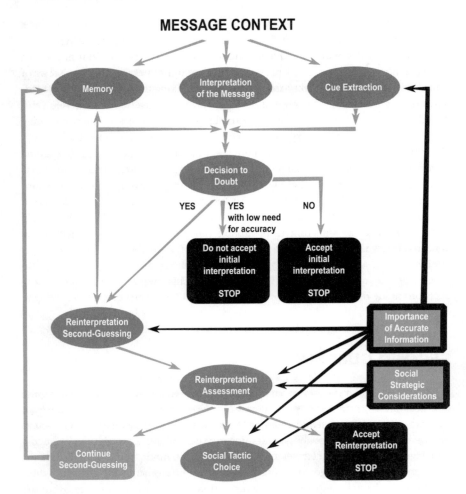

Figure 3.1 Hewes and Graham's model of the second-guessing process. Ellipses represent cognitive processes, standard rectangles represent causal variables, and black rectangles represent exit points. Thin arrows carry the results of a cognitive process to the next stage, whereas wide arrows show the causal effects of a variable on a cognitive process.
Source: Hewes and Graham (1989, p. 221).

face value. The more important it is that information be accurate, the more effort the gatekeeper expends to find a more plausible alternative interpretation.

In the *reinterpretation assessment* phase of second guessing, the gatekeeper evaluates the possible reinterpretations one at a time until the "best" reinterpretation is found. This re-working of the original information until the gatekeeper is comfortable with it causes an initial increase in cognitive processing and then, if she or he is satisfied, the second -guessing process stops. In an alternative scenario, however, second guessing continues if the gatekeeper is not satisfied with any of the reinterpretations. Eventually, the gatekeeper enters the fourth phase, _social tactic choice,_ in which additional information may be sought to verify or refute some of the various interpretations.

Second guessing's contribution to Gatekeeping Theory is its idea of the gatekeeper as an active information processor, and it improves our understanding of the cognitive processing that gatekeepers use in decision making. It adds to the elementary gatekeeping's pass/no pass decision, but it also explains how information can change qualitatively as it passes through channels and sections, gate by gate.

DECISION MAKING

Cognitive heuristics, sometimes called _judgmental heuristics_, are the rules of thumb that people commonly use in making decisions. Kahneman, Slovic, and Tversky (1982) have identified several judgmental heuristics that people use in solving problems and making decisions. They are generally and automatically applied without conscious consideration, somewhat related to what is called "common sense." These are deeply held beliefs about how the world works, perhaps hard-wired into the brain or the result of acculturation, or both (Nisbett & Ross, 1980, p. 18).

Two of these judgmental strategies include the _availability heuristic_ and the _representativeness heuristic_ (Nisbett & Ross, 1980). The _availability heuristic_ comes into play when people are asked to judge the frequency of objects or the likelihood of events: Items that are cognitively available (i.e., more accessible from memory or more easily imagined) are likely to be judged as more frequent or likely. The _representativeness heuristic_ helps people decide the category to which an event belongs: The more similar an event's characteristics are to those in the category, the more likely the event is to be placed in the category.

Such judgments are important because they affect behaviors (Nisbett & Ross, 1980). Although Nisbett and Ross did not study gatekeepers, we assume that the same cognitive processes that humans generally go through also apply to gatekeeping. Thus gatekeepers' cognitive judgments of a message affect their decisions about whether to allow information to pass through the gate. The availability heuristic makes more cognitively available messages (e.g., those that are more easily remembered) seem more frequent, thus potentially leading the gatekeeper to allow either more of them (_this information is always news_) or fewer of them (_this topic is overplayed_) to pass through the gates. The representativeness heuristic helps gatekeepers categorize information in a variety of ways but into at least two important categories: information we generally use versus information we do not. This approach acknowledges the active role of gatekeepers. They do not passively receive and watch messages flow through channels. Rather, they interpret the messages, resolve ambiguities, make educated guesses about things that they have not observed directly, and form inferences about relationships.

As Nisbett and Ross point out, however, when humans (not just gatekeepers) experience a rapid increase in the flow of information, their ability to make decisions about each message probably falls back on their knowledge about what the world is like instead of using rational decision-making processes. Such knowledge "structures" are sometimes referred to as frames, scripts, prototypes, or schemas. With reference to the gatekeeping process, we may ask, for example, if news gatekeepers use a "news schema" to evaluate whether a message qualifies as news (and passes the gate) or does not qualify as news. The nature of the gatekeeper's schemas may explain why some messages are allowed to pass the gate and others are rejected: A message may pass because it becomes associated with a news schema, or, conversely, one may be rejected because it is associated with non-news. The point is that gatekeepers almost never react to messages as unique or original; rather, messages are "assimilated into preexisting structures in the mind" of the gatekeeper (Nisbett & Ross, 1980, p. 36).

In contrast to judgmental heuristics, decision-making theories imply the conscious application of rules. Harrison states that decision making is the "most significant activity engaged in by managers in all types of organizations and at all levels" (1996, p. 46). He sets forth a process perspective on strategic decision making, which includes six components: (1) setting managerial objectives; (2) searching for alternatives; (3) comparing and evaluating alternatives; (4) the act of choice; (5) implementing the decision, and (6) follow-up and control. Gandy (1982) shows how decision-making theories can be used to study the selection of news items for transmission. From the point of view of the individual, the gatekeeping process is essentially a series of binary decisions—does the item pass through the gate or not? People take into account all the information they hold and then make a rational choice (Gandy, 1982, p. 21).

Classical and behavioral decision-making models, as McKenna and Martin-Smith suggest, position leaders as decision makers who use "rational, analytical and dispassionate" approaches, which include moral and ethical standards in the linear and deterministic decision-making processes (2005, p. 833). However, they argue that decision making is not a simple, certain process with clear phases that include problem detection, solution searching, evaluation, choice making, and implementation. They acknowledge the complexity and chaos in non-linear and unpredictable situations and redefine decision making as "a dynamic cycle set in a complex and chaotic environment, and influenced by the interactions between complex human beings" (p. 832). During the course of this, the decision is conditioned upon such moderating factors as the personality, motivations, and position of the decision makers, although they have handy resources to develop valid decision-making outcomes in many cases. "Personal resources such as time and attention are scarce in such positions, so it is understandable that managers use innate techniques such as simplification to improve their productivity" (McKenna & Martin-Smith, 2005, p. 833).

Rational and linear decision-making theories require recognizing a problem, discovering alternative solutions, evaluating them, and then making a decision according to a set of rules (Wright & Barbour, 1976). Although people are rarely so linear and rational, this sort of decision-making process is one taken by those who hope to influence gatekeepers and their audiences. Advertisers hope that people act either rationally or through some emotional process they understand and can predict.

Gatekeeping is similar to the consumer decision-making process because gate-keepers are consumers, producers, and distributors of messages. They "buy" some messages and reject others; also, some of the bought messages are later "sold" (liter-ally, in the case of the news services). An editor may become aware of an environ-mental problem in her local community. Once the problem has been recognized, she may conduct an information search to identify the dimensions on which environ-mental problems might be evaluated, such as in terms of aesthetics, economics, or health. At this stage, interested parties have the opportunity to create messages that influence the relative importance of such dimensions. The editor may assign report-ers to cover various aspects of the overall story; use messages that are available from another source, such as a wire service; or follow up on leads from sources, including public relations-initiated contacts.

Outside influence also is likely at the second stage of decision making—deciding among alternative solutions to the problem. Sources may constrain the range of information that is available or may emphasize some messages at the expense of others. As Wright and Barbour (1976) point out, if a source controls the range of information available to a communication organization, then the individual com-munication worker's decisions are influenced. Making some options more attractive than others is a way of increasing the likelihood that they pass through the gate, consistent with Lewin's (1947b) prediction concerning the role that positive and negative forces play in facilitating or slowing the passage of an item through a gate.

Next, the gatekeeper reviews all that he or she knows about the messages that are available for selection. Aspects of the decision process may include the gatekeep-er's overall impression of how useful the information is (Fishbein & Ajzen, 1981), an assessment of the probability that the message meets appropriate criteria, or even a relative evaluation of the criteria themselves. To return to the environmental exam-ple, the editor may have similar messages from a wire service, from a reporter, and from a public relations agency. If the editor globally questions the validity of public relations messages, then that option may be closed. Of the remaining two messages, the editor may feel that the news service story is more likely to meet acceptable standards of newsworthiness (because the news service has a long record of provid-ing quality stories) but still reject it because the editor gives more value to the inno-vativeness of the local reporter's story. Information that is linked with valued attributes is most likely to enter the gate.

At the final stage, the editor must apply a decision rule to determine which aspects of the environmental problem are covered. The rule chosen determines which information collected thus far is most influential in the ultimate decision, and it is likely that different decision rules are applied in various decisions. Such a clearly rational approach to decision making may not always apply to gatekeeping. In White's (1950) study, Mr. Gates' decisions were deemed by White to be highly subjective and involve the gatekeeper's own personal preferences. Mr. Gates' comments often seemed to represent a spur-of-the-moment decision rather than the linear and logical conscious process described above.

In gatekeeping, decision rules are established explicitly or implicitly by organizations, and therefore rules are also appropriately analyzed at the routine or organizational levels. The application of the rules is carried out by individuals, however, and so decision-making theories are still relevant to the individual level of analysis. Because people do not always execute rules in the same way, individual-level characteristics are important. When the rules are very explicit and exhaustive, variability in their application from one person to another is slight. Variability can be eliminated entirely if a computer makes decisions based on a programmed algorithm, thereby removing human error from the process (or at least holding it constant, because all decisions would be made using the same human-created program). Other variables that affect the application of rules include the extent to which their application is conscious or habitual, the person's ability to consider multiple objectives and decision dimensions at one time, the person's knowledge about how successful similar decisions have been in the past and how certain the person is that the decision remains valid in the future, the confidence the person has in the information that helped shape the decision, and the extent to which external sources of information are available (Gandy, 1982).

Theories about the rationality of decision makers have made a return with the emergence of game theory. De Almeida and Bohoris (1995) evaluate decision theory in maintenance decision making based on game theory and point out that decision theory has been a productive academic field in economics, statistics, psychology, and engineering. In their view, decision theory "is concerned with the identification of an action which is expected to provide maximum benefits to the decision maker" (p. 39).

Wright and Barbour (1976) outline several types of strategies through which a decision can be made: They call the first *affect-referral strategy*. The gatekeeper relies on vague feelings rather than comparing details about various units of information. The decision could be to pick the "best" message, but the gatekeeper might also pick one that seems "good" or good enough. For example, Berkowitz (1990b) found that, rather than consciously relying on news values, local television gatekeepers use their instincts to select news items. In the *compensatory* model, the gatekeeper subjectively evaluates the worth of each information item on a number of specific, weighted criteria and then creates an additive index of overall value. Positive and negative attributes neutralize each other. A television news gatekeeper might, for example, use two dimensions to decide which of the day's stories should be the lead: level of newsworthiness and the quality of the accompanying visuals. Although newsworthiness is overall the most important criterion, the lead story must have good visuals. A story of high newsworthiness but with poor visuals would get a moderate score under this decision-making rule and would be unlikely to be chosen as the lead.

The *lexicographic strategy* involves identifying one or more criteria on which the decision should be made and comparing all pairs of information items on the most important criterion. If no clear choice results using the most important criterion, then the next most important criterion is used as the basis for more pair-by-pair comparisons. Using this rule, a television gatekeeper concerned about visuals compares story A's visuals with those of story B, those of B with C's, and so on. The gatekeeper identifies minimum (and possibly maximum) desired values on each of the relevant criteria in the *conjunctive model*, and then evaluates the information items according to whether they fall within the acceptable range on each dimension. For example, the television gatekeeper has a minimum level of newsworthiness in mind; stories that do not meet the minimum are arbitrarily rejected. Some minimums and maximums may be fixed (as might be the case in determining how much to pay for information), but for others the standards may be relaxed if not enough messages meet the criteria. The television gatekeeper on a slow news day may pass information items through the gate that would be rejected on another.

In using a *risk model*, the gatekeeper evaluates the risk of losses or failures associated with each information unit, selecting the one that entails the least risk. For example, a television gatekeeper can select between information from two sources, one with a past record of dependability and the other of questionable trustworthiness. The risk model predicts the selection of the former. Finally, the *satisficing* model predicts that the gatekeeper accepts the first information item that meets the minimum criteria. In White's original study (1950), Mr. Gates rejected several stories late in the day because he had already selected similar ones. Having not looked at the entire array of stories before making his decisions, he often picked the first one that seemed appropriate.

Studying models of thinking, second guessing, cognitive heuristics, and decision making helps us analyze how the millions of events get culled into the day's news. Since models of thinking or decision making involve how human beings think and decide, their importance in studying gatekeeping is clear. Despite jokes to the contrary, all journalists are human beings and hence all would be expected to process input in much the same way. However, these theories do leave some room for variability. The representativeness heuristic, for example, gives gatekeepers an active role in interpreting messages, resolving ambiguities, and forming inferences. Even if there are only random differences in these judgments, they are differences nonetheless and lead to variability in news content. Wright and Barbour's (1976) typology of decision strategies represents another source of variation. Some journalists might be more likely to use an affect-referral strategy, others a lexicographic strategy or risk model. Could the picture of the world drawn by journalists be different from how other human beings might draw it? One possibility is that news gatekeepers use a "news schema" to decide what is and isn't news. If a news schema is different from the schema used by non-journalists, then their pictures of the world would indeed look different.

↳ if their schemas differ

CHARACTERISTICS OF GATEKEEPERS

Continuing our focus on individual gatekeepers, we look at who gatekeepers are and how this affects their decisions. White (1950) concluded, for example, that Mr. Gates relied on his own experiences and attitudes. More recently, Bissell (2000) found that photographic gatekeepers make decisions based on, for example, their personal political preferences and their ideas about what the audience expects.

Personality. Human beings have different personalities, by which we mean "enduring patterns of thought, feeling, and social behavior that characterize individuals over time and across situations" (Cervone & Mischel, 2002, p. 3). Henningham (1997) explored how the personality of journalists influences the production of news content. Journalists are more likely than the general population to have extroverted personalities, that is, to take energy from being with many people. This is likely an occupational asset. He concludes that extroverted journalists more often relate with the dissemination function of the media, whereas introverts take a more reflective and analytical perspective. The small number of introverts in journalism accounts for the small amount of reflective or contextual news items. Other similarities and differences in personality may influence gatekeeping. The classic Myers-Briggs typology includes other factors in personality in addition to extroverted-introverted (Quenk, 2000). Logic is more important when thinkers make decisions, but feelers also take into account the emotions of those the decisions impact. Sensors primarily rely on what they can see and feel whereas intuitives rely more on ideas and theories. Primarily based perceivers are more spontaneous, whereas judgers like to plan. These dimensions are continuous, such that a person can be more or less a perceiver and less or more a judger, or the person can be halfway between the two extremes.

The Holland Code (1997) is another personality typology used to assess suitability for various occupations. Personality types include realistic, investigative, artistic, social, enterprising, and conventional. Journalists usually have the enterprising personality type. They are less likely to fall under the realistic or investigative personality types, instead being better suited to a competitive environment where they strive to lead and persuade. This is consistent with Hess' (1981) argument that journalists typically are drawn to excitement.

This suggests that journalists do see the world differently than people in other types of jobs and may make different decisions about accepting or rejecting information items. It might also explain why some journalists produce more investigative content (investigative personality type), others more feature content (artistic personality type) and so on. Although persons who have certain personality types may gravitate to journalism as an occupation, there is a lot of variability. Personality typing alone cannot explain all gatekeeping decisions, but it is one of many individual characteristics that can be useful.

Background. A long tradition of media research has examined the background and demographic characteristics of individual gatekeepers (B. C. Cohen, 1963; Johnstone, Slawski, & Bowman, 1976; Weaver, Beam, Brownlee, Voakes, & Wilhoit, 2007; Weaver & Wilhoit, 1986, 1996). These characteristics include ethnicity, gender, sexual orientation, education, religion, and class. While it is true that ethnicity and sexual orientation are the result of a complex mixture of biological and social factors, every gatekeeper has a sexual orientation and an ethnicity. This makes these variables relatively easy to identify and measure, and so they are commonly used in studies of gatekeeping decisions and the kind of media content that results. An African-American hetereosexual woman from a middle-class background who graduated from an Ivy League university may go through a different decision-making process than a white gay man who comes from a working-class background and attended a small state university. To what extent do gender, sexual orientation, and socioeconomic status affect gatekeeping decisions individually and when combined? What other characteristics of journalists may be more difficult to study, and how do journalists and their audiences compare on such variables?

Weaver and his colleagues have examined these differences by comparing the background and characteristics of journalists and non-journalists. Because journalists self-select their career, as do other people, there is no reason to think that journalists' demographic characteristics should mirror the larger population's characteristics. The issue is in identifying how differences between journalists and the population affect their decision-making strategies. For some time media critics have labeled journalists as elites who differ from their audiences in ways that make them out of step with mainstream America (Weaver et al., 2007), but it turns out that such conclusions are largely untrue. If elitism is marked by high socioeconomic standing, the typical gatekeeper is not elite. Weaver and Wilhoit describe the typical journalist in the 1990s as "a White Protestant male who had a bachelor's degree from a public college, was married, 36 years old, earned about $31,000 a year, had worked in journalism about 12 years, did not belong to a journalism association, and worked for a medium-sized, group-owned daily newspaper" (Weaver & Wilhoit, 1996, p. 232). Weaver and colleagues' (2007) later survey confirms that the statistical profile of U.S. journalists in the early years of the 21st century is similar to that of 1990s. As with all averages, there is substantial variation within each characteristic: Journalists are not all alike.

Such diversity within the journalistic occupation can be studied. One way is to compare the demographic profile of journalists to non-journalists. For example, are journalists better educated, or less likely to be Protestant, or more likely to be female, than other occupations or the general population? Weaver and his colleagues (2007) did just that in 2002 and found that journalists were different from the general population on the typical dimensions. They are more likely to be men, less likely to be married, have fewer parental responsibilities, and are less often members of an organized religion. However, to discover such differences is not to say that journalists differ from most Americans in basic values and priorities. Unfortunately, such studies are more likely to find demographic differences and to make inferences about how such differences influence gatekeeping than to actually study the hypothesized effects.

Attempts to discover whether religious preference, gender, ethnicity and education affect gatekeeping decisions have been partially successful. Badaracco (2005) found that reporters who profess Catholic and evangelical Protestant religious connections sometimes write stories similar to their nonreligious colleagues, but there are also differences. Anecdotal evidence suggests that African-American journalists cover race differently than their Caucasian counterparts (e.g., C. P. Campbell, 1995), but Entman and Rojecki (2000) found in a study of 36 local news markets that there was no difference in reporting by African-American and white journalists. In the case of women's sports, gatekeepers may use gender either to promote or to reject stories about sporting events. Hardin (2005) found that newspaper sports gatekeepers make decisions about women's sports according to their own sense about audience interests.

Values. Gans (1979a) suggested that U.S. journalists share a set of eight enduring social values that guide the production of news. In sum, the values are progressive in nature, but not easily classified as either liberal or conservative.

Ethnocentrism describes the tendency of the U.S. mass media to frame and shape news events according to how well they match U.S. practices and values. Government reform in former communist or Middle-Eastern states is compared with the American system. Gatekeeping decisions use the United States as the standard against which to evaluate all other countries, assuming that the United States is most important, most valued, and most powerful (Wasburn, 2002).

However, the United States has no monopoly on ethnocentrism. Rivenburgh (2000) shows that journalists in Argentina and Denmark privilege their own national position when writing news. According to several studies (W. C. Adams, 1982; Bennett, 1994; Malek, 1997; Zaller & Chiu, 1996), ethnocentrism is especially evident when the topic is foreign affairs or international news. Journalists implicitly, and sometimes explicitly, side with their home country when it is involved in international conflicts. But ethnocentrism also causes news from other countries to be ignored—the home country is considered the only thing worth reporting (Wasburn, 2002). When foreign countries do make the news, those countries are likely to have significant economic ties to the reporter's home country (Kline, 1994). This explains why U.S. news typically ignores South America and Africa. Asian countries are included in news when U.S. dollars are to be made or lost.

Altruistic democracy represents politics and government as operating in the public interest. Because much of the world deviates from this ideal, gatekeepers generally choose stories that are negative in tone: ethics violations by politicians, inefficiency in government, financial corruption, nepotism, and racial injustice. Gatekeepers compare the day-to-day running of government with the ideals set forth by classical political theorists and almost inevitably find politics and government wanting. U.S. gatekeepers also portray ordinary citizens as politically naïve and passive—people who make a hero of any public figure who appears to act in concert with public needs (Wasburn, 2002, p. 13).

(3) *Responsible capitalism* holds that, while economic growth and fair competition are desirable, business should not pursue excessive profits or exploit customers or workers. Business sections of the print media are full of features on entrepreneurs and successful managers. Businesses that help the poor or jump on the "green" environmental movement are given favorable coverage. Underwood (1993) argues that responsible capitalism has become even more valued as economic rationalization has entered the newsroom. Meanwhile, what little coverage there is of labor unions portrays unions as a barrier to responsible capitalism (C. R. Martin, 2004; Puette, 1992).

(4) *Small-town pastoralism* favors both nature (in the battle against developers of urban areas) and smallness per se. Small towns are idealized as virtuous communities maintained via altruism and social cohesion. Media coverage of big cities emphasizes their problems, including violence, racism, and pollution, and such stories are contrasted with features of the relaxed, idyllic existence of small-town dwellers. Frank (2003) shows that journalists emphasize the values of small-town living even when the subject of the article is violence in small towns. Campbell (1995) notes how small-town pastoralism has been reflected in coverage of race issues in the rural south. As Andersen and Strate (2000) point out, small-town pastoralism becomes a value that even non-traditional news sources can and do invoke to get reporters to cover their causes.

(5) *Individualism* favors "self-made" men and women as well as those who have overcome constraints to their success, including poverty and bureaucracy. In the United States, the media look unfavorably on people who rely on others too much, such as those on welfare. The ideal person is self-actualized and self-sufficient, whereas dependent people are seen as being weak and psychologically underdeveloped (Shoemaker & Reese, 1996). Individual success or failure is typically explained in terms of a person's choices or character—the larger social or historical context is often ignored (Bennett, 1996). As Campbell (1991) argues, this sort of individualism was central to storytelling in the television series *60 Minutes* for decades. In fact, most investigative journalism invokes moral outrage by portraying the innocence or guilt of its subjects (Protess et al., 1991). Individualism is the media's dominant value; the media are no less than the "church of the cult of the individual" (Rothenbuhler, 2005, p. 91). Gatekeepers make decisions that accept information about moral dramas in which individual people act as either good or bad.

(6) *Moderatism* discourages excess or extremism in any form. The news media embrace political and cultural moderatism by outlining the contours of the mainstream

(Carey, 1988; Lull, 1995) and by marginalizing those entities perceived as deviant (Shoemaker, 1984). The more deviant a political group is, the less legitimately it is portrayed in the mass media. Shoemaker's study found that deviant groups (such as the Ku Klux Klan, the Nazis, and the Communists) were given negative labels, such as "self-righteous," "vehement," "killers," "a cabal of conspirators," and "a bunch of lunatics." Centrist groups (such as the League of Women Voters, the Sierra Club, and Common Cause) were given neutral or positive labels, such as "the club," "a nonpartisan group," "savvy," "hardworking," "intelligent," and "fair" (1984, p. 75). Privileging moderatism is not exclusive to news about political groups. There is moderatism and marginalization "in all aspects and all spheres of organizational life" (Ericson, Baranek, & Chan, 1987, p. 4).

⑦   *Social order* discourages public disorder, such as protest marches, and moral disorder, such as drug use. It should come as no surprise that journalists portray crime news as a threat to social order (Chibnall, 1977; Ericson et al., 1991). However, Gans (1979a) says that there are four kinds of disorder stories: natural, technological, social, and moral. Natural disorder includes earthquakes and floods, whereas technological disorder covers accidents caused by technology, such as a defect causing a plane to crash (see Berkowitz, 1992). Social disorder includes activities that threaten the peace. As an example, Gitlin (1980) described how the media marginalized demonstrations by the 1960s group Students for a Democratic Society by placing delegitimizing quotation marks around terms like "peace" march. Moral disorder covers normative violations that do not threaten social order, such as media calling public attention to young adults' novel hairstyles and dress (Shoemaker et al., 1987).

⑧   *National leadership* emphasizes moral and competent leaders, generally individuals, who have "made a difference" in some problem situation. Problems with leadership also make the news, as was the case when Bill Clinton was U.S. president and was caught in a sex scandal with an intern. Wasburn (2002) argues that Clinton's violation of the national leadership value explains the huge media attention given to the scandal. Gatekeepers are especially likely to accept information about a government official who has not performed his or her job perfectly. When New Orleans was devastated by a hurricane in 2005, the failure of anyone to step in and correct the problems was portrayed as a failure of national leadership. Public officials were personally attacked on television by gatekeepers, who inserted themselves into the story by voicing their personal wrath.

Information about violations of these values should be more likely to pass a gate than that which is congruent with the values, hence the perennial complaint that the media only cover "bad" news. In their study of how world events are covered by the *New York Times* and by ABC, CBS, and NBC, Shoemaker and her colleagues showed that deviant events are more likely to be covered and get more prominent coverage than events that demonstrate normal behavior—following laws and acting appropriately in public (Shoemaker et al., 1987; Shoemaker, Danielian, & Brendlinger, 1991). To the extent that deviant events represent threats to the status quo, the media may function as agents of social control when they publicize the events.

Publicizing deviance can set into action a corrective mechanism that punishes or eliminates the deviant actions.

Professional role conceptions. The gatekeeper's ideas about what his or her job entails can also affect gatekeeping choices. Cohen (1963) was the first to identify journalistic role conceptions affecting gatekeeping as the neutral reporter or the participant. Subsequent research expanded on Cohen's analysis, with Johnstone, Slawski, and Bowman (1976) describing what neutrals and participants were like. Neutrals were more likely to see their jobs as passively soaking up the news of the day, whereas participants believed that they needed to ferret out the truth. Weaver and Wilhoit (1986) and Culbertson (1983) found three roles during later research (disseminator, interpreter, and adversarial), and Weaver and Wilhoit (1996) added a fourth role (populist mobilizer) in their follow-up study. Weaver and his colleagues (2007) recently found support for all four roles.

Scholars expect that these roles lead gatekeepers to see different things and to evaluate them differently. *Disseminator* gatekeepers select information items that come to their attention as a regular part of their job, whereas *adversary* gatekeepers select stories about the misdeeds of government and business, probably at the expense of other kinds of items. Culbertson (1983) found a relationship between role conception and gatekeeping decisions. Stark and Soloski (1977) used college journalism students in a quasi-experimental design to judge whether role conceptions, among other factors, influenced news writing. The study found that role conceptions partially determined the kind of news story the student produced. Weaver and Wilhoit (1996) found that role conceptions affected the type of news stories which reporters considered their best work.

The emergence of public journalism reflects a shift of journalists' roles with more emphasis on community involvement and local news. However, Arant and Meyer (1998) show that most journalists adhere to traditional values and worry that public journalism presents a danger to the traditional professional values of independence and objectivity. Another study (Voakes, 1999) found strong support for civic journalistic practices, suggesting that journalists at smaller-sized papers, who pay more attention to community news and community involvement, are more likely to support civic journalism or public journalism. Role conceptions have also shifted with the arrival of online news media. Singer (1997, 1998) found that online journalists see their role as making sense of a huge amount of information. This can cause a relaxing of ethical standards when breaking news must be uploaded to online news sites and evaluated quickly (Arant & Anderson, 2001).

Types of jobs. Since not all gatekeepers have the same duties within a news organization, the type of job a gatekeeper holds affects how that person crafts information. Berkowitz (1993) argues that job types make a difference in television news work, with producers and news directors making decisions about what goes into the newscast. Reporters, on the other hand, are primarily information gatherers who bring raw materials to their supervisors for making decisions (Berkowitz, 1993).

Bass (1969) argued that differences in jobs shape print journalism, suggesting that news workers be divided into news gatherers (writers and reporters) and news processors (such as copy editors). Most gatekeeping research has been done on news processors, including the original Mr. Gates study. When a message reaches a news processor, however, someone else (a news gatherer) has already defined it as meeting a basic standard of newsworthiness. A full understanding of the gatekeeping process must include both roles. The amount of autonomy a journalist has also may influence gatekeeping. In addition, journalists working in remote news bureaus have more influence on what gets into their medium than do those who work in the central office.

Photo journalists and editors may differ from text editors in terms of their attitudes toward and perceptions of visual coverage. Fahmy's study (2005) of photo-journalists and photo editors revealed that most of them believe that the U.S. press differs from the foreign press in the visual depiction of human suffering, patriotism, political climate, and global reactions. The gatekeeping process for graphic photographs differs from decisions made for the majority of news photographs. When selecting graphic images of the Afghan War and the destruction of the World Trade Center in New York, political sensitivity played a dominant role, with less emphasis being given to readers' criticisms, taste, self-censorship, and personal ethics.

FORCES AT THE GATE

White's study emphasized the agency of his main actor, Mr. Gates. Since we have explored the individual level of analysis, we might expect that the agency or will of the individual gatekeeper is the force at the gate, pushing some items through or holding some information back. But as we have already noted, an individual level of analysis does not presume individual agency. Agency can be limited by the universality of human psychology, the ubiquity of certain environmental conditions in which gatekeepers operate, or the acculturation or standpoint of gatekeepers. Looking at the individual level of analysis does not assume that individuals unknowingly respond to deterministic conditions. Gatekeepers sometimes arrive at decisions consciously and strategically.

How gatekeepers think is, in some instances, simply a matter of how human beings think. Some thinking is essentially automatic. The force at the gates is a matter of biology or genetics. Human beings' cognitive processes are hard-wired in the brain through the process of human evolution. Thus, "individual differences in the functioning of these processes should be minimal if they are species-specific processes. Age, culture, intelligence, educational attainment, and other factors that strongly influence consciously controlled processes ought to be unimportant for innate automatic processes" (Kellogg, 2007, p. 80). Judgmental heuristics are perhaps the clearest example of such hard-wired thinking—they are understood as automatically applied without conscious consideration.

However, most psychological studies of how individuals think emphasize that the hard-wired brain tells only a small part of the story of the thinking process. Environmental factors play a central role. Theories of thinking acknowledge that when the information flow increases, the ability of gatekeepers to make rational judgments in the time allowed decreases. Environmental factors also interact with basic human biology. Since the human brain is limited in terms of what can be accessed from short-term memory, information processing is limited by channel capacity. Likewise, when gatekeepers use the availability heuristic, they rely on what can be accessed from memory. Environmental factors can play a strong role in the thinking process. For example, the use of the representative heuristic relies heavily on categories of news that are established by previous gatekeepers.

Environmental factors suggest a different kind of force at the gate. Individual gatekeepers are faced with an obstacle course of external factors. They generally seek the most efficient way through that obstacle course. Sometimes this means rationally calculating the most efficient path through a linear thinking process, employing a judgmental heuristic or applying rules to the decision-making process. Sometimes this means taking cognitive shortcuts to efficiently accomplish the steady flow of gatekeeping tasks, relying on an affect-referral strategy or a satisficing approach. After repeated negotiation of the same or similar obstacle courses, gate-keepers beat familiar pathways. Gatekeepers create news schema, for example, as a way of arriving at efficient decision making. A basic drive for efficiency forges famil-iar processes and that in turn can lead to similar gatekeeping over time and across gatekeepers. Variation in gatekeeping outcomes occurs when the obstacle course changes and new paths must be formed, or when "a complex and chaotic environ-ment" interacts with human complexity (McKenna & Martin-Smith, 2005, p. 832).

As we have noted in this chapter, human complexity takes many forms. Gate-keepers differ along gender, racial, religious, education, personality, and other lines. These differences highlight the ways that gatekeepers have been acculturated since birth into various social divisions. Strong socialization in a group leaves gatekeepers with the group's perception of reality. These differences have been identified histori-cally as sources of bias (Entman, 2007). Caucasian gatekeepers can craft stories that betray their bias; e.g., praising black athletes for their physical athleticism, but white athletes for their intellectual abilities and character traits (Rada, 1996). In other words, gatekeepers' rationality is bound by their socialization in various groups. Their decision making is degraded by deeply held, often subconscious, biases or, put differently, by "structural group-based miscognition" (Mills, 2007, p. 13). Group-informed biases, then, lead gatekeepers to shape news in predictable ways.

Another way of conceptualizing the force at the gate from these differences in gatekeepers' characteristics is through the lens of standpoint epistemology. Universal rationality is understood as a harmful myth, advanced as a tool of domination by elites (Gilligan, 1993). Advocates of standpoint epistemology acknowledge the "situatedness" of knowledge—"to the extent that an oppressed group's situation is different from that of the dominant group, its dominated situation enables the production of distinctive kinds of knowledge" (Harding, 2004, p. 7). Gatekeepers who are women, racial minorities, or members of marginalized religious groups are expected to understand the world differently than privileged white men. This is different than holding a "bias" because the standpoint approach denies that anyone can lay claim to unbiased knowledge—all gatekeepers are socially situated.

Individual gatekeepers are socialized or acculturated in other ways as well. They take on historically articulated role conceptions and come to embrace culturally articulated values. The differences in the ways gatekeepers embrace their role lead to variation in the construction of media messages. Meanwhile, the near universal acceptance of American cultural values leads to similarity in the kind of messages that make it through the gates of U.S. media. In either case, individuals have been socialized to do their work or see their world in certain ways. The strength of the socialization, of course, can vary. Gatekeepers with exposure to different nationalities, for instance, may be less ethnocentric than those who have not had such exposure. Whether the newsroom has a countervailing socializing influence is the subject of the next chapter.

4 The Communication Routines Level of Analysis

As Lewin described the gatekeeping process, movement through a channel from gate to gate is controlled either by a gatekeeper or by a set of "impartial rules" (1951, p. 186), which we refer to as "communication routines." Routines are "patterned, routinized, repeated practices and forms that media workers use to do their jobs" (Shoemaker & Reese, 1996, p. 105). Such routines exist not only for the news gathering, processing, and transmission process within the mass media (e.g., deadlines, inverted pyramid, news beats) but also for interpersonal communication (e.g., some subjects and words are commonly judged as inappropriate for a mixed gender group). Thus, frameworks such as White's (1950), which emphasize the agency of the individual gatekeeper, can obscure the constraints placed on individual journalists. Epstein (1973) argues that organizational values consistently take precedence over the individual values of journalists. He concludes that "network news is not simply determined by the personal opinions of newsmen. The picture of events that correspondents and commentators present is constantly questioned, modified and shaped by technicians, news editors, producers and executives with quite disparate values and objectives" (Epstein, 1973, p. 231).

Routines are crucial in determining which items are moved through the channel and which are rejected, and the distinction between individual influences and communication routine influences on gatekeeping must be made if we are to evaluate the extent of each separately. Even when an individual appears to be a gatekeeper, we must ask about the extent to which the individual is merely carrying out a set of routine procedures. When routines are more important, we should see uniformity in selection decisions across gatekeepers. Variation across individuals would indicate that characteristics of the individuals are more important. Shoemaker, Eichholz, Kim, and Wrigley (2001) weighed the influences of individual and routine level factors in newspaper coverage of congressional bills, and conclude that journalism routines are a distinct explanatory factor of news content. The study, which included two sets of surveys and a content analysis of news stories on congressional legislation, finds that routine "news values" were a better predictor of how prominently the bills were covered than the characteristics of the people who wrote them. Cassidy's (2006) study arrives at a similar conclusion—routine level forces exerted more influence on the professional role conceptions of journalists working for both print media and their online versions than did individual level forces.

A body of literature has emerged to support the independent influence of routines. For example, Sasser and Russell's (1972) study of news judgments in a newspaper, two television stations, and two radio stations showed little agreement on event selection, length, and position *except for the most prominent news items*. This suggests that routine guidelines on selection influenced gatekeepers' decisions for major news but that, for less prominent news items, gatekeepers' individual preferences (or medium differences) were more important. Hirsch (1977) has suggested that the media's selections of *categories* of news items more closely parallel each other than is the case with *individual* news items. An earlier study by Stempel (1962) found high agreement among newspapers as to what categories of news should be published. Two decades later, Stempel (1985) again found substantial agreement among three television networks and six newspapers on the "mix" of events covered by category, but he found disagreement about which specific news items should be used. Routines seem to dictate the overall pattern of events, and individual gatekeepers decide which particular news items are used within that standard framework. In contrast, Flegel and Chaffee (1971) found that newspaper reporters said they were influenced more by their own opinions than by those of readers and editors. Reporters make decisions, but they underestimate the extent to which a standard framework makes many choices for them.

In its "routine" form, gatekeeping engages norms of selection that have evolved over the history of mass communication. When gatekeepers allow norms—patterns of established behaviors—to guide their selections, they represent their profession or society more than act as individual decision makers. This does not mean, however, that individual decisions cannot affect the gatekeeping process. As Homans (1950) points out, an individual's "orders" may guide future behavior. That is, today's individual gatekeeping decision may become tomorrow's selection norm. In fact, Kurpius (2000) shows that television news departments with a commitment to public journalism have been successful at intentionally altering newsroom routines.

Shoemaker and Reese (1996) see routines emerging from three distinct sources: the journalists' orientation to the consuming audience, the external sources upon which journalists rely for news, and the organizational culture and context in which news is crafted. Each represents a different kind of routine or pattern, but, as we describe later, each exhibits a similar underlying logic of explanation.

[handwritten margin note: Each represents a different kind of routine]

ORIENTATION TO THE AUDIENCE

Individual journalists have modest exposure to their audience. Journalists no doubt encounter readers, listeners, or viewers on occasion, and news items increasingly come with an email address that allows the audience to send comments to reporters.

However, Gans (1979a) and others (e.g., Schlesinger, 1987) show that journalists have only an abstract, second-hand sense of what the audience wants from the news media. Journalists rely instead on well established routines to produce news it is believed will appeal to the intended audience. One such routine is journalists' reliance on "news values" as an abstraction of what the audience values. Journalists come to internalize these news values through a process of socialization (Breed, 1955; Tuchman, 1978).

Standardized news values are used to determine what will pass through the gate. News values work as rules to guide the choice of which details of a message will be emphasized or omitted. They are "the criteria of relevance which guide reporters' choice and construction of newsworthy stories" (Chibnall, 1977, p. 13), and they are based, in part, on assumptions about the audience. "Is this important to the audience or will it hold their attention? Is it of known interest, will it be understood, enjoyed, registered, perceived as relevant?" (Golding, 1981, p. 74).

A glance at several newspapers' renditions of world events suggests that gate-keepers' definitions of news hold much in common (Shoemaker & Cohen, 2006). But what are these news values? Although there is now general agreement that newsworthiness is multidimensional, the number and type of news dimensions seem to vary by study. Factor analysis has been used for decades to identify groups of stories that are given similar play in the media. Stempel's (1962) analysis of 156 national news stories in 25 newspapers distinguished six factors of newsworthiness: suspense-conflict, public affairs, human interest, timeliness, positive events, and controversy about politics and government. Buckalew (1969b) found five dimensions of newsworthiness: normality, significance, proximity, timeliness, and visual availability. Badii and Ward (1980) found four dimensions: significance, prominence, normality, and reward. Although proximity is often mentioned as an important news criterion, Luttbeg (1983b) found no evidence that proximity influenced news decisions in a study of 75 newspapers.

Deference to audience interests drives news in other ways as well. Market research sometimes determines which events make it past the gate (Berkowitz, Allen, & Beeson, 1996). The introduction of market surveys and focus groups to television news organizations played an important role in broadcast journalists moving beyond conceptions of a mass audience and constructing news for specific segments of the socioeconomic strata (Allen, 2005). Nevertheless, studies have found that news reporters and editors generally ignore or reject market research on audience taste or interest and rely instead on their own stylized versions of audiences (Gans, 1979a; Jacobs, 1996). Sumpter's (2000) study of the work routines of newspaper editors shows that editors construct typifications of audiences. A typification is constructed through newsroom interaction or interaction with one's immediate circle of family and acquaintances as a generally reliable guide for how the world is to be understood. Audience typifications, then, are imagined groups of readers. Sumpter (2000) concludes that editors used these typifications to help them match news items to various audiences.

Therefore the audience has come to influence news content in as much as journalists develop routines based on assumptions or intuitions about the audience. To the extent that newsrooms employ news values such as conflict or human interest, news content will characteristically display conflict and human interest. To the extent that newsroom workers believe audiences value drama, news content will be dramatic. In fact, Bennett (1996) concludes that journalists will find drama even where little really exists—"the journalist can choose from a stock of plot formulas that are used so often they become unconscious models for transforming ongoing life into 'news reality'" (p. 36).

ORIENTATION TO EXTERNAL SOURCES

Gatekeepers have no shortage of tools or avenues for gathering news. But as Sigal (1973) has pointed out, journalists rely on a relatively predictable set of routine news gathering channels. For example, reporters typically gather news from official government proceedings, news releases, news conferences, and non-spontaneous events such as ceremonies and speeches. Or, reporters can use informal channels, such as leaks and background briefings. Sigal also identifies enterprise channels, where reporters initiate interviews, do original research, or cover spontaneous events; however, these channels account for a surprisingly small amount of the news. He concludes that reliance on routine channels leads to news that is dominated by official sources. These official sources are typically government related, but can also come from other major institutions—political parties and groups, leading corporations, education, and health professions. Some institutions, such as think tanks, exist in no small part to offer information and interpretation for the news media (A. Rich & Weaver, 2000).

Boorstin's (1987) work adds a distinction between pseudo-events (see Chapter 6 for more) and the larger body of non-spontaneous events. These events include contrived activities that have little purpose other than to get media attention. When a candidate for public office delivers a speech to a crowded auditorium, the event, if it results in winning votes from the crowd, serves a productive purpose. If the candidate tours a local farm with the media in tow, the event may appear to be aimed at getting the farmer's vote but its real purpose is to get media attention for the candidate's agriculture policies. Boorstin concludes that even informal channels, such as leaks, become formalized and thus function as pseudo-events. Regardless, official sources dominate the news channels. Livingston and Bennett (2003) hypothesize that given the technological advances which allow for more and easier coverage of event-driven news—news based on spontaneous events—gatekeepers rely less on official sources than the more routine channels. However, their findings show the opposite: "When an unpredicted, nonscripted, spontaneous event is covered in the news, the one predictable component of coverage is the presence of official sources" (p. 376).

Schiffer's (2006) look at news media coverage of the so-called Downing Street memo controversy underscores that most media are dependent on official news channels. Schiffer concludes that coverage of the memo "on the news pages of large papers tracked closely with Bush administration statements. Even clearer was television's reliance on official sources, with almost half of all mentions coming within 24 hours of two official actions" (p. 506). This is not strictly an American phenomenon, however. Traquina (2004) finds a predominance of official sources in the coverage of HIV and AIDS in four countries.

As new media channels open, some scholars have suggested that reliance on elite sources will wane (B. A. Williams & Carpini, 2004). Lower economic barriers mean alternative media outlets can grow, and alternative media, by definition, rely on alternative sources. Atton and Wickenden (2005) found that alternative media do indeed make more use of non-elite sources than their mainstream counterparts. However, they find use of a "counter-elite"—sources recognized for their ideological expertise, authoritativeness, and legitimacy. This amounts to a pattern of sourcing not unlike the mainstream media.

Routine reliance on official sources can shape the news in a variety of ways—it privileges those in power (Bennett, 1996), it narrows viewpoint diversity (Hallin, 1989; Liebler, 1993; Schiffer, 2006), and it reinforces gender stereotypes (Armstrong & Nelson, 2005). For example, Zoch and Turk (1998) show that news sources are still predominantly men, constructing a world in which men are more authoritative than women. Simply put, <u>content turns out in predictable ways because gatekeepers share routines for information gathering and processing</u>.

Increasingly, according to Soley (1992), the news media rely not only on a standard set of news makers, but also on an elite group of "news shapers" (Soley, 1992), whose "sole function is to provide commentary or analysis, although their statements are never described as such" (p. 2). According to Soley (1992), news shapers are part of an exclusive group—they number less than 100 and share the same ethnicity, gender, and educational and associational pedigree. Print and broadcast reporters regularly lean on this "power elite" as a ready source of opinion, interpretation, and evaluation. Soley points to some news items that are "based entirely upon these news shapers' statements" (p. 153).

Finally, another external source of gatekeeper routines is other gatekeepers. As Grey (1966) pointed out in a study of a Supreme Court reporter, in part a journalist's decision about what to let in the gate depends on what other journalists are doing and saying. Journalists feel compelled to validate their own news sense by showing that others are interested in the same event.

ORGANIZATIONAL CONTEXT

Organizations settle into routines to "impose a structure upon time and space to enable themselves to accomplish the work of any one day and to plan across days" *to claim objectivity*

(Tuchman, 1978, p. 41). Routines also develop as a way to minimize the organizational risk of being involved in a libel suit and to protect individual communication workers from criticism by their peers. For example, Tuchman (1972) has identified four strategic procedures that journalists routinely follow in order to claim objectivity: giving conflicting evidence ("both" sides of a conflict), presenting supporting "facts" (anything commonly accepted as true), quoting what other people say or using quotation marks to call the legitimacy of groups or events into question (e.g., "peace" march), and structuring information into the inverted pyramid format (i.e., hierarchically arranging the news item with the most important information first). In short, organizations develop routines as a way of accomplishing a variety of collective tasks and goals. They rely on an interchangeable workforce to meet deadlines, fill the daily or hourly news hole, and cast events as news. All of this, plus organizational hierarchies, meetings, teams, and technology, affect the gatekeeping process.

Communication routines are well established throughout the industry. Bantz, McCorkle, and Baade compared a local television news operation with a "news factory," pointing out that news work is highly standardized, with "nearly identical reporters and photographers [used] to produce a uniform product within a limited period of time" (1981, p. 385). This factory system, the authors suggest, "reduces a newsworker's personal investment both in the segment he or she helps produce and in the entire newscast. This is a consequence of the interchangeability of newsworkers and the newsworkers' lack of control over the final product" (Bantz, McCorkle, and Baade, 1981, p. 382).

Even the presence of routine deadlines within a communication organization can affect choices. When a deadline is imminent, gatekeeping is probably limited to those messages already on hand, but when more time is available, the organization may follow up news tips and seek information that does not routinely come to the organization (Whitney, 1981). In White's (1950) study, Mr. Gates was also affected by his deadline. As the deadline neared, because of limited space he rejected many items that would otherwise have been selected.

Hence the daily task of filling the news hole generates its own routines. Gieber's (1956) study of telegraph editors found the editors to be passive, task-oriented communicators, making no evaluation of the incoming copy other than in terms of how it fitted production goals, bureaucratic goals, and relations with others in the newsroom: "The most powerful factor was not the evaluative nature of news but the pressures of getting the copy into the newspaper" (Gieber, 1964, p. 175). A reporter must write a number of news items each day, which also creates pressures. Dunwoody (1978) has shown the significance of this for the construction of news. News written by the science reporters she studied was influenced by the number of items the reporters had to file and by the frequency of deadlines. Roshco (1975) and Breed (1955) contend that a paper's news hole results in news becoming a value, i.e., the constant pressure to fill the news space makes getting more and more news the central goal for gatekeepers.

When journalists are faced with seemingly limitless information from which to fashion news, they make the task manageable by invoking frames. Frames, according to Gitlin, are "patterns of cognition, interpretation, and presentation, of selection, emphasis, and exclusion" (1980, p. 7). By using frames, journalists enhance their ability to process information. Once an event is recognized as having news potential, frames determine how it is categorized and packaged. Gitlin believes that frames are an inevitable part of journalism.

Routines are functional in communication organizations because they make manageable the unmanageable—the "task of transmuting the events of the world into news" (Golding, 1981, pp. 64–65). Routines are developed by all organizations, because routinization helps control the flow of work. It is for just such a purpose that journalists categorize events into five categories: soft news, hard news, spot news, developing news, and continuing news (Tuchman, 1974).

Gatekeepers use news values for "transmuting the events of the world into news." Thus, while news values orient organizations to an audience, they also aid in accomplishing an organizational imperative. According to Golding, news values are designed to assess "fit" (1981, p. 75). An event is a good fit with news organizations if it pragmatically can be produced, meets technological requirements, meets basic expectations for a news item and can be made news within the constraints of the mass medium.

Similarly, Galtung and Ruge (1965) specify nine characteristics of a news event that determine its chances of passing through the various media gates. Events should coincide with the *time frame* of the medium. Events of great *magnitude or intensity* are more likely to be selected, especially if they are increasing in magnitude. Events are less likely to pass through news gates if their meaning is ambiguous—*clarity* is a positive force. The media are most likely to accept news events that have close *cultural relevance* for the intended audience. Passage through gates is more likely if events are *consonant* with expectations. *Unexpected* and unusual events are often selected, as are those that are judged as having *continuity* with past events. Because gatekeepers look at the day's news in its entirety, as a *composition*, some news items are selected merely because they contrast with others. And finally the *values* of both the gatekeepers and their societies influence selection, above and beyond the other eight factors.

It is clear, however, that news values and the characteristics of events must still be processed by gatekeepers in organizations. Clayman and Reisner (1998) examined how newspaper editorial staff discuss the news values or newsworthiness of potential front-page stories during editorial conferences or staff meetings. Since the managing editor does not have direct knowledge of the candidates for front page placement, he or she is reliant on the summations of editorial staff. According to Clayman and Reisner, "what matters in the gatekeeping process is not just the news values that editors have internalized, but also what they say and do publicly in the relationally consequential forum of the editorial conference" (p. 197). They concluded that the rhetorical practice of understated support for news items positively affects gatekeeping outcomes while also maintaining collegial relations with fellow editorial staff. Sumpter (2000) also studied editorial meetings but found little interaction related to newsworthiness. He found editors mostly discussed how best to market the news.

The presence of ethical procedures and style guidelines also takes large and small decisions out of the hands of individual journalists and makes them routine matters. Anderson and Leigh (1992) show that newspaper editors and broadcast news directors make an attempt to communicate ethical guidelines to reporters as a means of avoiding problems and streamlining decision making (see also Anderson, 1987). Keith (2005) has shown that copy editors play a role in policing ethical lapses. While such ethical decision making shapes how news items turn out, it also affects the selection of news. Anderson and Leigh (1992) suggest that some important events have not become news simply because journalists are increasingly sensitive to ethical issues. Routine reliance on stylebooks also streamlines decision making. For example, the *AP Stylebook* specifies the language to be used when referring to racial minorities, thus removing a sensitive issue outside of the realm of individual judgment.

Management decisions establish routines in other ways. Bennett (1996) shows how television stations that have invested in satellite truck equipment or a news helicopter then routinely cover those events that justify the investments. Gunter (2003) describes how news items are often prepared using software programs, particularly financial and sports news where statistical data are used to generate standardized news. And Salwen (2005) describes how Google used algorithms to select news, the placement of news, headlines, and photos. Any technological innovation, once adopted, offers routine paths for news organizations to select and shape the news. According to Pavlik (2000), new technology, particularly the internet, has changed how newsrooms operate, how journalists do their jobs, and what information makes it through the gates. For example, the introduction of email created new routines for newsroom communication, gathering news, and interaction with audiences.

EXAMPLE = council

The news media not only use technology—media are technology. Different technologies—print, broadcast, or internet—may shape routines. In fact, some have noted that internet-based journalism represents nothing less than a paradigm shift. However, the emerging scholarship regarding online media does not present a consensus on the nature of gatekeeping routines in their new institutional settings. On one end, Williams and Carpini (2004) argue that the online media environment challenges the very assumptions of Gatekeeping Theory. The massive influx of online media outlets challenges elite domination of the channels of news. Gates are disappearing (see also Levinson, 2001). Williams and Carpini (2004) conclude: "Even the informal standard operating procedures, routines, and beats that determined newsworthiness have come under serious rethinking" (p. 1213). On the other end, Singer argues that even though the gatekeeping function is changing in the online news environment, "it seems unlikely to lose all relevance any time soon" (Singer, 1998).

In fact, Singer's (1997, 2005) studies of how traditional print-based news organizations have adapted to publishing news online show that routines established in the print-based organizations remain powerful in the online setting (see also Arant & Anderson, 2001; Cassidy, 2006). In the middle, some scholars, such as Bruns (2005, 2007) and Levinson (2001), note the unique ways in which collaborative news sites select and construct the news. Bruns calls these production routines *gatewatching*, i.e., "observation of the output gates of news publications and other sources, in order to identify important material as it becomes available" (2005, p. 17).

Findings suggest that online news media—whether major news sites, social or collaborative news sites, blogs, forums, or social media—have some routines that differ from traditional media. While traditional media have built routines around an orientation to the audience, social news sites accommodate the audience in a much more direct way. For example, on *digg.com*, submissions are voted on by users in a decision-making process that determines which items appear on the front page. This process is so rapid and continuous that an item stays on the front page on the site typically between one and two hours (Wu & Huberman, 2007). While the submissions include links to news items on major news sites, other submissions may include blog posts, photographs, or video. Lerman (2006, 2007) describes this routine process as *social filtering* or *social information processing*—the collaborative activities of users on social news sites to sift through the internet and find content. According to Rodriguez and Steinbock (2006), collaboration has facilitated two kinds of online networks: a trust-based social network, linking individuals to those they trust with decision making, and a vote-based social network, linking individuals to rank-ordered content.

The use of collaboration in the construction of news, as novel as it may be, still constitutes a routine. Wood and Gray define collaboration as a process that "occurs when a group of autonomous stakeholders of a problem domain engage in an interactive process, using shared rules, norms, and structure, to act or decide on issues related to that domain" (1991, p. 141). If we conclude that routines differ from one organizational setting to another—from print organizations to online organizations—then this is more specifically an organizational rather than a routine factor. Hence we return to this issue in the next chapter.

THE FORCES AT THE GATE

The production of news is a collaborative effort—not just on social sites on the internet, but in any news organization (Clayman & Reisner, 1998). An organization may have many gatekeepers, but producing even one newspaper, one newscast, or one web site at a time is a collective accomplishment. Routines play no small role in that accomplishment. But concluding that news workers rely on routines to accomplish the selection and construction of news stops short of specifying how forces at the gate let some information through and keep some out.

Some explanations seem to lean on a vaguely functionalist logic: Routines are necessary for an organization to achieve its work. As Breed put it, "the paper keeps publishing smoothly as seen both from the newsroom and from the outside" (1955, p. 333). With chaos as the alternative, organization is a necessity. In other words, routines arise from and meet "organizational requirements" (Gans, 1979a, p. 78). Routines are also necessary to meet the needs of elite sources, upon which media are so reliant. Elite organizations promote some events as newsworthy to advance their view of the world. As Molotch and Lester conclude: "The work of promoting occurrences to the status of public event springs from the event needs of those doing the promoting" (1974, p. 103). They also conclude that these needs "routinely coincide" with the organizational needs of media gatekeepers (p. 107).

Other explanations rest on a logic of socialization. As gatekeepers are socialized into their roles, they learn to use norms and rules for the selection and construction of news (Tuchman, 1978). For example, while socialization is conceived as an informal process, routines can also emerge from formal channels as well. Ethics and style considerations can be taught or policed in the newsroom. Once the founding values and norms of the news profession are internalized, gatekeepers achieve a kind of self-reinforcing solidarity of belief and action (Schudson, 2001).

Most of the explanations, however, highlight the efficiency of routines. News organizations and news workers are faced with an overwhelming stream of events and information that must be culled and crafted into news. Routines economize effort. According to Golding, routines simplify the task of news judgment—events that are more easily accessible, "manageable technically," or "ready prepared for easy coverage" than others will routinely be told as news stories (1981, p. 75). As Sigal (1973) showed, news content is much more likely to come via routine news channels than through enterprise channels, which involve additional work on the part of news workers. Likewise, official sources are often readily available, making for efficient news gathering. Human nature suggests that people will seek out and settle into efficient rather than inefficient processes.

This is also true for cognitive efficiency. Routines make for more efficient mental processing. For example, Tuchman notes that typifications are used to "decrease the variability of events as the raw material processed by newsmen and news organizations" (1997, p. 188). Or journalists use frames as an efficient way to "process large amounts of information quickly and routinely" (Gitlin, 1980, p. 7). Psychological mechanisms are at work in maintaining such routines.

Finally, we should consider economic efficiency. Routines make for faster and thus cheaper work. Routines, by steering journalists to familiar paths, also minimize risky behaviors, therein avoiding everything from flak, which might require response time from management, to lawsuits, which likely require expensive legal representation. Established routines allow for an interchangeable workforce, thus creating economic efficiencies for news organizations (Bantz, McCorkle, and Baade, 1981). The marketplace rewards efficient behavior, whether that behavior is rationally pursued or stumbled upon by accident. News organizations may forgo short-term efficiencies to craft new routines if they believe the new routines will ultimately produce more profits (investing in an investigative reporting team to enhance the organization's reputation) or some positive externality (adopting public journalism procedures to improve audience participation in public life). This suggests that routines, while a force at the gate, do not determine gatekeeping choices. Other positive and negative forces are also pushing at the gates.

5 The Organizational Level of Analysis

→ the key difference between Ch. 4 and Ch. 5

Since communication routines are developed by communication organizations to conduct their business, why treat routines and organizational factors as two levels of analysis? We see the routines level as including communication practices that are common across many communication organizations, whereas we reserve the organizational level for those factors on which communication organizations may vary. In other words, in the first case we study the effects of practices that are common across organizations, and in the latter we look at the effects of variables that describe differences between organizations. In addition, we locate within the organizational level a consideration of how groups' decision-making strategies affect gatekeeping choices.

It is essential to study gatekeeping at the organizational level. Although individuals and routines generally determine what gets past the gate and how it is presented, the organizations hire the gatekeepers and make the rules. The ability to hire and fire is one of the greatest powers of an organization (Stewart & Cantor, 1982), allowing it to shape its future and change its past. From the organization's point of view, a successful gatekeeper is a person who can perfectly represent its interests. If an organization doesn't like the way the gates are operated, it can fire the gatekeeper.

An organization is "a bounded, adaptive, open, social system that exists in an environment, interacts with elements of it, and engages in the transformation of inputs into outputs having effects on its environment and feedback effects on itself" (J. S. Adams, 1980, p. 322). As Bantz points out, organizations are "constituted in communication" and exist not as "activity systems" but as "symbolic realities" (1990a, p. 503). As an organization selects events from among the population of available events, it creates its own symbolic environment. For example, if a news editor fails to select an item about a fire, for the purposes of the newspaper (and even perhaps for its readers) the fire fails to become part of the symbolic environment. For the newspaper, it is as if the fire never happened. As such selections are made, the nature of the organization itself evolves, being continuously changed by its communication behaviors.

FILTERING AND PRESELECTION SYSTEMS

Organizations, including the mass media, act as cultural gatekeepers for the larger society, according to Hirsch (1970), who points out that a gatekeeping-type function (he calls it *preselection*) is probably necessary for all industries. "There are always more goods available for possible production and marketing than there are actually manufactured, promoted and consumed." Some organizations use test marketing to decide which products to carry into production, and the test results act as an organizational gatekeeper. For other organizations, however, including the popular music industry, conventional market research procedures are unreliable, and *preselection systems* have been developed as a substitute. Such a system "filters the available products, insuring that only a sample of the available 'universe' is ever brought to the attention of the general public" (p. 5).

Regardless of the industry, the preselection system has clearly differentiated roles and functions (Hirsch, 1970, 1977): The *artist* provides the creative material, which is identified by an *agent*, who acts like a talent scout for the *producer*, who supplies the capital necessary to get the product under way. The *promoter's* job is to create and manage anticipated demand, while the *gatekeeper* stands between the industry and its consumers, deciding which products will be recommended or publicized to the *public*, the ultimate consumer of the product. The success of online music services such as iTunes has put more power in the distribution of songs, and less in the production of physical albums. This technological development transformed the music industry by changing its profit structure.

[handwritten margin note: Example Music Industry*]*

ORGANIZATIONAL CHARACTERISTICS

As noted at the outset of this book, while the mainstream press all but ignored the Downing Street memo, some alternative media outlets kept the story alive. The differences between mainstream and alternative media underscore the important ways in which one news organization can vary from the next: management styles, goals, news policies, size, newsroom cultures, and staffing arrangements, among other factors.

[handwritten margin mark: ✳ *]* The way a newsroom operates, as noted in the previous chapter, influences how news is selected and shaped. Needless to say, not all newsrooms operate in the same way. The traditional management style has "stressed authoritarian control, an inflexible chain of command, and a downward flow of directives from managers to subordinates." It has also "stressed division of work into component parts, unity of command, and centralized authority" (R. C. Adams & Fish, 1987, p. 155). When a newsroom is run in this way, an individual's position within the organization affects the influence he or she has in the gatekeeping process (Hickey, 1966). Gatekeepers who are central in an organizational network (e.g., publishers or station managers) have the highest status and may be valued more by the organization. Centrally located gatekeepers

have more power to develop organizational policies—written or unwritten—that may influence message selection. For example, Donohew found a high correlation between publisher attitude and newspaper content and concluded that "publisher attitude appeared to hold up as the greatest single 'force' operating within the news channel" (1967, p. 67). Chomsky's (2006) archival research of mid-20th century memos between the publisher and editor of the *New York Times* shows that the publisher explicitly intervened with news content on a routine basis. The study shows how a publisher's policy can make its way onto the pages of a paper without the reporters' awareness of the intervention.

The influence of such organizational policy is not uniform, however; communication workers may interpret or perceive policy in very different ways (Gieber, 1960). Organizations that do not have a rigid bureaucratic structure may permit more latitude in individuals' gatekeeping decisions than those that have a clear hierarchy of authority and decision making. In an organization of hierarchically arranged communication workers, lower-level employees try to second guess superiors' judgments to increase their own probability of success in getting their messages transmitted (Tuchman, 1972). This is evidence of a gatekeeping process within the organization—some reporters' stories are used more than others.

As Sumpter (2000) and others have pointed out, newsroom practices have evolved over time. Many studies of newsroom management styles do not examine news content, but they nonetheless show important variation in newsroom practices. Gaziano and Coulson (1988) explored the differences in the authoritarian and democratic newsroom management styles of two newspapers. They found little difference in journalists' attitudes or perceptions, except that reporters in the more democratic newsroom got along better with their editors. Esser (1998) also explored two newsroom styles—centralized and decentralized—but saw the difference related to national factors, a subject we return to in the chapter on system-level influences. R. C. Adams and Fish (1987) identify four distinct management styles in their study of local television newsrooms: exploitive authoritarian, benevolent authoritarian, consultive, and participatory group. They found that the participative style, marked by the involvement of management and workers in decision making, goal setting, and control, resulted in greater stability and higher productivity.

Many newsrooms have embraced elements of a participative style, namely by initiating a team approach to news gathering, writing, editing and/or design. Schierhorn, Endres, and Schierhorn (2001) document the rapid rise of the team approach at newspapers. They found "those papers with teams think and act very much the same, regardless of newspaper circulation or staff size" (p. 13). Russial's (1997) case study of the *Oregonian's* use of a team approach for science and health reporting found a marked increase in front page placement and amount of science and health items. In contrast, Hansen, Neuzil, and Ward (1998) examined newspapers that replaced old, hierarchal organizational structures with a team approach. They found that journalists chafed under the new approach—reporters felt their routines were disrupted and individual authority diluted, leading to a lower quality paper.

The top-down structure of newsrooms, if nothing else, is conducive to bending reporters to newspaper or publisher policy (Breed, 1955). Policy directives, although associated with old-style newsrooms, have not necessarily gone away. Bissell (2000) found that decisions about photos' publication passed through a chain of gate-keepers, but that "the publisher's perceptions of racial equity were filtered down through the newsroom, resulting in a staff that did not actively seek to equally represent gender, race and age" (p. 90). Reisner (1992) found that even though journalists discuss stories in terms of news values, a newspaper's policy and editors' own ideology play a role in news selections. In her investigation of editorial cartoons during the 2000 presidential campaign, Proffitt (2001) found that the majority of presidential campaign cartoons reflected moderate, conservative policies, suggesting that editorial news policies do influence the choice and content of the cartoons.

Most of these studies note that policy is handed down from a publisher, but what happens to news content when the "publisher" is a corporation? The ownership structure of a media outlet is another important source of variation in media organizations. Demers (1995) looked for differences between corporate newspapers and entrepreneurial newspapers. Although he did not find widespread differences in attitudes between the types of staffs, findings suggest that news stories "at corporate organizations are more highly controlled and edited" (p. 106). Several studies have examined the effect of chain ownership on the newsroom environment and news content. Results do not paint a uniform picture. On the one hand, studies by Gaziano (1989) and Wackman, Gillmor, Gaziano, and Dennis (1975) show that chain and independent papers differ in how they endorse candidates—chain papers are more homogeneous in their endorsements. Likewise, Glasser, Allen, and Blanks (1989) found that newspapers owned by the Knight-Ridder chain gave more play to a scandal involving presidential candidate Gary Hart than other newspapers. On the other hand, Blankenburg concluded that while independent papers generally devoted more pages to news-editorial content than chain papers, "general trends in costs and revenues across newspapers warrant as much attention as the ownership distinction" (1995, p. 639). In other words, chain ownership may not be the most important factor in understanding some news content but it has accounted for some variance in the endorsement of candidates.

Differences between media outlets, whether they are independent or owned by corporations and chains, may simply reflect a difference in organizational goals. Some organizations aim to maximize profits and are oriented to the economic marketplace, whereas others have advocacy or public service goals and are oriented to the marketplace of ideas. News media that use market research to discover customers' content preferences are generally understood to be driven by a profit motivation or goal (Beam, 1998), the logic of market research being to then give readers what they want. This differs from the historically rooted goal of many news media to pursue normative news standards as a means of social leadership (McManus, 1994). But does this really explain significant variation in news content? The evidence, thus far, is mixed.

Some influence on news content is relatively obvious—research shows that market-driven newspapers use research findings to create special sections that meet consumer interests or offer more specialized content in general (Attaway-Fink, 2004; Beam, 1998). Market-oriented journalism results in "proportionally fewer items about government and public affairs and proportionally more items about private life, coping, sports, and amusements" than public service-oriented journalism (Beam, 2003, p. 380). McManus (1994) concludes that market-driven television news is less informative and leads to less public understanding than normative-driven news. Television news prioritizes images over ideas and emotion over insight and analysis. The market orientation also shows up in how newsrooms operate; e.g., there is more interaction between journalists and other newspaper workers, such as advertising staff members (Beam, 1998). But research also shows many striking similarities in content between strongly market-oriented news media and those that are not. Beam (1998) concludes that market-oriented newspapers retain a strong commitment to "public-affairs content" and "journalistic excellence." So-called hard news or public affairs news is bountiful in strongly market-oriented newspapers (Beam, 2003).

The terms "market-driven" and "market-oriented" are often used interchange-ably in this body of research. But organizations must always interpret market research, with some news media acting on the findings in ways that are different from others. As Beam (2002) points out, how strongly or weakly an organization is oriented to the market is a matter of management or organizational goals. Achieving any management goal is an organizational accomplishment. Demers' research shows that newspapers which rationalize their organizational decision making—typically corporate-owned newspapers—are generally good at achieving their established goals (1996), "including placing less emphasis on profits as an organizational goal and more emphasis on producing the highest quality news product" (1995, p. 106). The irony is that corporate-owned newspapers are less driven by the marketplace in some respects than other newspapers, apparently because they are also more likely to rationalize their organizational structure. It is the organizational structure that insulates them from market demands (Benson & Neveu, 2005).

News organizations may have a variety of goals beyond economic motives that end up shaping media content. Hirsch (1981) indicates that some organizations con-centrate on the creation and production of information (e.g., a newspaper), whereas others concentrate on distribution (such as a radio station that plays hit music). These two types of organizations together act as "gatekeepers of ideas and symbols. Cultural change and innovations usually develop within the production sector, and are made known and diffused to wider publics by the distributor organizations" (Hirsch, 1981, p. 187).

Organizational size also may play a role; for example, gatekeepers in larger newspapers might be required to apply organizational rules more and depend on their own idiosyncratic logic less than gatekeepers in smaller newspapers (Bergen & Weaver, 1988; Demers, 1994; Trayes, 1978). If the newspaper is shorthanded, gate-keeping may take the form of selecting and processing existing messages; if resources are more plentiful, the gatekeeping process may be extended to following up on potential stories, so that a story is "created" and selected all in the same process (Gieber, 1960; Whitney, 1981). However, newspapers with plentiful resources do not necessarily use a different array of sources than other papers. Ramsey's (1999) study of sourcing in science stories in eight newspapers found that more resources do not lead to more variety in use of sources.

Size also makes a difference for media chains, not for just individual organizations. Akhavan-Majid and Boudreau explored differences in chain-owned and independent newspapers and concluded that the organizational size of chains was the "major determinant of editorial values" (1995, p. 871). Meanwhile, a survey by An and Bergen showed that "advertising directors at small chain-owned newspapers are ... more susceptible to advertisers' pressure than those at large independently owned newspapers" (2007, p. 119).

An organization's culture is built by and affects gatekeeping activities. For example, Bantz (1990a) says that an "elite" organization is likely to define its staff in terms of elites and non-elites (e.g., "stars" and "experts"). Such an organizational culture influences individuals to base their decisions more on criteria developed within the organization than on those from outside—hence few reports from other media organizations or press releases would be used. Individuals in elite organizations develop a collective consciousness that results in an organizational interpretation being placed on new information (Weick, 1979).

Thus, for example, elite organizations such as national television networks exhibit a different disposition to international news than do local television stations. Foreign news is valued more by national than local stations; Kim (2002) found that network journalists think about international news differently from their local counterparts. Network journalists take a global view and tend to select international events with diverse themes, whereas local television is more likely to cover international events only when they are relevant to the local community. Kim concludes that the journalist's "mindset operates in tandem with organizational structure and goals" (p. 449). Chang and Lee (1992) also point to organizational variation in the selection of foreign news, noting how organizational differences in editorial policy and the availability of space and news services influence gatekeeping. Berkowitz suggests that the gatekeeping process in local television news is partly decided by "organization demands such as resource constraints and newscast formats" as well as "group dynamics" in news organizations (1990b, p. 66).

Other organizational characteristics, such as the percentage of women or ethnic minorities in the news organization, may also exert an influence on the news. Craft and Wanta (2004) studied how the percentage of women in newspapers' editorial positions influences the issue agenda and story focus. In newspapers with a high percentage of women editors, male and female reporters cover similar issues. In contrast, in newspapers with a low percentage of women editors, male and female reporters cover different issues, with men more likely to cover politics and women more likely to cover education stories. Other characteristics of newsrooms may also shape news; e.g., some television newsrooms have a stable workforce and some have a high rate of employee turnover; some have stable formats and some alter formats frequently; some rely on consultants and some do not (R. C. Adams & Fish, 1987).

The nature of the organization—whether a newspaper, newspaper bureau, or news service bureau—may also explain variation in news content. Fico and Freedman (2001) found that the use of sources varies by the nature of the organization. They showed that news items about a gubernatorial campaign written by statehouse bureaus rely more on issue experts, a "horse race" frame, and unattributed "reporter leads" than do newsroom-based or news service items. Newsroom-based items were more likely to lead with candidates' statements.

While one print organization may differ from another and thus create different news content, it is perhaps a more obvious point that different kinds of media have different gatekeeping routines: Television gatekeepers are more likely than their newspaper counterparts to reject news items that do not have good visuals (Abbott & Brassfield, 1989). Newspaper journalists have more autonomy in their work than television journalists (Pollard, 1995). News service editors have been found to slow their rate of accepting news copy before the deadline, probably because they fill up their allocated space early and retain only enough for late spot news (Jones, Troldahl, & Hvistendahl, 1961). Bloggers in the online media have established their own routines, ignoring traditional routines by embracing partisan viewpoints, using non-elite sources, and keeping stories on the news agenda longer than their print and broadcast counterparts (Lowrey, 2006). Simply put, some organizational routines are medium specific.

It would be an overstatement, however, to conclude that the medium determines organizational routines. Hansen, Ward, Conners, and Neuzil found that newspapers that adopted new information technology were able to locate more sources easier and faster, but those sources represented "the same power structure and news frames as before" (1994, p. 567). Perhaps more importantly, research has looked for ways in which technological adoption affects news organization (Johnsen, 2004). The conclusions generally highlight the importance of the organizational context in which technology is integrated into news production. Boczkowski (2004) showed how three newsrooms with online newspapers faced the same technological innovations but adopted them in different ways. The organizational environment of the newsrooms refracted technological adoption in distinctive ways. For example, the extent to which the traditional newsroom was present in the online newsroom resulted in different adoption practices. And the configuration of online newsrooms around either traditional editorial control or around user-generated content made a difference in how online technology was adopted.

ORGANIZATIONAL BOUNDARY ROLES

Boundary roles, as Adams (1980) sees them, are composed of the activities that take place among individuals in the organization and people in the environment.

These include buying materials from vendors and gathering information from sources, filtering information to and from the organization, gathering information from the outside, acting as the face of the organization to the outside world, and protecting it from external threats. Those who engage in these activities are *boundary role persons*, and those who engage in filtering inputs and outputs are called gatekeepers. For example, Associated Press (AP) editors filter outputs when they decide which messages to send on to subscribing newspapers. The newspapers' news service editors filter inputs when they decide which of the messages sent to them by the AP will actually be used.

From this perspective, gatekeeping amounts to a series of transactions between the organization and those external to it. *Inputs* are messages about some of the events that come to the attention of the communication organization, and *outputs* comprise the news items that are prepared and transmitted. A boundary role person selects and rejects input messages according to criteria established inside of the organization. In contrast, deciding what the organization should output requires that a boundary role person select and reject from among the prepared news items, using criteria established by those external to the organization. For example, a news service reporter is offered information from various sources. This gatekeeper selects information and prepares messages that will be communicated to the organization, using the organization's criteria. Within the organization, the messages are manipulated in a variety of ways—edited, rewritten, material added or deleted, emphases added or deleted, and so on—to become the set of news items that can be sent to its clients. According to this organizational model, a subset of the input messages will be selected for outputting, using criteria established by its clients. The news service organization's own criteria for processing and considering news items are compared to the criteria of its clients. In the same way, media advertising directors see news content through the eyes of advertisers and sometimes advocate within the news organization for priorities based on advertisers' criteria (An & Bergen, 2007).

This approach is quite different from that of the routines level. Although several studies have looked at the extent to which news service and newspaper patterns of selection are similar (e.g., Gieber, 1956; Hirsch, 1977; McCombs & Shaw, 1976; Todd, 1983; Whitney & Becker, 1982), the assumption of studies conducted on the routines level is that causality runs from the news service to the newspaper, that is, newspapers adopt whatever pattern of selection the news service offers. In contrast, the organizational boundary approach suggests that news services transmit items in patterns of selection congruent with their perception of what the newspapers wish to receive. The news service pattern of selection becomes the dependent variable.

This organizational model is indirectly supported by Whitney and Becker (1982). They found support for their hypothesis that the distribution of news service copy across categories serves as a cue for newspaper editors' selections, but there was no evidence that news service editors and newspaper editors share underlying news values. They concluded that their study "supports the idea that news as routinely transmitted in stock categories is indeed 'uncritically accepted' in newspaper and television newsrooms" (Whitney & Becker, 1982, p. 65). In contrast, the boundary roles perspective predicts such a finding not because newspaper editors are uncritical, but because news service editors know what newspaper editors want. Patterns of selection are congruent because the news service gives the newspaper what it knows the newspaper wants. News values differ, because the news service editors' news values influence only inputs to their organization. Outputs to the newspaper are influenced by news service editors' perceptions of what the newspaper editors values. Using this perspective, it is quite possible that wire service editors' news values can be different than those of newspaper editors and still result in similar patterns of selection.

In an early study, Cutlip (1954) looked at how a technological change in the way the AP transmitted information to newspapers—specifically, the change from all-capital-letter teleprinter wire to teletypesetter—affected the mix of news that several Wisconsin newspapers offered their readers. This technological change was followed by decreases in the proportion of local news and increases in the amount of AP copy run by several of the papers. Although Cutlip suggested that the power to make the change was in the newspaper editors' hands, he did not explain why a technological change in wire copy transmission should result in a decrease in local news. The boundary role perspective suggests that the newspapers began using more AP copy because AP suddenly began doing a better job of giving the newspapers what they wanted.

Although the boundary activities approach views gatekeepers as following someone else's rules—either their own organizations' rules or those of an external organization—there is still individual variation in application of the selection criteria, which Adams refers to as "filtering errors" (1980, p. 338). From the organization's point of view, any deviations from established rules for selection are seen as errors in either acceptance or rejection procedures. False positives include inputting or outputting messages that should not have been selected, according to the established criteria. This may be most likely on a "slow" news day. As Stempel (1989) has suggested, the fact that government offices are usually closed on the weekend means that less news is generally available and, therefore, more marginally newsworthy stories pass the gates on these days. False negatives occur if messages that should have been input or output are instead rejected. For example, an editor may decide not to send someone to cover a press conference on the assumption that it would be unimportant, only to find out later from the competition that something extraordinary happened.

An organization views such deviations from prescribed rules as having two types of costs: direct losses and opportunity costs (J. S. Adams, 1980, p. 338). There is a tendency for boundary role people to make more false negative than false positive errors, and studies show that gatekeepers omit, exaggerate, and systematically bias their choices (1980, p. 340).

Much of the research on boundary spanning roles has involved public relations—where public relations practitioners mediate between the information transmitting needs of an organization and the information receiving needs of the news media. For example, by surveying both newspaper editors and cardiac surgeons in Pennsylvania, Ankney and Curtin (2002) examined the boundary spanning role of medical public information officers in media coverage of medical stories. A majority of cardiac surgeons and editors believed that hospitals should have a formal protocol for handling newspaper relations, but neither group supported a policy allowing public information officers to monitor physician interviews with daily newspaper reporters. The study suggested editors understand that hospital public information officers are boundary spanners, but they resent their dependence on the hospital communications staff for information about a topic on which they cannot do their own research (Ankney & Curtin, 2002, p. 239). The public information officer must bridge the organizational output needs of hospitals with the input needs of editors.

ORGANIZATIONAL SOCIALIZATION

Learning the norms and values of the organization is called organizational socialization, and a number of stages have been suggested (Jablin, 1982). First, prearrival or anticipatory socialization involves the person forming expectations about what the job will be like. Next, in the encounter stage, the person enters the organization, the result sometimes being "role shock," a conflict between what was expected and organizational reality. The final stage is metamorphosis, in which the person tries to be accepted as a full member of the organization. The person may take on a new self-image, establish new relationships with people, take on new values, and learn new behaviors (Jablin, 1982). Or the person may leave the organization.

Some studies, such as Breed's (1955) analysis of "social control in the newsroom," consider how a journalist is socialized to learn the editorial policies of the organization. Journalists learn from observation and experience what is newsworthy (in other words, acceptable to the employer) and how to avoid libel suits and criticism from peers; Tuchman (1972) says they learn the "strategic rituals of objectivity." The journalist's socialization as a media professional gives him or her what Sigal calls "a context of shared values" with other journalists (1973, p. 3). Nevertheless, socialization can also be specific to the organization. Kim's (2002) analysis of broadcast journalists found their attitudes about international news to be shared with others in their place of employment. For example, all six CNN journalists in the study displayed the same attitudes or values about media coverage of international news.

As gatekeeping decisions are made, this context of shared values comes into play. Therefore, not only do gatekeepers make decisions based on their personal criteria (individual level of analysis) and on those routines of communication work that pervade their profession (routines level), but they also make decisions based on an organizational mindset that is the result of organizational socialization. Thinking in terms of cognitive heuristics (Kahneman et al., 1982; Nisbett & Ross, 1980), we can see that gatekeepers' judgments are formed not only by their personal experiences but also by their professional and organizational lives.

In some instances, socialization may only be "skin deep"—the employee suppresses dissident values in order to keep the job or perhaps even to work behind the scenes to further a goal. This was apparently the case with A. Kent MacDougall (1988), a journalism professor who says that he held socialist political views during a decade of employment with the *Wall Street Journal* (Reese, 1990). He writes: "I made sure to seek out experts whose opinions I knew in advance would support my thesis ... Conversely, I sought out mainstream authorities to confer recognition and respectability on radical views I sought to popularize" (MacDougall, 1988, p. 23). In response, the *Journal* noted that its careful editing process would have caught any such manipulations—an explanation from the routines level.

THE GROUPTHINK PHENOMENON

Another factor in a gatekeeper's presentation of the day's events is the group dynamics of media workers, particularly their level of social cohesiveness. Janis coined the term *groupthink* to "refer to a mode of thinking that people engage in when they are deeply involved in a cohesive ingroup" and the pressure for unanimous decisions is stronger than that for considering alternatives. "Groupthink refers to a deterioration of mental efficiency, reality testing, and moral judgment that results from ingroup pressures" (Janis, 1983, p. 9). Janis's central proposition is that organizational cultures emphasizing friendly relations among employees create the conditions in which "independent critical thinking will be replaced by groupthink." In addition, the cohesion of the ingroup may create conditions in which "irrational and dehumanizing actions [are] directed against out-groups" (1983, p. 13).

Are gatekeepers subject to the groupthink phenomenon? This depends largely on whether journalists form a cohesive relationship with others in an organization. Janis divides <u>symptoms of groupthink</u> into three categories. First, group members overestimate their group's power and morality. If journalists feel they are invulnerable, they may take more risks than usual. Some journalists consider themselves protected from lawsuits by the First Amendment, whereas others may believe that they are exempt from physical harm. Sometimes the former find themselves in jail for not producing notes as directed by a judge, and too often the latter are killed in war zones. Journalists may also assume that their actions are inherently moral, and, therefore, they may not question the ethical consequences of their actions. The public's "right to know" can be a defense against journalists' violations of ethics and provide a moral base from which they produce content that responsible citizens need to know.

Another set of groupthink symptoms involves closed-mindedness. Journalists may ignore information that counters their proposed actions and conceive of all their critics as evil, weak, or stupid. To the extent that journalists consider themselves the

correct arbitrators of what the public needs to know, they will be closed to alternative points of view.

The final symptoms involve pressures on the group's members toward uniformity. Each member of the group self-censors doubts about the group's actions, and a
majority decision is accepted as representing unanimity. If a member dissents, direct
pressure for conformity is applied by other members. Some members of the group
take on the role of *mindguards*—those who protect the group from contrary information. Pressures toward uniformity may be especially prevalent among communication workers. Journalists do tend to socialize with other journalists (Johnstone,
Slawski, & Bowman, 1972) and tend not to be personally involved with nonmedia
organizations. Editorial meetings decide the newspaper's editorial policy on issues,
and journalists have a strong tendency toward "pack journalism," with news gatekeepers validating their own selections by observing what other gatekeepers do
(Crouse, 1972). This results because journalists have an ever-present need to validate their own news sense. Bernard Cohen describes the job of foreign affairs correspondents as going "hand in hand in quest of news, looking everywhere together, yet
each one also looking on his own and hoping that his narrow channel of the broad
front will yield a different, or an original, or the first, discovery" (1963, p. 83).

On the other hand, gatekeepers may not be subject to the groupthink phenomenon if any of three antecedent conditions is absent: The group is insulated, with few
sources of alternative information or evaluation. Group leaders use their power and
prestige to influence others in the group. There are no norms about how to make
decisions. Comparing these conditions to the world of 21st century gatekeepers, few
journalists can be isolated in the world of the internet. To the extent that a gatekeeper relies on a restricted group of sources, he or she can be isolated and more
susceptible to groupthink. As for the influence of leaders, most communication
organizations are hierarchically organized, with people in managerial positions
imposing their decisions on those beneath them. However, the many norms that
exist to guide gatekeepers in handling messages minimize the influence of group
leaders. This suggests that the groupthink phenomenon may only apply to communication gatekeepers in situations where few routines exist to guide decision making.
Tuchman (1997) suggests that journalists are not able to anticipate every potential
event and message, although most newsroom procedures are designed to "routinize
the unexpected" (p. 173). In these unexpected situations, such as a highly newsworthy event, journalists may be most subject to groupthink and may thereby provide a view of reality based on incorrect assumptions. Once journalists are able to get
more outside information, however, the groupthink effect may subside.

FORCES AT THE GATES

A variety of forces work on the organizational level to influence media content. Some
of the literature emphasizes the power of those in key organizational positions to

shape media content, thus accounting for variation from one organization to another. Organizations are structured to achieve the goals of management and/or ownership. News content should thus be expected to reflect the instrumental goals of those in charge. This is the assumption behind critics' charges that news media are driven by the profit-seeking goals or greed of management (for example, Herman & McChesney, 1997). As noted above, evidence suggests that management and ownership have some success in placing their stamp on organizational output. Those in charge may be responding to external factors—for example, taking advantage of a marketplace niche by setting a goal of offering socially conservative or liberal content—in which case this is less a matter of agency than it might appear.

Other forces are at work here as well, and these complicate managements' and owners' ability to unambiguously manage content. A host of organizational characteristics—ranging from management style to the organization's size to the gender makeup of the staff—bound the agency and dilute the power even of those in charge. The management of a small independent television station may pursue a goal of national political influence, but its material endowments will likely limit reaching that goal—limited financial resources, limited expertise, limited broadcast power, and so on, are substantial barriers.

Management also faces the obstacle of getting everyone in the organization to participate in a collective task. The force typically at work here is the tendency of workers to consciously or subconsciously learn the organization's ways of doing things. Breed (1955) explains the many ways in which gatekeepers learn organizational goals, values, and procedures. Individuals conform to organizational policies not only because they are explicitly told to do so, but also through subtle and explicit means of communication. A reporter tries to fit in, feels admiration for veteran journalists, hopes to get promoted, or fears sanctions from those up the hierarchy. Socialization naturalizes the decision-making process, leading to a workforce that makes news judgments in predictable ways.

Socialization does not leave workers powerless, however; nor does it make management all powerful. Workers, to the extent they are conscious of and perhaps even cynical about the socialization process, may actively resist some management directives. As noted above, a *Wall Street Journal* reporter says he tried to use the occupation's own routines to subvert editorial policy, a form of counter socialization. Counter socialization is limited by the fact that management can hire *and* fire gatekeepers. Open subversion is not tolerated.

The socialization process can also produce unintended consequences for those in charge—it influences content in ways that management may not anticipate. Thus, a profit-oriented company, because it is strongly rationalized, may forgo some profit maximizing actions. Socialization reinforces organizational culture to the extent that it acts as a force at the gate. The organization that sets up some reporters or anchors as stars creates a newsroom that may give deference to those stars. Invested with power, stars can use that power in ways the organization does not anticipate.

If socialization is "too successful," it can lead to the errors in thinking and processing inherent in the groupthink phenomenon. Group dynamics, according to this school of thought, are so strong that individuals' rational abilities may be altered. And so we see that organizations are human-made environments which take on a life of their own, producing their own forces at the gates—forces that can both accomplish and confound the intent of human actors.

6 The Social Institution Level of Analysis

Although we have defined gatekeeping as an activity performed by a communication organization and its representatives, we also recognize that communication organizations exist within a social system alongside other social institutions, many of which affect the gatekeeping process. We discuss several of these, showing how each may influence both the selection and the shaping of messages as they approach and pass or do not pass through news gates.

≈ MARKETS ≈

In profit-making organizations, the gatekeeping process is part of the overall process of maximizing income. Markets are the mechanism whereby supply and demand are brought into balance. The marketplace rewards news media which produce a product that meets market demand (A. Alexander, 2004; Hoskins, McFadyen, & Finn, 2004). If the market demands sensationalism, that's what it gets. If the market demands a particular political interpretation of events, that's what it gets. Put another way, the news media that provide sensationalism or a particular political spin are rewarded financially, while those media who do not supply these goods receive fewer financial rewards. To the extent that media organizations respond by seeking to maximize income, markets will dictate media content.

This is simple media economics. And it's an economic model that has some empirical support. Gentzkow and Shapiro's (2006) study explores the level of "bias" in over 400 U.S. newspapers but conclude that the bias had much less to do with ownership than with the characteristics of the marketplace. They conclude that "consumer demand responds strongly to the fit between a newspaper's slant and the ideology of potential readers, implying an economic incentive for newspapers to tailor their slant to the ideological predispositions of consumers" (p. 43).

However, as nearly all scholars readily admit, media economics is considerably more complicated than it may first seem. The central complication is the definition of the media *market*. Media face a "dual-product marketplace" (Napoli, 2003, p. 4). "The media enterprise commonly sells media products to audiences and sells audiences to advertisers" (Baker, 2002, p. 11). Since these two markets do not always want the same thing, specifying the nature of the market is an important step in understanding how markets shape content. This can be made even more complicated by the consideration of other markets. McManus (1994) identifies two additional markets—the stock market and the market for sources. Media corporations and conglomerates must keep an eye on how content decisions might influence the value of their stock in the stock market. And since media trade in information, content decisions can also be driven by the need to appease suppliers, i.e., sources.

One key characteristic of the media marketplace is the number of media outlets in the market. Since the regulation of supply and demand is achieved through competition, the relative level of competition can end up affecting the supply, i.e., what makes it past the gates. Rosse (1980) offered an umbrella model of newspaper competition where metropolitan dailies, satellite-city dailies, suburban dailies, and weeklies each took up different roles within a single marketplace. Subsequent research has documented the decline in this type of competition, but still suggests some market differentiation is at work (Bridges, Litman, & Bridges, 2002; Lacy, Coulson, & Cho, 2002). For example, Hallock (2006) shows that in some of the remaining competitive markets, differences in editorial page content can be found.

Meanwhile, Bagdikian (2004) has famously chronicled the monopoly conditions in many media markets. A daily or weekly newspaper that has no direct competition can escape the "correction" the market is supposed to provide. He concludes that monopoly leads not only to less content, but also to a narrowing diversity of political and social viewpoints. The broadcast news marketplace has often been described as an oligopoly (Bagdikian, 2004; Litman, 1980; Moran, 2006; Prisuta, 1979). Each market is served by a handful of network affiliates with minor variations in the products offered. Others have argued oligopoly has become less the case with an increase in outlets, competition from other sources, and differentiation of programming. Powers (1990) points instead to a rise in monopolistic competition; i.e., many sellers serve the marketplace, but each carves out its own niche. Such a market structure leads to differences in media content; e.g., stations not only differ in time spent on feature and human interest stories, but they typically have little duplication in news stories. And, as Powers points out, some stations have lengthened their newscasts as a means of differentiation. The news media have also responded by using language targeted to specific lifestyle groups (Niblock & Machin, 2007). Not everyone is willing to concede a post-oligopolistic media marketplace. Bagdikian acknowledges some differentiation but concludes the five dominant media firms operate more like a cartel. Media firms compete on some fronts, but cooperate on others. He concludes that "major media maintain their cartel-like relationships with only marginal differences among them, a relationship that leaves all of them alive and well—but leaves the majority of Americans with artificially narrow choices in their media" (2004, p. 7).

Competition for market share appears by some accounts to be alive and well in many broadcast markets. One response to competition has been sensationalism (Vettehen, Nuijten, & Beentjes, 2005). For example, Harmon (1989) showed that local television news gatekeepers admitted to planning sensational, sex-related content for ratings "sweeps" weeks as a way of attracting a larger share of the market to their stations. Ehrlich (1995) found similar behavior during sweeps at a large market television station, highlighting a management memo of "sleazy" topics to run during the sweeps period. However, Ehrlich also found a medium market station less willing to use sensationalistic programming during sweeps.

Marketplace competition can have a variety of effects other than sensationalism. In fact, competition, according to market theory, should lead to innovation, not uniformity. Some research bears out the theory. For example, a shift to competitive commercialism in New Zealand's media marketplace led to greater diversity in cited sources and an increase in non-elite and enterprise sources (Comrie, 1999). A study of rising commercialism in Norway's news media concludes that commercialism stimulated the use of investigative journalism (Rolland, 2006).

Implicit in many of the market analyses referenced above is that market forces change over time and place. The rise of the internet as a news medium is just one of many notable changes in the marketplace for news. Not only has market competition waxed and waned, but the news media's relative insulation from the marketplace has also changed over time, as noted by concerns over rising commercialism (Kuttner, 1997). These historical changes are sometimes a function of political economy, which points us toward the role of government, which we explore below, or a system-level influence, which we take up in the next chapter.

⌇ AUDIENCES ⌇

In the United States and other late-capitalist or post-Fordist economies, the audience is both a market and a product. Because the audience's attention is sold to advertisers, the size and composition of the audience is important to media gatekeepers. Media that do not give audiences what they want will have less "product" to sell to advertisers. Hence, media rely on audience research or ratings not only to measure their relative success in offering content that generates a large audience, but also to measure the audience that can be sold to advertisers (Napoli, 2003). In its simplest form, economic theory suggests that the audience gets what it wants—it dictates content and becomes the gatekeeper. News is filled with "crime, car wrecks, kicker stories, and 'news you can use'," because the news media are giving the audience what it wants in order to maximize audience shares (Allen, 2005).

More elaborate theories point to the complications of the audience-as-market economic model. The complications begin with the nature of the audience. Direct knowledge of the audience is limited; hence gatekeepers rely on knowledge of the measured audience and the predicted audience (Napoli, 2003). The predicted audience drives gatekeeping decisions, but this process is fraught with uncertainty and hence risk. "The inability of media organizations to confidently anticipate the audience size and composition of individual media products compels these organizations to duplicate content that already has proven successful" (p. 62). In the news business, that can mean relying on crime and car wrecks as reliable formulas. Ultimately, then, this adaptation to the audience relies more on gatekeeping routines than some objective market force.

Regardless of whether the audience is a market force, scholars disagree about whether audiences can affect gatekeeping decisions. Gieber says that news selection "has no direct relationship to the wants of readers"—being instead influenced by socialization to the communication organization (1960, p. 204). Donohew (1967) found that community opinion was unrelated to gatekeeper behaviors. On the other side of the argument, Pool and Shulman (1959) show that reference group theory may explain how audiences affect communicators: "The messages sent are in part determined by expectations of audience reactions. The audience, or at least *those audiences about whom the communicator thinks*, thus play more than a passive role in communication" (Pool & Shulman, 1959, p. 145, original emphasis). This conclusion finds support from Hardin's (2005) survey on the coverage received by women's sports, which suggests that newspaper sports editors choose content based more on their own judgments about audience interests than on the audience itself. Hardin concludes this sense of audience is driven by personal beliefs and the hegemonic ideology about women's sports, thus pointing to factors beyond the actual audience.

In Pool and Shulman's (1959) study, good news was reported more accurately than bad news, possibly because the transmission of good news is seen as a favor to the audience and is received with gratitude. Reporters may fear that bad news will alienate the audience, and the reporter "may therefore distort it, either to soften its edge or because anxiety engendered by having to report it makes him less efficient" (1959, p. 156). This idea is more recently supported by Fahmy's (2005) survey of photojournalists and photo editors: Visual journalists' coverage of human suffering in the Afghan War and the events of September 11, 2001, was influenced by readers' criticisms.

Although Gieber (1963, p. 9) says that "it would be a testament of folly to assume ... that the newsman knows his readers with any realistic degree of intimacy," he also suggests that *introjective* journalists—those who take on the values and feelings of the audience—will be influenced by their perceptions of what the audience wants. Introjection occurs when the audience's values and feelings are internalized, changing the journalists' cognitive system. On the other hand, the *projective* journalist assumes that the audience's values and feelings are similar to his or her own. Projective gatekeepers follow their own judgments, assuming that the audience will agree. Introjective gatekeepers—probably fewer in number—"catch" the concerns of their audiences, and gatekeeping is then more influenced by the gatekeepers' perceptions of what the audience wants than by the gatekeepers' own values and feelings.

Organizational theories about boundary activities (J. S. Adams, 1980) suggest that gatekeepers who perform *output* tasks—those who decide which news items, from among those available, are sent to the audience—make selection decisions based on criteria established by those external to the communication organization, including audiences. Therefore, gatekeepers' perceptions about what the audience wants should be important in guiding their decisions. This idea was offered earlier by Westley and MacLean (1957). Media gatekeepers (represented by the letter C in Figure 1.3, page 17) transmit messages that give the audience what it needs or wants. Why? Because a mass medium survives only to the extent that it serves the audience's needs. Many media are in competition with one another for the audience's attention; the one that best meets the audience's needs is most successful (also see the section on markets in this chapter). The media act as *agents* for the audience, providing the audience with "a more extended environment" (Westley & MacLean, 1957, p. 34). Journalists justify their foreign affairs gatekeeping choices by saying "we print what we know the public will want to read," even though their ideas of what the public wants vary dramatically (Cohen, 1963, p. 125).

In his investigation of U.S. television journalists' attitudes and selection criteria regarding international news, Kim (2002) found that local journalists select events based on audience demands, choosing international news with a local angle. International news is an endangered species as journalists use audience demand to justify their inadequate reporting of international news—audiences are not interested in international news, and so there is no need to cover it.

ADVERTISERS

For mass media that are supported primarily by commercial sponsorship, advertisers can exert substantial influence on what gets into the channel, including what is selected and how it is shaped. As Altschull asserts: "The content of the press is directly correlated with the interests of those who finance the press. The press is the piper, and the tune the piper plays is composed by those who pay the piper" (1984, p. 254). Mass media gatekeepers—both entertainment and news—frequently select shows both to attract a large audience and to maximize advertising dollars. However, the audience has less power than it may seem.

As we've already noted, both audiences and advertisers are markets for the media. But audiences are generally less well equipped than advertisers to influence content. Baker (2002) conceptualizes advertisers' influence as differential, based on their budget, knowledge of media routines, and how the topic is covered. "Having an audience that values the product in multiple ways but with different degrees of knowledge about how well it performs each is a context that enhances the opportunity for the other purchaser, the advertiser, to influence content away from what the audience wants in the dimensions about which the audience finds knowledge most difficult to obtain" (Baker, 2002, p. 14). Thus, the audience does

It is a way they make money [handwritten margin note]

not always get what it wants. Advertisers, on the other hand, have substantially more power.

In fact, "the audience" is a misnomer. The move away from conceptualizing the audience as a mass market to viewing it as multiple smaller targeted markets means that some members of the larger audience are more important than others (Baker, 2002). Advertisers value audiences with purchasing power and young audiences, who generally have fewer brand loyalties (Turow, 1997). Some newspapers have cultivated high-income readers by "intentionally structuring our news content primarily for [them]. [They] also market selectively, concentrating circulation drives in the right neighborhoods—those predicted to yield high demographics" (Fink, 1989, p. 40). The result, according to Turow, is "lifestyle-specific news (and) information" (p. 4) and "a portrayal of the world that is more the ideal vision of the corporate establishment sponsoring them than a reflection of competing visions of various publics" (p. 3). Again, advertisers are left with more power to shape content. How do they use that power?

Advertising can directly influence news content when advertisers use the power of the purse to make demands. There is evidence that many newspapers delete or change news items under pressure from advertisers, real estate and automobile advertisers having the most influence, probably because they account for a big chunk of newspaper ads (Soley, 2002). The pressure is much the same in broadcast journalism, although network correspondents report relatively minimal pressure (Price, 2003). Nevertheless, the pressure takes a variety of forms. The simplest, and by some accounts the most common, is for advertisers to withdraw ads while citing disagreeable news content (Kaniss, 1991). Other forms of pressure include: organizing advertiser boycotts of media, using control of retail spaces to hinder distribution, and establishing ad policies which warn media in advance about the types of content that the advertiser finds problematic. The consequences of advertiser pressure on gatekeeping are many (Soley, 2002): news items may be pulled, the offending content is buried where it is least likely to be seen, offending reporters are fired, positive or puff stories are run, entire sections—such as automotive sections—can be handed off to the advertising department, and gatekeepers engage in self-censorship.

Types of pressure from advertisers

With industry polls showing direct advertiser pressure is widespread (Soley, 2002), advertisers, even if they are small in number, have created a culture of influence, meaning that the card of direct pressure only occasionally must be played. Indeed, when a reporter is fired for angering advertisers, the action becomes part of the lore of the newsroom, which socializes gatekeepers to avoid angering advertisers in the future. Note that countervailing heroic tales of standing up to advertiser demands can also be told in newsrooms (Kaniss, 1991). Gatekeepers have been socialized to accept advertisers' interests as the media's own best interest or even as the public interest. Flattering news coverage can be justified as supporting hometown merchants or the local economy. Or news web site in-text links to advertiser web sites can be defended as simply providing audiences with information (Craig, 2007).

The force of socialization may come out of the shadows only when the advertising spigot is turned off. A case study of *Ms.* magazine shows that its editors were surprised to learn about the many subtle ways advertising had influenced content—a realization that fully came only when the magazine decided to do away with advertising (Cunningham & Haley, 2000). Even if the pressure is not direct, editorial gatekeepers make decisions knowing that advertising is responsible for the financial health of their publication. Bad news about advertisers is slighted, good news about advertisers is magnified, and news that puts audiences in a buying mood becomes more valuable (Baker, 2002). Gatekeepers can also agree to "advertising-disguised-as-news in advertorials" (Lacher & Rotfeld, 1994, p. 288) or so-called feature ads—those designed to look like editorial content (Cameron & Haley, 1992).

The magazine industry has its own unique record of pressure from advertisers. Hays and Reisner (1990) found widespread and consistent pressure from advertisers on farm-related magazines. As they point out (see also Soley, 2002), specialized media typically come with a narrow advertising base, where one or two advertisers account for a large percentage of magazine income. This makes advertiser displeasure more important than it might be at consumer magazines, with their more diversified advertising bases (p. 941).

Consumer magazines operate under a different kind of pressure. For example, Kessler's (1989) study showed that gatekeepers at women's magazines apparently have self-imposed constraints against running stories about the health risks of smoking. The study investigated the editorial and advertising content of six major women's magazines (e.g., *Cosmopolitan* and *Good Housekeeping*) to see whether the presence or absence of tobacco advertising would relate to the amount of editorial content about the health hazards of smoking—"the number one cancer killer of women" (Kessler, 1989, p. 319). Although women's health was a major topic in the magazines, there was almost no editorial content about any health hazards of smoking, even in *Good Housekeeping*, which did not accept tobacco advertising. The *GH* health editor told Kessler that plans for coverage of the health hazards of smoking were stopped several times because lung cancer was seen as controversial and not appealing to the audience (1989, p. 322). As Kessler pointed out, even though *GH* could not lose tobacco advertising income, it might lose advertising revenue from non-tobacco subsidiaries of the tobacco conglomerates.

In a different kind of deference to advertisers, *Vanity Fair*'s editor pulled the magazine out of an economic slump in 1984 by running articles on fashion designers who were the magazine's major advertisers. The April 1989 issue carried 37 pages of ads from people who had previously been given favorable editorial coverage in the magazine (Lazare, 1989).

Advertiser pressure can come in the form of quid pro quo agreements—news media commit to editorial space for advertisers based on the purchase of advertising space (Gossage, Rotzoll, Graham, & Mussey, 1986). Advertiser "pressure" can also be formalized via contractual means, as is sometimes the case with internet search engines. Hargittai (2004) points out the role of commercial interests in categorizing and presenting online content to users: Web sites can achieve good positioning by paying a fee. Commercial sites may show up right on the top of the results list even if they don't have much relevant information for the search keywords. This is not a new phenomenon. Nineteenth century newspapers had contracts with advertisers to provide positive news coverage or to run "reading notices," ads made to look like news content (Baldasty, 1992). In the early days of radio, whole programs were contractually developed and produced by advertising agencies to provide a showcase for their products. Advertiser control over television's daytime soap operas remains strong (Cantor & Pingree, 1983).

Advertisers do not necessarily have to breach a high "wall of separation" between the advertising and editorial functions of the media organization. On one front, corporate advertising directors are, in their boundary spanning role, surrogates for advertising clients. An and Bergen's (2007) study of advertising directors shows their willingness to, among other things, use regular advertisers as expert news sources and display advertisers' logos prominently in news photos. In addition, since management has to be complicit for advertiser influence to work, the relationship of owners and managers to advertisers is an important empirical detail. Advertisers may have the ear of publishers, given the common circles in which they move, such as both belonging to local chambers of commerce (Soley, 2002). Advertisers already reside within the walls of media organizations by virtue of corporate ownership of media and their membership on boards of directors (J. Cohen & Solomon, 1995; Croteau & Hoynes, 2006). As Bagdikian (2004) has documented, some media corporations have flirted with lifting the wall of separation altogether. A new CEO of the Times Company decreed that a representative of the advertising department would have a direct say about news content, a decree that had to be rescinded despite early approval by stockholders. The factors cited point to closely related organizational level factors. In fact, some studies have found openness to advertiser demands dependent in some ways on organizational characteristics (An & Bergen, 2007; Kaniss, 1991).

⇆ FINANCIAL MARKETS ⇆

Media organizations get their money not only from advertisers; capital also comes from stock dividends and sales and from financing. Whereas media companies were once family-owned businesses, they are now regularly part of larger conglomerates publicly traded on the stock market. Up to 50 percent of newspaper circulation in the U.S. comes from publicly traded media-related conglomerates (Cranberg, Bezanson, & Soloski, 2001). Boards of directors are bound by law to maximize stock value for stockholders, typically under the watchful eye of large institutional investors. Thus, the major media conglomerates expect to see the value of their stock increase on the stock market, and this simultaneously increases the income of top executives through their ownership of stocks (Bagdikian, 2004). In addition to stock options, executives earn bonuses based on profit margins. However, the real media owners, according to Cranberg, Bezanson, and Soloski (2001), are the stockholders. Public ownership via the stock market provides instant feedback about the economic health of the organization and leads them to focus more on short-term decisions than long-term goals. The change in value of a corporation's stock is a clear example of Lewin's idea that positive and negative forces facilitate and constrain movement of events through gates. Public ownership breeds structural and human gatekeepers who are highly sensitive to such data.

Corporations' and conglomerates' primary goal is to make more money for stockholders, which often involves buying other companies. To the extent that the acquisition process involves borrowing money, the organization needs the cooperation of financial suppliers and must maintain a strong credit rating. The less solvent the organization is, the more influence financial institutions have, increasing their presence on the organization's board of directors. As long-term debt and interest payments increase, the board of directors acts to stabilize its sources of cash, which in media companies comes mainly from advertising revenue (An & Jin, 2004).

Such forces create their own pathways of influence on content, including a change in the relative market orientation of the news media. When increasing cash flow becomes a major goal, there is no insulation from market demands. Wall Street's influence therefore is largely a matter of pushing media firms to be more oriented to the marketplace (An & Jin, 2004). That can include making media organizations more risk averse, subsequently relying on standard genres and eschewing journalistic innovations (Napoli, 2003).

Cranberg and colleagues' (2001) study of publicly traded media firms concludes that a parent company's financial goals affect virtually everything in a news medium, from staff size and quality to the type and amount of news. Such decisions often come after research about the audience and subsequent market segmentation. For example, a case study of a Canadian news organization by Edge (2003) provides compelling evidence that financial markets influenced both the organization and the news it produced. Shares in a company once controlled by the Southam family became widely distributed, allowing a rival known for its tight budgets to gradually buy the stock. But the acquisition of the Southam newspapers so strained the rival's financial stability that it eventually sold them to yet another company. According to Edge, the cycle then repeated itself, because the third firm bought the newspaper company's shares at the height of a stock market boom—market forces precipitated staff cuts, affecting news coverage. In the end, the new owners asserted "overt political motives" at the newspapers (p. 234).

⇒ SOURCES ⇒

In Westley and MacLean's (1957) model (Figure 1.3), media are the channels through which information passes on its way from the source to the audience.

However, as Sigal points out, channels are also "the paths by which information reaches the reporter" (1973, p. 120). Because in many cases media workers do not themselves experience events, the version of reality as processed by sources is extremely influential in determining what comes to the attention of the media.

As we noted in Chapter 4, the procedures that journalists use to identify and select sources are an important part of the gatekeeping process (see also Chibnall, 1975, 1981). But, the sources' own vested interests also affect what they make available to the media worker. Economically and politically powerful sources have more access to the media and, therefore, more opportunity to insert messages into media channels (Gans, 1979b). Grabe, Zhou, and Barnett (1999) conclude that white male elite sourcing still dominates television news magazine programs (see also Zoch & Turk, 1998). Although only about 10 percent of sources are affiliated with government, sources from academia and business appear more than five times as often as working class people in the news magazine programs. Resource-poor groups often have to resort to deviant acts to attract media attention (Gitlin, 1980; Goldenberg, 1975). Such events enter the news channel with a positive force, but the attention the groups get in the news tends to delegitimize them by emphasizing how the groups break laws or behavioral norms, challenge existing power groups, and/or are odd (Shoemaker, 1984). Advocates of civic journalism have promoted the use of non-elite sources in regular news coverage; however, at least one study concludes that the increase of non-elite sourcing has been so light that readers do not really notice (Massey, 1998). To the extent that journalists rely on elite sources, such as government officials or experts, gatekeepers are vulnerable to the agendas of elites (T. Koch, 1991).

Sources may either facilitate or constrain the movement of information through channels they control, thus affecting the introduction of an item into the media channel or into a section of the channel. The extent to which the source's and journalist's frames of reference overlap determines the formality of communication between the source and journalist (Gieber & Johnson, 1961). When reporter and source frames of reference are completely separate, communication is more formal than when there is overlap. Sources believe that reporters should be "open" gatekeepers, essentially just passing unmediated information straight through the gate. Reporters, on the other hand, want sources to be "open-door" informants, giving the reporter all the information available and letting the journalist decide whether and how information passes through the gate (Gieber & Johnson, 1961, p. 297).

A coorientational model (Dyer & Nayman, 1977; McLeod & Chaffee, 1973; Shin & Cameron, 2005; Stegall & Sanders, 1986) may also be used to study relationships between journalists and sources. Both sources and gatekeepers benefit from their mutual relationship, with the sources getting access to target audiences through the mass media and gatekeepers getting access to someone who can regularly provide credible information. The gatekeeper's need for regular, credible information results in a dependence on bureaucratic sources (Gandy, 1982), but identification with the source may be an important contingent condition for the extent to which the source controls content (Donohue, Tichenor, & Olien, 1972). For example, gatekeepers who identify with the police are more likely to allow the police to influence what passes through the gates.

We should not assume, however, that gatekeepers uncritically accept all information provided by sources. Kuhn (2002) concludes that the media are not merely passive recipients of information from sources; instead they may critically scrutinize sources' definitions of issues or events. Because sources have their own agendas to push, gatekeepers have to actively filter out falsehoods and interpret messages in light of what is known about the source, event, or issue (see "second guessing," Hewes & Graham, 1989). According to the coorientational model, journalists' suspicions of sources may or may not produce accurate perceptions of information. Journalists and sources may arrive at a consensus regarding information; at a false consensus when journalists and sources think they agree but really do not; or at a "false dissensus" when journalists and sources "believe that they disagree more than they actually do" (Shin & Cameron, 2005, p. 322).

⌣ PUBLIC RELATIONS ⌣

Public relations departments and personnel are often the means for how sources and organizations get media attention. All kinds of organizations conduct public relations campaigns, targeting the mass media with news releases and media kits, setting up interviews or news conferences, organizing events, providing photos or video, maintaining online newsrooms and blogs, and generally doing what's necessary to generate publicity for an organization. Public relations efforts also help organizations that are not able to afford paid advertising, although the cost of a major public relations campaign rivals that of advertising (Levine, 2008; Wilson, 2004). Media gatekeepers, of course, are under no obligation to use any of the materials that public relations firms or divisions generate or to participate in public relations activities. In fact, gatekeepers routinely treat public relations efforts with suspicion (Sallot & Johnson, 2006).

Surveys of journalists and public relations practitioners find that both professions perceive a strong influence of public relations on the news (Sallot & Johnson, 2006; Sallot, Steinfatt, & Salwen, 1998). Public relations practitioners see a somewhat greater influence of public relations in shaping the news agenda than do journalists, but even journalists on average estimate that 44 percent of news content is influenced by public relations activities (Sallot & Johnson, 2006). Studies using content analysis put the percentage at over 50 percent (VanSlyke Turk, 1986b). Even with huge numbers of reporters and editors, large newspapers such as the *New York Times* and the *Washington Post* obtain more than half of their daily materials from press releases and press conferences by government agencies, public relations firms, and interest groups (McCombs, 1994). However, in broadcast news, where the news hole is much smaller, the use of news releases is lower (Berkowitz, 1990a).

The news (or press) release has been at the heart of public relations efforts for many decades (Scott, 2007), but these public relations initiatives have evolved over time. Organizations and groups maintain online newsrooms, which can provide news releases, organizational histories and mission statements, policy statements or papers, and an organization's other publications (Reber & Kim, 2006). They may also contain blogs by organizational staff and leadership (Gillmor, 2004; Holtz, 2002). Organizations that fail to offer a full array of online public relations initiatives stand to lose ground to those that do (Christ, 2005). Thus, one effect of expanded public relations activities is the increased likelihood of affecting the media's news agenda—a likelihood that comes at the expense of poorer organizations.

Organizations, particularly political organizations, aim to "manage" the news. Political campaigns manage the news by tightly controlling media access to candidates and by creating events for the press to report (Norris, Curtice, Sanders, Scammell, & Semetko, 1999). To the extent that political organizations can script a campaign, they give reporters little else to report on other than the script (Skewes, 2007). Ironically, the more scripted the campaign, the more reporters look for the nonscripted moments. In turn, "the campaign communication game becomes ever more control oriented and managed" (Bennett, 2005, p. 368).

Another way to get a message across is by designing and holding events that the news media will cover, such as demonstrations and protests (Wolfsfeld, 1984). Pseudo-events occur only because someone planned or incited them, and their primary purpose is to get media coverage (Boorstin, 1971). The pseudo-event lasts only as long as the media remain to cover it and is generally timed to coincide with media deadlines, for example, the last moment in which something can happen in order for it to appear on the evening television news show. Twenty-four hour television news operations also organize their time schedules to produce content for specific target audiences, and pseudo-events are scheduled to reach specific viewers. The pseudo-event fills both the group's need to reach the public and the media's need for news. Well-managed pseudo-events include good visuals, which makes them particularly attractive to television and streaming video on the internet.

To the extent that these campaigns are successful, media content is affected directly (through the publication of press releases) and indirectly (by calling the media's attention to the problem). Public relations efforts can succeed for a variety of reasons. Gandy (1982) argues that public relations materials operate as an information subsidy for news organizations. Public relations agencies that gather information, write newsworthy stories, or provide pictures hold down costs for the news organizations. Curtin's (1999) research bears out Gandy's point. Newspapers create specialized sections as a way to attract certain types of readers, but often do so without additional financial resources. Public relations material often fills the void. But as Curtin (1999) points out, editors, particularly at large chain-owned papers, still harbor significant distrust of public relations products and hesitate to use them in other sections of the newspaper.

Public relations practitioners also impact media content by maintaining access to media gatekeepers. Practitioners cultivate professional relationships with reporters and create a gatekeeping channel that can be used when the occasion arises (Howard & Mathews, 2006). For example, campaign news secretaries keep in close contact with reporters to correct mistakes, refute charges from opponents, and provide constant interpretation of campaign events (Bennett, 2005). Lee and Berkowitz (2004) found a similar practice in Korea, which they call "third gatekeeping." Korean public relations practitioners screen a newspaper's first edition to identify problems. When they find problems in articles, they call newspaper reporters or even personally visit the newspaper office to address the problem. However, in her study of public relations and media access, Yoon (2005) found that public relations expertise does not necessarily lead to increased media access.

⸗ GOVERNMENT ⸚

Even in a late capitalist society where markets, rather than governments, are seen as the most legitimate means of regulating the media, government nevertheless influences gatekeeping. In fact, government institutions and actors have a variety of means at their disposal. They engage in news management or public relations efforts, but they also set and apply a variety of laws, policies, and regulations aimed at the media.

The kind of news management used by political campaigns has also been in evidence in government–media relations (Cook, 1998). In Rivers' analysis of "the news managers" in Washington, D.C., he writes that the "control of information is central to power" to make his point about how the government attempts to control the mass media by managing the flow of information (1965, p. 129). This is clearly not a new phenomenon. Franklin Roosevelt was so savvy in his understanding of news that Arthur Krock of the *New York Times* said: "He could qualify as the chief of a great copy desk" (cited in Rivers, 1965, p. 134). For all of Harry Truman's being known as honest and open, the size of the Executive Branch's "information" and "editorial" jobs doubled during his presidency. They doubled again during Dwight Eisenhower's first four years in the office, and his chief publicist, James Hagerty, made decisions about what would and would not be released (see also Foerstel, 1998). This is what news management is about—government officials decide which information is doled out to the news media and what is not. This is not an American phenomenon. Research shows similar management of the news in Great Britain, Spain (Sanders, Bale, & Canel, 1999), and India (Thussu, 2002).

In the case of Britain, recent governments have actively formulated media strategies to influence the news agenda (Kuhn, 2002). For example, the first Blair government set up a Strategic Communications Unit at Downing Street, which included former journalists, to coordinate its news management activities. The Blair government conducted both proactive and reactive media strategies, with the former playing a major role in its news management. Proactive media strategies include "creating news stories, staging events for media coverage and controlling the release of information," whereas reactive strategies are intended to contain the impact of news stories criticizing the government (Kuhn, 2002, p. 49).

The American military, particularly since the Vietnam War, has actively sought to manage news coverage. The military has restricted movement of the press corps while at the same time feeding reporters with a constant flow of images supportive of military perspectives (Perlmutter, 1998). The U.S. Defense Department prohibited media coverage of coffins of the war dead in Iraq. Similar controls were placed on photojournalists in the first Persian Gulf war (Ottosen, 1992). Later, the military controlled access to the battlefield by "embedding" reporters with troops. "Newspaper coverage by embedded reporters during the invasion and occupation [of Iraq] were significantly more positive toward the military than those of nonembedded reporters" (Haigh et al., 2006, p. 149).

Gatekeepers can also demonstrate some resistance to government attempts to dictate coverage. Althaus' (2003) examination of evening news broadcasts during the 1990–91 Persian Gulf crisis found that information sources outside of the American government produced more criticism of American involvement in the Gulf War than the usual politicians who act as official sources. Althaus concluded that journalists exercised considerable discretion in giving voice to oppositional opinions, going beyond previous source patterns.

Like interest groups, government bodies can also resort to advertisements when other forms of news management seem less likely to succeed. Advertising works as a form of inter-media agenda setting and as information subsidies (Young, 2006). Great Britain and Australia have established traditions of government advertising (Deacon & Golding, 1994). In fact, the Australian government is the country's largest advertiser (Young, 2006). Such expenditures give governments the same power as big corporate advertisers—they can threaten to withdraw advertising when gatekeepers displease those in government. Such a threat can be made even with American-style First Amendment protections in place (Bernabe-Riefkohl, 2000).

In the United States, where the First Amendment creates a barrier to government regulation of media, law and public policy still influence news content. Libel law, for example, applies across the mass media and establishes a real possibility of a lawsuit should gatekeepers publish or transmit information that wrongly harms someone's reputation (Carter, Franklin, & Wright, 2005). Although libel law strongly favors the news media, news organizations' lawyers are often loathe to green light any news content that even approaches gray areas of the law (Barendt, 1997). And since libel laws in other countries offer less protection than in the U.S., multinational news corporations in the U.S. may hold back on news content that spans borders. Likewise, laws regarding invasion of privacy set boundaries on media behaviors, shutting the gate to some news content. That said, journalists often operate with little or no sense that their actions might precipitate legal action (Skolnick, 1968; Voakes, 1998). One other form of U.S. content regulation has usually been minor, but became a major political and legal issue during the George W. Bush presidency. The law stipulates that the identity of undercover intelligence agents cannot be published. Thus, when the media were complicit in the outing of an agent whose husband had been critical of the Bush administration's rationale for war in Iraq, a complicated legal investigation followed (N. Chomsky, 2006).

Other laws address content less directly, but nevertheless create conditions that can influence eventual news content. Ownership regulation is one such example. In the case of broadcasting, the government maintains nominal influence over station ownership through its licensing authority. Since stations ostensibly receive a license based on their ability to serve the public interest, convenience, or necessity, broadcast stations have had to offer news programming to the public. Initially, this meant a kind of news geared to a broad general audience, bereft of content that might be considered offensive to the American mainstream (Benjamin, 2001; McChesney, 1993). However, licenses are routinely bought and sold with little attention to a public interest standard, and the Federal Communications Commission (FCC) has shown little interest in the presence or nature of news content (Aufderheide, 1999; Horwitz, 1989).

Thus, ownership regulation is largely a matter of how many or what kinds of outlets a corporation owns. Regulators attempt to structure the marketplace so that competition shapes news content. The idea, as we noted above, is that wider distribution of ownership creates more competition, which leads to more voices entering the marketplace of ideas (Baker, 2007). National ownership limits apply to broadcast outlets (E. D. Cohen, 2005), and print media consolidation is subject to antitrust regulation (Carter, Franklin, & Wright, 2005). The FCC has also largely prohibited cross-ownership of newspapers and broadcast outlets within a market (Carter, Franklin, & Wright, 2003), a prohibition, like all FCC regulations, that is subject to change. In fact, critics (e.g., Sturm, 2005) have argued that relaxed ownership restriction leads to greater economies of scale for news gathering operations, thereby leading to more and/or better news. Research by Napoli and Yan (2007) dispute this contention, showing that increased ownership concentration had resulted in less local news production.

A variety of other media-related policies influence the gatekeeping process. Shield laws protect journalists in some circumstances from divulging anonymous sources (Fargo, 2006), whereas access provisions have kept cameras out of courtrooms and legislative assemblies and denied access to some public records (Graber, 2006). Fair use laws create modest barriers to the use of copyrighted material in the news media (Olson, 2004), and equal access provisions stipulate that if one candidate for public office receives airtime, then all other candidates must get time as well. The equal access provision has evolved, however, and news programming has long been exempt. Problems occur as the definition of news programming expands (Paglin, Hobson, & Rosenbloom, 1999; Vos, 2005). Congress and the president, meanwhile, play a role in regulation, largely by threatening new policy to address perceived news media shortcomings (Krasnow, Longley, & Terry, 1982). The threat performs a chastening function, meant to influence future news media behavior and content.

≈ INTEREST GROUPS ≈

An interest group, such as Common Cause, the Sierra Club, or Accuracy in Media, is formed by individuals who want to communicate their position on issues. Individuals united around a single issue believe they have a stronger voice together than individually. Three types of interest groups are relevant to gatekeeping: those involved in promoting their issue stance, those attempting to alter media content, and those that do both.

Groups such as Mothers Against Drunk Drivers use the media to get information out about their programs and issue positions. They try to persuade media gatekeepers not only to include messages about their groups, but also to ensure that the messages are favorable (Russell, 1995). They sometimes use public relations as a tool to reach their target audiences by influencing media gatekeepers (Rose, 1991), and they can be very successful. By studying the interest group Christian Coalition, Huckins (1999) shows a significantly strong relationship between the Coalition agenda and the media agenda, with the group's targeted issues getting significant newspaper coverage.

Accuracy in Media, an example of the second type of interest group, exists for the express purpose of changing media content (Herman & Chomsky, 1988). These groups criticize the media and/or individual gatekeepers and try to affect the gatekeeping process (Bryski, 1998). They exert a double influence on content: Not only do their criticisms get on the news agenda (thereby replacing messages that would otherwise have been selected by a gatekeeper), but they also may cause revisions of media practices or policies. Their goal is to increase the "cost" of a media practice the group deems offensive or problematic by forcing the gatekeeper to deal with "flak" (Herman & Chomsky, 1988). "Public decency groups exercise power over the things they keep watch over, through unremitting observation and exhaustive inquisition, sensitive to any violation, drawing attention to peculiarities and describing them in intimate detail" (McCabe & Akass, 2007, p. 64). The American Family Association (AFA), for example, specifically targets media gatekeepers, describing itself as a Christian organization promoting decency on television and in other media. AFA members send protest postcards to companies that advertise on television programs that the AFA deems offensive.

The third type of interest group uses the media to promote a position and also occasionally tries to influence the gatekeeping process, sometimes by providing "guidelines" for covering topics of interest to the group. For example, in 1968 the American Bar Association (ABA) adopted its "fair trial–free press" guidelines: By 1976, 23 states had adopted voluntary press–bar guidelines that specified how the media should cover crime and trials. In their study of compliance with the ABA guidelines, however, Tankard, Middleton, and Rimmer (1979) found that newspapers operating under a voluntary press–bar agreement were no more likely to follow the ABA guidelines than were those that had made no such agreement. Dixon and Linz (2002) found ABA guidelines on pretrial publicity, particularly guidelines on portrayals of race, also seemed to have gained little traction with the news media. Likewise, the International Chamber of Commerce has promoted guidelines for advertising content, as have other associations, but they have met with little success (Boddewyn, 1991).

Interest groups, regardless of the type, have also resorted to becoming advertisers as a supplement to other tactics for influencing media content. According to Soley (2002), the move has met with mixed success—activist advocacy groups are frequently turned away by news media, while business-sponsored groups are more typically welcomed. Soley's somewhat impressionistic conclusion is supported by Falk, Grizard, and McDonald's (2006) study of issue advertising in the Washington, D.C., television market. Business-related interest groups outspent other advocacy groups by a five to one ratio.

⤨ OTHER MEDIA ⤨

The distribution of competing media in a marketplace shapes content in several ways. Media compete for audiences, sources, and advertisers. These competitive pressures encourage gatekeepers to monitor one another. Media try to scoop the competition on big stories, but once a big story is exposed, other media must pick up the story as well (Gans, 1979a). Although media organizations often compete, journalists from competing media often collaborate with their peers. For example, political reporters discuss what was newsworthy about a campaign event, thereby leading to similarity in content (Crouse, 1972; Skewes, 2007). Monitoring other media is widespread, but some media are monitored more than others. This sets up an inter-media agenda setting effect.

Just as some journalists set the agenda for others, some media organizations set the agenda for others (Bantz, 1990b). The *New York Times* seems to be especially influential in leading to other media's coverage of a topic, as Reese and Danielian (Danielian & Reese, 1989; Reese & Danielian, 1989) showed in their studies of inter-media agenda setting on the drug issue. Other influential media include the *Washington Post*, the *Los Angeles Times*, and the *Wall Street Journal* (Bantz, 1990b). These newspapers are read every day by thousands of journalists who look for information that they could turn into their own messages.

The influence of competing media on gatekeeping may be particularly important in situations where other influences are slight, such as when individual gatekeepers lack strong personal opinions about the topic or no selection norms exist (B. C. Cohen, 1963). A lack of organizational resources can also affect inter-media agenda setting. For example, international news gathering is too costly for small television stations, so they rely heavily on television news agencies like Reuters Television to cover international events (Paterson, 2001). Through a comparison of newscasts from around the world, Paterson (2001) finds that smaller broadcasters use 80 percent or more of non-local stories from television news agencies, whereas broadcasters with more resources use news agency coverage to supplement their own reporting of international events.

To what extent do news services determine the topics that newspapers cover? Stempel (1959) found six Michigan dailies' selection of wire service stories agreed only about a third of the time. Todd (1983) found some agreement between the *New York Times* service and newspapers in news selections, particularly among the top stories. Harmon (1989) found substantial agreement between newspapers and local television news in the same market, suggesting that not only do the gatekeepers all begin from roughly the same set of events but they also pay attention to each other's news decisions.

A different sort of media agenda setting can also occur when advertisements set the agenda for news coverage—political advertising can set the news agenda for both print and broadcast news (Roberts & McCombs, 1994). In his investigation of inter-media agenda setting in the 1996 presidential election, Boyle (2001) found that presidential campaign advertising does set the agenda for network news coverage and newspaper prestige press coverage. Other research shows that advocacy group advertising also seems to influence the news agenda (B. Miller, 2006).

⊰ NEWS CONSULTANTS ⊱

Some media organizations seek advice from consultants, such as Frank Magid Associates or McHugh Hoffman, in formulating strategies to enhance their ratings and competitiveness (Allen, 2005; Bantz, McCorkle, & Baade, 1981; Berkowitz, Allen, & Beeson, 1996). They are especially influential on local television stations. Berkowitz and his colleagues (1996) concluded that although news consultants are not involved in daily newsroom decision making, they can influence media content by offering recommendations on how and which events the station should cover if it wants to be successful in the news business. For example, consultants for television stations recommended more live reporting or visuals in the news, and these recommendations were carried out in media coverage (Bantz et al., 1981; Tuggle & Huffman, 1999). Consultants also played an important role historically in orienting local television news to the marketplace (Allen, 2007), pushing stations to "predictably portray police, children and pets, celebrities, and 'team' coverage of fleeting events" (Allen, 2005, p. 378). Content studies show that stations using consultants aired less government and political news and more news about crime, weather, and human interest topics (Allen, 2005).

The influence of news consultants, however, is subject to a decision by the newsroom to follow their advice or reject it. In this sense, journalists' perception of consultants is an important factor that determines consultants' impact on news content. Journalists' work roles and attitudes about journalism have been shown to influence their views about consultants (Berkowitz, Allen, & Beeson, 1996; Tuggle & Huffman, 1999). By surveying news managers in 16 local television news departments, Berkowitz and his colleagues (1996) found that news managers with stronger ties to the business success of their news organizations were more supportive of consultants. In contrast, managers who were more concerned with their journalistic ideals were more critical. Tuggle and colleagues (1999) examined journalists' views about the influence of consultants on the newsroom's decisions on live reporting. Their study shows that reporters are more likely than news directors to agree that news consultants influence their station's decision to go live.

FORCES AT THE GATE = "SUMMARY"

This chapter began with a consideration of how market forces shape the news, but it is not always clear which market forces are important. Some analyses see markets as a kind of ontological force, as a force of nature. For example, to say that "market forces have picked up considerable momentum" (McManus, 1994, p. xiii) could be a metaphor or it could be describing a real force. Metaphors are unavoidable, but some capture the nature of the force at the gate better than others.

Hence, markets are included in this chapter mostly as part of an institutional reality that creates the contours of a social or institutional landscape. The introduction of legal protection of markets in the United States and other countries changes the social landscape, creating an environment more hospitable to some media behaviors than others. Markets operate "on their own internal logic" (Baker, 2002, p. 95), but it is a logic that is institutionally created. To the extent that media actors seek to maximize profits, their behaviors in the media marketplace are somewhat predictable. If information subsidies help hold costs down, then we can expect gatekeepers to make optimum use of news releases. News releases are used until the loss in dissatisfied readers or viewers offsets the gains in economic efficiency. If sensationalism draws audiences that advertisers desire, then we can expect the amount of sensationalism to reach some optimal level. Structural features of the institutional environment present some pathways that are more logical to travel than others. Or as Baker puts it, "influence tends to flow in particular directions" (2002, p. 14). For example, given the variety of markets in which the media operate, and the lack of "knowledge" from audiences, market pressures from advertisers will be most germane to gatekeepers.

Forces in front of the gates are at times conceptualized as being similar to human nature, with gatekeepers seen as having an innate human capacity for greed or rationality. Bagdikian casts the Gannett newspaper chain's actions as "acts of greed and exploitation" (2004, p. 178). The desire to maximize profits is generally understood in standard economics as flowing from human rationality. But the human capacity for reason does not really explain the forces in front of the gates, because gatekeepers have been known to leave some profits on the table to achieve other, equally rational, goals. What we perceive as rational is often just socialization or enculturation. As natural as the desire to maximize income may seem, it is still a culturally rooted desire (Kuttner, 1997).

Rationality can take a backseat to expediency—local television stations trust the recommendations of consultants, not because they have knowledge of a full range of options, but because they defer to what they believe is expertise (also see Chapter 3 regarding decision making and rationality). When gatekeepers face uncertainties, market rationality often fails to deliver a clear course of action. Inter-media agenda setting may or may not help a small organization's bottom line, but it is a social arrangement that solves the problem of uncertainty about news judgments. Thus when a path through the institutional landscape has been beaten, the need for efficiency leads to the familiar path. Although following a familiar path can be described as rational, it should be remembered that the path was created through socialization.

Socialization is apparent in a variety of other settings. When gatekeepers operate with notions of what the audience wants, they do so not from direct or accurate knowledge of the audience's interests, but based on their socialization in newsrooms. When gatekeepers have done battle or been told of battles with advertisers, they try to head off future fights by not making the same "mistake" again. As a Chrysler executive put it, "editors know 'what our advertising guidelines are'" (Soley, 2002, p. 211). Restraints eventually become "self-imposed" (Kessler, 1989). Socialization is also apparent when journalists and sources are coorienting—they arrive at shared ways of understanding their environment.

The institutional level of analysis also presents forces that appear as naked power. For example, political, government, and other sources can manage the news by using their position to dictate what gatekeepers should do. But power is not absolute—tight news management does not leave journalists without options. Journalists tell the meta-story of how sources manage the news (Fallows, 1996), seizing on unscripted moments that are bound to occur (Bennett, 2005; Skewes, 2007).

Another form of seemingly naked power is the government's ability to criminalize certain behaviors. Gatekeepers are threatened with lawsuits, fines, and jail time for disobeying laws and regulations. But this power is also less absolute than it appears, since journalists both knowingly and unknowingly flout the law. Thus, even when shield laws fail to protect journalists, they may still choose to go to jail rather than turn over their source (Pracene, 2005). Gatekeepers also actively stretch the laws and regulations, pushing for new interpretations of laws that maximize media flexibility (Krasnow, Longley, & Terry, 1982). In other words, gatekeepers often calculate the costs and benefits of how they respond to government or other power. The force at the gate relates as much to cultural attitudes about the costs and benefits of a course of action as to brute ontological force.

Finally, the force at the gate has also been conceptualized in functionalist terms. For example, when Gandy (1982) says that journalists' need for regular, credible information leads to a dependence on bureaucratic sources, he is seemingly offering a functionalist explanation—the effect seems to create the cause. And while the language here does borrow from functionalism, Gandy is really telling a different kind of story. Gatekeepers are reacting to an institutional landscape where market forces reward certain behaviors. Thus, the more complete formulation of the operative force in Gandy's explanation is that gatekeepers will lose audiences and subsequently profits if they choose to ignore official sources. In fact, it is a choice some alternative publications have made, the term "alternative" generally coexisting with small circulation.

7 The Social System Level of Analysis

The news of war in Iraq that was carried on Al Jazeera, the Qatar-based Arabic satellite channel, differed from the news reported by American media (Aday, Livingston, & Hebert, 2005). The difference came not just from the fact that Al Jazeera and CNN or Fox News Channel are different news organizations or face different social institutional influences. Media organizations in Qatar and the United States obviously operate in very different contexts: News is as different in the Middle East and the United States as are governments or economies. Different places in the world may produce different institutions, but explaining the source of those differences is not straightforward.

For decades, studies (e.g., Emery, 1969; Hachten & Hachten, 1999; Head, 1985; Shoemaker & Cohen, 2006) have examined the national contexts in which media messages are created. However, the nation-state per se is typically not conceptualized as the source of the differences. Head, for example, examines "national" media systems but posits: "A country's broadcasting system mirrors national character, expressing a particular political philosophy and cultural identity" (1985, p. 2). So, what is the source of different media messages? Do we call this a difference in social systems? Or, if not social systems, how about social structures, ideologies or cultures? This is not a matter of semantics. These options are not synonyms—each comes with theoretical presuppositions and each points to different empirical sites of investigation.

This chapter explores how social systems, social structures, ideologies, and cultures may explain the choice and shaping of media messages. We note how each formulation has been used in mass communication scholarship, the presuppositions of each of these formulations, and the underlying forces at the gate. The chapter concludes by exploring how these approaches may contribute to Gatekeeping Theory.

SOCIAL SYSTEM

Some of the classic works in U.S. mass communication have highlighted the role of social or cultural contexts in shaping media systems. The canonical text *Four Theories of the Press* (Siebert, 1956; Siebert, Peterson, & Schramm, 1973) pointed to the ways in which the news media reflects the organizing philosophy of a society. The book states unequivocally "that the press always takes on the form and coloration of the social and political structures within which it operates" (Siebert et al., 1973, p. 1). To understand media form and content "one must look at the social systems in which the press functions" (Siebert et al., 1973, p. 2). The news media in authoritarian societies have been found to create different content than the press in so-called libertarian, socially responsible, and communist societies. The formulation of these four particular social systems has been questioned by subsequent scholarship (Nerone, 1995). Nevertheless, the idea that social systems influence content has not gone away.

Gans, in *Deciding What's News*, makes a similar case that the social system matters. "Perhaps journalists perform unintended or unrecognized (latent) functions for nation and society as a whole, which are necessary enough to force journalists to act as they do" (1979a, p. 290). Thus, in a democratic society where political parties have been weakened through progressive and subsequent reforms, the media have been forced to fill a void (see also Patterson, 1993). Journalists hold candidates to intense scrutiny, culling weaker leaders. According to Gans, journalists also function as a sounding board for policy makers, playing an integral role in the formulation of public policy (see also Cook, 1998). Likewise, in a secular state—in a society that has disestablished a state church—the media are compelled to serve as "moral guardians" and even as "prophets and priests." The media may play the role of "story tellers and myth makers," activities formerly played by select tribal members in pre-modern societies (Gans, 1979a, pp. 292–294).

The idea is that a functional society requires a variety of roles, some of which may be filled by the news media and their employees. For example, Strohm suggests that the content of the African-American media can be explained by understanding the role they play in the overall social system and the role they play relative to other media. "The long-recognized 'protest' role of the black press may also be part of a broader internal and external social control function" (1999, p. 60). The news media produce different content because the media play different roles relative to each other in the social system.

The content of the media may be similar because actors in media organizations perform the same function relative to other social actors. A social system with weak political parties may make different demands on its news media than a system with strong parties. In a system with weak political parties, such as the United States, the news media play a weeding out function, producing content that "handicaps" the candidates within a "horse race" narrative (see Kuhn & Neveu, 2002). In a system with strong parties, such as the Netherlands, the content focuses on policy differences among candidates (Ostergaard & Euromedia Research Group, 1992).

Although effects of social systems probably exist, there is little empirical evidence to support this. Because scholars stand within their own systems, they cannot escape and look at them objectively, a well recognized shortcoming of systems or functional analysis. "(T)he systems focus ... lends itself well, at the theoretical more than at the practical or empirical levels, to the complexity of interrelationships between the features of given systems; it is not well-suited to the subtleties and ambivalences of social, cultural and economic processes" (Boyd-Barrett, 1995, p. 73). Gans is explicit about the limitations of functional analysis, even calling his own observations "speculative." "Whether journalists perform necessary functions can be studied only if all news media were suddenly to disappear for a time" (Gans, 1979a, p. 291).

Gans, Boyd-Barrett, and others are discussing the shortcomings of a systems analysis that is rooted in theoretical assumptions. The tradition of studying the social system in which news media operate has been influenced in no small part by functionalism. In fact, many of the studies cited above do come with a functionalist logic. Functionalism has all but disappeared as a viable theoretical approach (Huaco, 1986), but various forms of functionalism remain. The social system as a level of analysis is perfectly valid and does not require functionalist assumptions. Hence it is important to understand when functionalist assumptions are present and when they are not.

Forces at the gate. The basic logic of functionalism is that a social system has a finite number of integrated roles or social needs. Just as in an ecosystem, a change in one part of the environment affects other parts of the system. The system needs to stay in balance to remain functional. If the system gets out of balance, if a need is not met, a vacuum is created. Since nature abhors a vacuum, it is only natural that the vacuum be filled. The vacuum, to use Gans' words, forces "journalists to act as they do" (1979a, p. 290). So what exactly is the force that compels media to select particular content? Critics of functionalism argue that the nature metaphor has been overplayed. The main issue, according to some, is that functionalism fails to specify the actual mechanism that necessitates actions or outcomes (Mahner & Bunge, 2001). Subsequent generations of scholars have looked to culture or ideology or institutional pressures to account for why a vacuum or need is filled, or even for why something is perceived as a need.

SOCIAL STRUCTURE

Closely related to the idea of social system is that of social structure. Examinations of social structure typically look at similar phenomena, but avoid the functionalist suppositions. Hallin and Mancini argue that "one cannot understand the news media without understanding the nature of the state, the system of political parties, the pattern of relations between economic and political interests, and the development of civil society, among other elements of social structure" (2004, p. 8). Simply put, the social environment's structure makes a difference in media content.

News media do not exist independently of the larger public sphere. Media institutions often share "common historical roots" with political institutions, which "shape the development of both media and political systems" (Hallin & Mancini,

2004, p. 46). Also, to the extent that public policy and funding mechanisms are established for the news media, the news media are structured accordingly. For example, Humphreys shows how changes in political parties and a move toward *laissez-faire* economics in Europe following the Second World War "brought about a later 'depoliticisation' of the press" (1996, p. 41). Hence, the historical co-evolution of social institutions leaves a mark on news media content.

A study by Donahue, Olien, and Tichenor (1985) showed that editors' opinions changed over 20 years to reflect the increasing diversity and pluralism of the society. Another study by the same authors (Donahue, Olien, & Tichenor, 1989) showed a relationship between a community's degree of pluralism and both news and advertising content. Similarly, Humphreys draws a distinction between media content in *consensual* and *majoritarian* democracies (1996, p. 11). The difference in state structure leads to a difference in media structure and ultimately to a difference in the relative pluralism of media voices—consensual democracies afford greater pluralism (see also Hallin & Mancini, 2004).

Hindman, Littlefield, Preston, and Neumann (1999) examined the impact of community structural pluralism and ethnic pluralism on newspaper coverage of ethnic minorities. Structural pluralism, defined as "the degree of specialization and differentiation within the community" (p. 256), significantly predicted only whether editors included ethnic minorities on a list of most important news sources. Meanwhile, the study found that the greater a community's ethnic pluralism, the more likely editors were to view the coverage of ethnic minority stories as important.

Common structures produce common content. Varied structures produce varied content. Chang, Wang, and Chen (1998) show how different social structures in China and the United States shape notions of newsworthiness in different ways, ultimately producing different television news content. Likewise, a change in the social structure can lead to changes in media content. Sun, Chang, and Yu (2001) show how economic reforms and changes in "open-door" policies in China eventually led to changes in both domestic and international news, in part because news media responded to changing audience expectations.

While some studies, such as those comparing the United States and China, look to countries, others do not equate social structure and nation-state. In fact, many studies compare media content based on broad political, economic, or social differences. Head, for example, compared broadcast program content based on three social systems, "First, Second, and Third Worlds" (1985, p. 322). Hallin and Mancini (2004) identify three "political systems"—systems which interact with economic and technological factors—that shape the structure of the media and ultimately media content. They differentiated among a Mediterranean or polarized pluralist model, a North/Central European or democratic corporatist model, and a North Atlantic or liberal model, examining how 18 countries fit these three models or social structures.

Forces at the gate. The logic of how social structure might shape news content stresses the way in which social institutions create "constraints and opportunities to which media organizations and actors respond" (Hallin & Mancini, 2004, p. 296). These constraints and opportunities emerged given the shared historical development of political, economic, and media institutions. Media content is similar within a social structure to the extent that actors respond rationally to the same constraints and opportunities. Since the institutional environment may create more than one rational path, we might expect minor variation even among rational actors. Room for agency exists, but agency will be bound by the ways in which social structures create constraints and opportunities. Some scholars take a more sociological or cultural approach to institutional logic (P. A. Hall & Taylor, 1996), which stresses the way in which actors are socialized into particular institutional roles and behaviors based on the way social structure has shaped media institutions.

IDEOLOGY

The cultural studies tradition, whether in its British (e.g., Turner, 2002) or American (e.g., Warren & Vavrus, 2002) incarnations, has called attention to the role that ideology plays in the construction of media messages. The notion has been absorbed into media sociology as a powerful tool for explaining commonality in media messages at a society or national level. For example, Ferguson (1998) points out that European notions of race have left a unique imprint on television, radio, film, and newspaper messages. Entman and Rojecki argue (2000) that American ideas of race shape messages in American news publications, television, films, and advertising. For example, Weill concludes that "gate keeping of information" by white editors in Mississippi in the 1950s and 1960s "usually eliminated any positive aspect of civil rights activity" (2001, p. 559). Most scholars of the media agree that ideas about race matter a great deal to the creation of media messages. But although ideas and ideology matter, we must pay close attention to how ideology is conceptualized.

As noted earlier, some invoke ideology as an individual-level influence. For example, in Entman and Rojecki's (2000) study of race and media, ideology is one variable among others, such as age, education, and knowledge, that explains why individuals hold certain racial attitudes. Ideology is operationalized by "self-designation as liberal, moderate, and conservative" (p. 24). This approach makes sense within the positivist tradition—ideology cannot be observed as a "social fact" (Morrison, 1995), only by how it manifests itself in individuals. Ideology as a society-level phenomenon was thought to be alien to the positivist enterprise.

Williams defines ideology as "a relatively formal and articulated system of meanings, values and beliefs, of a kind that can be abstracted as a 'world-view' or a 'class outlook'" (1977, p. 109). Swidler offers a nearly identical take, referring to ideologies as "explicit, articulated, highly organized meaning systems" (1986, p. 278). According to Becker, "ideology is an integrated set of frames of reference through which each of us sees the world and to which all of us adjust our actions"

(1984, p. 69). Each clearly posits ideology as a society-level influence, and each points to the explicit and the integrated, organized, or systematic nature of ideologies.

These definitions of ideology raise an important empirical issue: Can we identify ideologies in the United States or other countries that rise to the level of explicitness and integration or organization suggested by the definitions offered by Williams, Swidler, and Becker? It has been difficult to identify a coherent and integrated set of ideas that represents a single American ideology. Indeed, American history is just as likely to be about conflicting ideas as about ideological consensus. For example, many of the conflicts in American history reflect the inherent incompatibility of ideas about racial inequality and ideas about liberalism, which ostensibly sees all human beings as equal. This brings us back to the point about systems made above, that society may be less systematic than it appears, but it also points us to the historical nature of ideology.

Gans has reminded us that ideology "changes somewhat over time" (1979a, p. 68). Indeed, ideological labels widely in use at one time fall out of favor at other times (Eisinger, Veenstra, & Koehn, 2007). Swidler makes such changes central to her understanding of ideology's impact on culture. She argues that a society can go through settled and unsettled periods, with a greater diversity of ideas flourishing in settled periods. She sees the development of more explicit or systematic ideologies as a response to the contested power relations characteristic of unsettled periods.

While it is useful to note the relative settledness or unsettledness of a society, it should be pointed out that Swidler is in agreement with a notable theorist of ideology, Gramsci, on at least one important point: Ideology is constructed and maintained by the powerful elite as a means of reinforcing existing power relations. Gramsci's theory of hegemony (Gramsci, Hoare, & Nowell-Smith, 1971) suggests that the media serve as agents of the powerful, creating a false consciousness for the audience (see also Lewis, 1999) that maintains the dominance of the powerful elite.

Creeber (2004) shows how, despite the incredible geographical, racial, religious, cultural, and linguistic diversity of the United Kingdom, the British Broadcasting Corporation has maintained a narrow view of "Britishness"—a view that resembles the United Kingdom's powerful elite. Such depictions marginalize oppositional voices (see also Richardson, 2001). But Creeber points out that this narrow Britishness is losing hold as new media channels challenge notions of a common culture. Most scholars are less likely to be encouraged by the presence of more media channels (Carter, 1998). Since a dominant ideology colonizes the language and myths used in public discourse (Barthes, 1972), it is not likely to be easily uprooted. Others argue that corporate control of the media explains control by the dominant economic class (Bagdikian, 2004; McChesney, 1997).

Some messages may be selected because they reinforce the status quo, but others are selected because they point out potential dangers that need to be dealt with if the status quo is to be maintained. Media coverage of the Watergate scandal during the Nixon presidency was highly critical of Richard Nixon and his advisers, but the media did not question the legitimacy of the American political system; the scandal was framed in terms of the individuals' crimes. As Gitlin (1980) points out, the entire affair ultimately celebrated the American system—*it's so good it can survive the crimes of its caretakers.*

Thus, theories of hegemony suggest that gatekeepers sometimes select messages that are critical of the status quo; in fact, to retain their legitimacy as news organizations the U.S. media have to be adversarial, within certain ideological bounds. For example, Burch and Harry (2004) studied how four California newspapers covered pesticide issues and concluded that activists opposed to dominant pesticide use practices were quoted more than neutral sources or pro-pesticide sources. "The findings give weight to the general idea that news media as mediating institutions drawn to conflict-rich stories, are, or at least can be, anti-hegemonic, while still playing their functional role as part of the ruling hegemony, as an important subsystem within the larger political-economy" (Burch & Harry, 2004, p. 566).

A pitfall in hegemony theory is its apparent lack of falsifiability. If the dominant ideological line controls news media coverage, then hegemony is supported. If an anti-hegemonic line is advanced, then the theory is also supported. What sort of test can be devised to separate hegemonic effects from others, or to test whether a hegemonic effect is stable across time?

Some scholars have questioned the strength of a U.S. hegemony in the 21st century. Entman (2003) argues that elites do not have the power that theories of hegemony suggest. He concludes that "the collapse of Cold War consensus has meant differences among elites are no longer the exemption but the rule" (Entman, 2003, p. 5). More specifically he argues that U.S. presidents no longer have the ability to frame all foreign policy for the White House press corps. In other words, ideology is no longer as integrated, organized, or systematic as it once was. Granted, others have argued just the opposite, that a conservative hegemony has only been strengthened in the 21st century. Kellner writes that "the tremendous concentration of power in the hands of business groups who control powerful media conglomerates has intensified corporate control of vital news and information" (2004, p. 31).

Forces at the gate. Ideology or hegemony shapes news content when it leads gatekeepers to select items that gain the consent of the governed and thus serve the purposes of powerful elites. A dominant ideology is not established on the basis merely of the power of the ruling elite to dictate things such as news content. Elites gain hegemonic hold by articulating a "worldview that accommodates a broad range of interests, not merely the leading group's interest" (Condit, 1994, pp. 206–207). The logic of this approach holds that a dominant worldview shapes how gatekeepers see events and write news. The dominance of the worldview is such that gatekeepers understand the world and power relations as natural (S. Hall, 1989). Hence, the agency of gatekeepers is bound by the ideology that they have internalized through enculturation and education.

CULTURE

The cultural studies tradition has, as the name would suggest, also paid close attention to the role of culture in the construction of media messages and, in the process, breathed fresh life into an old concept. *Culture* is invoked in a variety of ways. It can be understood as a largely national phenomenon—many cross-cultural studies are studies across countries (e.g., McCann & Honeycutt, 2006). It can also be studied at an organizational level—studies look, for example, at the culture of newsrooms (see Marcellus, 2005). Culture can refer to common social practices; for example, the culture of consumption (see Milner, 2004) or the culture of beauty makeovers (see McGee, 2005). In fact, at some level all of these examples refer to culture as a set of common or shared social practices. These social practices constitute a "way of life"—patterned, regular, unified, and systematic ways of doing things (Bourdieu, 1977). Culture finds its regularity and unity, in part, through shared symbols, rituals, values, and norms, all of which give meaning to life.

These approaches to culture point to some of the same issues raised by notions of ideology. For example, how unified or systematic must a culture be? Cohen (1974) argues that once a simple society becomes more complex, culture becomes more heterogeneous. In fact, Swidler argues that cultures are not unified, but rather contain "diverse, often conflicting symbols, rituals, stories, and guides to action" (1986, p. 277). Culture provides a tool kit of various "cultural elements" that can be used to "construct diverse strategies of action" (p. 281). The tool kit contains things such as values, ideas, symbols, norms, and rituals, and therefore it is incorrect to say that a nation embodies a single culture. While scholars might talk about the American creed—a distinctly American set of values, ideas, and norms—the fact remains that various values, ideas, and norms are often in conflict.

Thus studies of culture use a variety of analytical approaches. For example, some studies examine how cultural values influence news content, such as Ravi's (2005) argument that differences in coverage of the Iraq War in newspapers from five countries reflect the different cultural values and practices in those countries. Ravi concludes that "newspaper coverage seems to reflect notions, values, and ideas that resonate within particular societies" (p. 59). Baysha and Hallahan (2004) studied the Ukraine's 2000–2001 political crisis to understand the nature of mass media coverage. They conclude that the media used Ukrainian cultural values to construct a portrayal of reality that called up "feelings associated with fascism, Civil War, Cold War, Stalin's repressions, etc." (p. 245). The cultural tool kit available to gatekeepers is limited because "[c]ertain packages have a natural advantage because their ideas resonate with other cultural themes" (p. 245).

Some cultural values are highlighted more than others in news content. Larson and Bailey (1998) identified the types of prominent people and values portrayed in five years of ABC World News Tonight's *Person of the Week*. American values such as individualism, heroism, and unselfishness were more commonly portrayed than values of populism, capitalism, and patriotism.

The cultural tool kit is not limited to cultural values. Corner, Schlesinger, and Silverstone argue that "cultural norms should not be underestimated" (1998, p. 4). Roach declares that "news narratives … tend to gravitate in predictable ways toward established cultural norms" (1995, p. 32). McCargo (2003) argues that, even in the absence of legal regulations, the mass media in Asian countries are regulated by cultural norms, a form of regulation that is probably felt in all countries.

Culture both influences the kinds of items that are allowed to pass through a gate and is influenced by them. Just as Lewin (1951) found that some foods are appropriate for some cultures and not others, the value placed on news items varies across cultures. Although some news items are objectively available, they are not culturally available. For example, at one time in the United States, newspapers did not cover rape and child abuse in the open manner with which the topics are discussed today (Thomason & LaRocque, 1995). In many countries, these topics are still not reported.

Forces at the gate. The logic of culture's influence on news content is that gatekeepers adopt meaning systems from their cultural environment. These meaning systems or tool kits, which include cultural values, norms, ideas, and the like, provide gatekeepers with both constraints and opportunities (Geertz, 1973). Thus, culture "locks man into a certain approach to life but also provides answers to the deepest questions about the meaning of life" (Laitin, 1986, p. 13). Gatekeepers make choices that seem natural, right, or rational. Cohen (1974) offers a different perspective on culture's logic of explanation: "The constraints that culture exerts on the individual come ultimately not from the culture itself, but from the collectivity of the group" (p. 85). This implies an element of cultural coercion. Gatekeepers act as they do because they feel compelled to do so. Here culture is understood in terms similar to hegemony—elites use the cultural tool kit to affect false consciousness as a means to achieving their own ends. "Political entrepreneurs recognize that through appeals to culture they can easily attract a mass following" (Laitin, 1986, p. 11).

SOCIAL SYSTEM AS LEVEL OF ANALYSIS

The terms *social system*, *social structure*, *ideology*, and *culture* are conceptualized in different ways and draw on different logics of explanations. Indeed, although these concepts have been championed by different research traditions, they can still be fitted together to theorize about gatekeeping. Although studying the social system as a level of analysis has functionalist assumptions, and, frankly, functionalist baggage, we hope to rehabilitate it here. The social system needs to be understood primarily as a level of analysis, referring to society-level influences on news media content—those influences include social structure, ideology, and culture. Put another way, social structure, ideology, and culture are all indicators of social systems. In social scientific terms, as a level of analysis the social system has within it social structure, ideology, and culture as variables. One social system is different from another based on differences in culture, ideology, and/or social structure.

The choice of the term *social system* as a description of this level of analysis is not without some complications. "System" may suggest an organized, unified, or inter-related whole, again bringing up the issue of heterogeneity and homogeneity. How homogeneous must a social system be for it to be a system? The question does not have easy answers; but a few points can be made: First, "system" may imply an organized and unified entity in some contexts, but the first definition of the term stresses it is an "assemblage" or "combination of things" that make up a whole. Unity or internal organization is not central to the meaning of the term. Second, although a system is indeed a whole, we expect that competing values, norms, and ideas exist within it. Third, scholars have studied social systems that are both smaller than and larger than nation-states. The important thing is that scholars, as most do, specify how it is that the system being studied is a "whole."

Although ideology and culture are considered here as indicators of a social system, the point made by Gans (1979a) and Swidler (1986) bears repeating—ideology and culture may be in a state of change. One cannot assume that ideas constituting a dominant ideology at one point in time constitute the same ideology at another. Cultural values that hold sway at one moment may fade as a formative force. Any talk of an American creed, for example, needs to be treated skeptically or, better yet, specified empirically.

Finally, scholars who wish to explore how a social system shapes the gatekeeping process should explain their logic in detail. For example, functional theory has been out of vogue for years, based on the idea that it only favors the stability of a social system. In fact, however, functional explanations are common when talking about social change. The mass media are sometimes understood as functioning to support the status quo. For example, when studying the case of U.S. President Richard Nixon being forced to resign because of his crimes, Gitlin (1980) described the news media's actions as reinforcing the political system. Instead of questioning whether such crimes required revisions in the political system, Gitlin describes the media's actions as glorifying the ability of the existing system to survive the crimes of an individual and still continue without a revolution. By interpreting Nixon's actions as those of an individual and not as the result of a problem with the executive branch's power relative to the legislative and judicial branches, Gitlin interprets the media's enterprise reporting and revelation of the crimes as supporting the social system and thereby the stability of the United States. He said that although the news media were critical of Nixon and his crimes, the news never questioned the viability of the social system.

Stinchcombe (1987) shows that such tensions in or threats to social system stability are entirely in line with studying the extent to which a social system is homeostatic, that it contains social institutions whose job it is to maintain the stability of the status quo. For example, the People's Republic of China deliberately introduced social change in order to enter the world market economy in the last quarter of the

20th century. A functional explanation fairly well fits the government's actions: It built modern, large cities from villages (a small fishing village, in the case of Shenzhen, near Hong Kong), educated people to fill information-age jobs, and created a middle class in 20 years, while at the same time changing laws to hold back social change, to brake its speed. Freedoms were encouraged and then swept away as people were jailed and then encouraged again in a different way. China's government, which had managed a homeostatic system for 5000 years, introduced these tensions or threats within its own social system, a form of controlled social change. Although the government introduces change, its hold on power is a function of its ability to control the speed of change. Out-of-control change becomes revolution, whereas micromanaged change is a strategy to continue the power of the Communist Party. The party's success lies in its ability to also change in ways that are consistent with changes in the country. Thus internally sanctioned social changes affect not only the country, but also the government that approved them.

These examples suggest that gatekeepers within a social system can be used either to stop social change or to manage its speed and direction. Factors such as the social system's ideology and culture shape what gatekeepers understand to be the natural world, but the complexity of social systems does not produce gatekeepers who must act alike. We discuss this more in the next chapter.

Part III Theorizing about Gatekeeping

Although Kurt Lewin is considered one of the fathers of communication study (Schramm, 1980) and the father of gatekeeping research (Reese & Ballinger, 2001), he had little to say about news in his definitive examinations of gatekeeping (1947a; 1951). Lewin elaborated on the "generality" of his theory only after he had explored gatekeeping through the example of how food made its way from the grocery store or garden to the dinner table. "This situation holds not only for food channels but also for the traveling of a news item through certain communications channels in a group, for movement of goods, and the social locomotion of individuals in many organizations" (Lewin, 1951, p. 187).

Lewin's understanding of field theory evolved over decades and was not well explained in any one of his publications, possibly because he died before writing the definitive work. After reading many of Lewin's articles and book chapters from his early career forward, however, we believe that understanding the field theory of Lewin in the early 1950s is necessary to understanding the role of gatekeeping in the 21st century. Scholars such as Pierre Bourdieu & Johnson, 1993, 1998) are returning to field theory to understand the selection and construction of news, but how similar is the field theory of Lewin to that of Bourdieu? And how can both help continue the development of a theory of gatekeeping?

8 Field Theory and Gatekeeping

The main idea behind field theory is to look broadly for explanations of social behavior, rather than test single hypotheses. Since theories are by definition a set of interrelated, logically consistent statements (Shoemaker et al., 2004), it is obvious that Gatekeeping Theory can become more powerful and larger in scope if gatekeeping is considered as one phenomenon within a larger field of related variables.

LEWIN'S FIELD THEORY

Lewin was a young scholar at an exciting time in the development of psychology as a social science. When he graduated from the University of Berlin in 1910, the dominant paradigm in psychology was philosophical, and psychologists commonly held joint appointments with departments of philosophy instead of forming multiple psychological sections. Gold (Lewin & Gold, 1999), who wrote an intellectual biography of Lewin, says that the field of psychology when Lewin was a young scholar concerned itself only with things that could be observed. While a graduate student, Lewin was greatly influenced by scholars who argued that *ideas* were part of reality and could be important constructs to use in forming hypotheses and developing theory. Although they could not be seen, ideas were introduced as theoretical constructs that could be defined both theoretically and operationally.

Lewin was a student of Ernst Cassirer, a leader in developing this philosophy of science, and soon became known as a proponent of Cassirer's paradigm of "constructivism" (Lewin & Gold, 1999, p. 8). Cassirer and Lewin argued that anything, any construct that could be theoretically conceived, could be measured and that such constructs could be related with one another in such a way as to build theory. This perspective, radical in the 1920s, is today the basis of most social science research.

As Lewin became a young psychologist following the First World War, the idea that constructs could be causally related was popular, as was holism, the idea that sets of related constructs considered simultaneously could explain social behaviors. It became the basis of gestaltism. Lewin became disenchanted with holism as limited to the theoretical level—"waving one's arms broadly in explanation of a puzzling phenomenon" (Lewin & Gold, 1999, p. 9)—but he retained the idea of broadly looking at explanations for behaviors.

Ultimately Lewin used mathematics to develop equations that could be tested with quantitative data. Although testing bivariate relationships was important, Lewin's equations reflected gestaltism by including numerous variables, each with a coefficient to express its force in the overall situation. This was consistent with the then new idea of logical positivism, which held that the only worthwhile theoretical statements were ones that could be tested. Lewin and other scholars became convinced that if psychologists could identify the right constructs and measure them as variables in equations, such equations could be used to develop psychological laws as valid and reliable as any in the physical sciences.

As he grew as a scholar, Lewin began referring to field theory in his publications, although its meaning was not explained. As we followed Lewin's intellectual development across his publications, we came to realize that field theory is essentially what today's scholars routinely practice—multivariate analysis. When trying to establish a causal relationship between two concepts, we identify and statistically control for multiple alternative explanations for the bivariate relationship. In other words, we try to understand the overall—or holistic—situation in which the relationship occurs. If doing research today, Lewin would develop theoretical models and use structural equation modeling to test whether the data support the theory. His concept of forces is consistent with the role of beta coefficients in regression equations.

So the "field," according to Lewin, is the complex environment in which a phenomenon occurs. His gatekeeping model showing how food gets to the table (Figure 1.1) reflects gestaltism in that he considers multiple situations in the field (channels and sections) and demonstrates that a formula predicting food usage would reflect choices and decisions (gates or variables), each affected by various forces.

GATEKEEPING RESEARCH AND THEORY

Although David Manning White, a student of Lewin, placed Gatekeeping Theory on the mass communication research agenda with his 1950 case study of a newspaper wire editor, White omitted field theory in his description of gatekeeping. Because of this, subsequent gatekeeping scholarship was both fruitful and frustrating. A frenzy of gatekeeping research emerged from the 1950s through the 1970s; however, theorizing about gatekeeping developed in fits and starts.

Lewin's field theory or ecological perspective received little attention from early communication scholars, appeals for a return to Lewin's theory notwithstanding. Brown (1979) argued that leaving field theory behind left holes in Gatekeeping Theory.

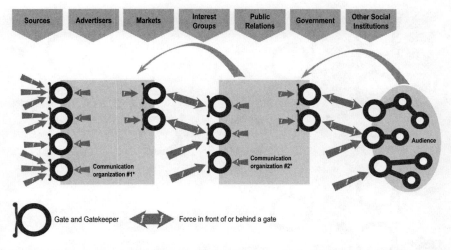

Figure 8.1 Gatekeeping between organizations is embedded in the social system ideology and culture and is influenced by social and institutional factors. As an example, communication organizations could include news services, online media, public relations agencies, television networks, or newspapers.

Notes: * See Figure 8.2 for a detailed version of gatekeeping within an organization.
    ** See Figure 8.3 for a detailed version of gatekeeping within an individual.

A sociological turn in news media scholarship, marked by the likes of Gans (1979a) and Tuchman (1978), filled some of those holes by examining individual gatekeepers in their organizational and social context.

Shoemaker (1991) returned to Lewin's holistic approach in her introduction of levels of analysis to gatekeeping and built several models to show the primary factors in the gatekeeping field. These levels of analysis represent a significant step forward in theorizing about gatekeeping in that studies, variables, and findings can be compared more easily. We include these holistic models, and we additionally show how constructs on these five levels of analysis function together as a field.

Figures 8.1, 8.2, and 8.3 synthesize what is known about gatekeeping, based on the levels of analysis we have discussed. Figures 8.2 and 8.3 are not independent models but represent enlargements of portions of Figure 8.1. The overall process is shown in Figure 8.1 but without detail within communication organizations and within individual gatekeepers. Figure 8.2 shows the gatekeeping processes within a communication organization, and Figure 8.3 shows the intra-individual psychological processes within one gatekeeper. In Figure 8.1 circles represent individual gatekeepers, vertical bars in front of gatekeepers are gates, and the arrows in front of and behind each gate represent the forces that affect a message's entrance into the gate and what happens to it afterward. The large squares are communication

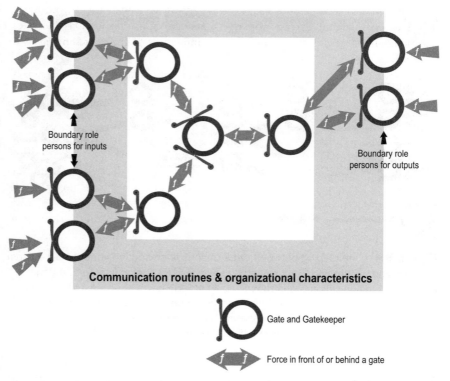

Boundary role
persons for inputs

Boundary role
persons for outputs

Communication routines & organizational characteristics

Gate and Gatekeeper

Force in front of or behind a gate

Figure 8.2 Gatekeeping within an organization is embedded in communication organizational characteristics.
Note: See Figure 8.3 for intraindividual gatekeeping processes.

organizations, and small rectangles represent social and institutional factors. One or more channels lead to and from each gate and gatekeeper, each carrying one or more messages or potential messages.

The process starts with a variety of potential messages traveling through multiple channels to any of several types of communication organizations, such as a news service, a blog, a public relations agency, a newspaper, or a television network. An organization may have multiple staff members operating in boundary role input positions, each with the power to control which potential messages actually enter the organization and the power to shape the message.

Moving to the organizational enlargement (Figure 8.2), we see that, within a complex organization, the boundary role gatekeepers in charge of inputs may channel selected messages to one or more internal gatekeepers, who may exert their own selection processes and who also may shape the message in a variety of ways. The surviving, shaped messages are then transmitted to boundary role gatekeepers for final shaping, selection, and transmission directly to the audience or to another communication organization (see Figure 8.1). As the feedback loop from organization 2 to organization 1 (and from the audience to organization 2) indicates, selection of messages for outputting is heavily influenced by the selection criteria of the receiver. As Figure 8.2 shows, the gatekeeping processes internal to the organization are embedded in the organization's communication routines and characteristics, which affect the decisions organizational gatekeepers make. Figure 8.2 also provides for the "groupthink" phenomenon (Janis, 1983), particularly among socially cohesive groups of gatekeepers.

Figure 8.3 identifies various psychological processes and individual characteristics that can affect the gatekeeping process, including cognitive heuristics, models of thinking, socialization, second guessing, values, attitudes, decision-making strategies, role conceptions, and type of job. Just as the broader gatekeeping model is embedded in social system ideology and culture, within-organization gatekeeping is embedded in communication routines and organizational characteristics, and individual-level gatekeeping processes are embedded in the individual's life experiences.

Thus we see the complexity of the gatekeeping process. The individual gatekeeper has likes and dislikes, ideas about the nature of his or her job, ways of thinking about a problem, preferred decision-making strategies, and values that all impinge on the decision to reject or select (and shape) a message. But the gatekeeper is not totally free to follow a personal whim; he or she must operate within the constraints of communication routines to do things this way or that. All of this also must

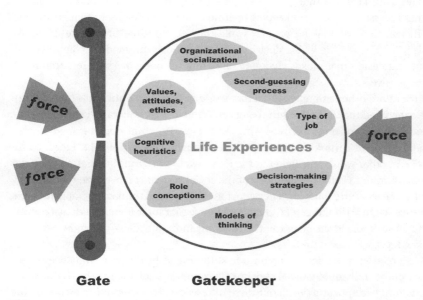

Figure 8.3 Intraindividual gatekeeping processes are embedded in life experiences.

occur within the framework of the communication organization, which has its own priorities but also is continuously buffeted by influential forces from outside the organization. And, of course, none of these actors—the individual, the routine, the organization, or the social institution—can escape the fact that it is tied to and draws its sustenance from the social system.

In fact, this model is made more complex when we realize the ways that these various factors can operate in conjunction with one another. As we have noted in previous chapters, in some cases the effects can be additive—at each point that an item passes through a gate, the chances increase that this information is selected and shaped as news. The conjunction of factors may also have interpretation or interaction effects (Shoemaker, Tankard & Lasorsa, 2004).

Simply put, examining factors from this model in isolation is not enough. For example, to what extent are individual communicators responsible for gatekeeping selections? "There will always be much room for the exercise of discretion by journalists" (Tunstall, 1971, p. 23). However, that latitude may vary according to the type of communication organization being studied. Abbott and Brassfield (1989) found that individual television gatekeepers seem to have more decision-making autonomy than their newspaper counterparts. And the decision-making styles of journalists can also be shaped by organizational routines. For example, Wright and Barbour (1976) conclude that a decision maker may select either the first item that meets minimum criteria or the most recent one (i.e., the newest news). Organizational routines will be important in determining whether the first or the most recent message is selected. Although gatekeepers can consider an unending stream of potential messages, most gatekeepers operate under fixed deadlines that encourage an efficient decision-making process while they at the same time prize newness. Primacy may be a more viable decision-making option with modern computerized layout and design that makes changing one's mind about a message less traumatic and expensive.

There are other examples of factors working together. Paul and Elder (2002) have concluded that individual thinking can often be egocentric, driven by the presumed rightness of one's own thinking. But they also point out that media gatekeepers' egocentric thinking extends to "sociocentric thinking" (Paul & Elder, 2002, p. 195), in other words, the belief in the rightness of our group's or nation's actions and justifications. Thus, the ideology of the social system can override the decision making of egocentric thinkers. They conclude that critical thinkers are able to resist such socio-centric thinking. It is possible of course that some ideologies may be more conducive to some levels of egocentric thinking and some ideologies more resistant to some levels of critical thinking.

As noted in a previous chapter, one study found little direct influence of the gender of the individual journalist on media content (Liebler & Smith, 1997). Journalistic routines appear to wash out these differences. However, it is worth examining the journalistic role conception of the gatekeepers—those who hold an interpretative role conception might be different than those who hold a disseminator role conception. Based on feminist epistemology (see e.g., Tanesini, 1999), which suggests that women see the world differently than their male counterparts, we might expect to see different interpretations of events and ideas in the news writing of female gatekeepers than male gatekeepers. If Duran (2001) is correct that feminist epistemologies vary by social system, then the social system might be another source of variation in news output by male and female reporters with an interpretative role conception. The enactment of the interpretative role conception can also be limited by the audience's reluctance to tolerate anything other than a disseminator role conception (Schudson, 1978). In turn, audience attitudes may vary by the type of news organization—interpretation is often better tolerated from magazines and blogs than newspapers and television networks. Interpretation is also better embraced by audiences in some social systems than others.

When examining how a number of factors shape gatekeeping, the temptation can be for interpretation; i.e., when we believe one factor is 'prior' to other explanatory variables, leading to the so-called short-circuit fallacy. Interpretation is not a fallacy; it just needs empirical verification. McChesney (2004) argues persuasively that the ideology of the economic elites shapes the news. However, ideology can appear at times to explain the whole gatekeeping process—we have the kind of news we do because news "stems directly from the system of profit-driven journalism in largely noncompetitive markets" (McChesney, 2004, p. 57). Herman and Chomsky's (1988) hierarchical model of influences on news, while invoking a number of factors that "filter" the news, also emphasizes the primary role of ideology in shaping the news. Their explanation for news coverage on Central America focuses on the American government's intentional use of lies and propaganda in the service of killing many innocent Central Americans. But their account says little about the media's role in communicating this content to the public, except to chide the media for being lapdogs—"the media were so closely wedded to U.S. government goals and perceptions that they never sought to learn the facts" (Herman & Chomsky, 1988, p. 194).

Thus, while ideology may indeed be a powerful factor in explaining news content, particularly in juxtaposition to individual-level factors, its power is tempered when the routine and organizational levels of analysis are considered. According to Gans, American journalism "is not simply a compliant supporter of elites or the Establishment or the ruling class; rather, it views nation and society through its own set of values and with its own conception of the good social order" (1979a, p. 62). We can avoid the short-circuit fallacy by accounting for a range of factors across the five levels of analysis.

The value of exploring factors over different levels of analysis is that it brings detail and nuance to our explanations of gatekeeping. The downside of examining a range of factors is that we can lose sight of the big picture by staring at the details, or we lose sight of the forest for the trees. The wisdom of field theory is its attention to the big picture, to the forest. In other words, field theory explores how a variety of interrelated factors form an environment in which gatekeeping occurs. If we are to do more than catalog explanatory factors across levels of analysis and actually theorize about gatekeeping, a return to field theory is essential.

FIELD THEORY AND GATEKEEPING TODAY

The void created when journalistic studies of gatekeeping left field theory behind has been filled by Pierre Bourdieu's concept of the field. Lewin and Bourdieu are not interchangeable, but both have much to offer. Some differences between the two theorists are obvious, such as Lewin's belief that mathematics could measure the forces before and after gates, terminology that Bourdieu ignores or avoids. Some differences are more subtle. For example, the individual is at the center of the field in Lewin's theory, while the media organization is more central to Bourdieu's field theory, a difference that reflects Lewin's psychological background and Bourdieu's more sociological approach.

Some similarities also exist. In both approaches, the *field* ranges conceptually from the micro to mezzo to the macro levels, and both emphasize the need to study many variables to understand a single phenomenon. In addition, both address the relationship among levels of analysis. Field theory of the 21st century "is concerned with how macrostructures are linked to organizational routines and journalistic practices, and emphasizes the dynamic nature of power" (Benson & Neveu, 2005, p. 9). Individual gatekeepers' range of decisions is limited by those macrostructures, organizational routines, and journalistic practices. Macrostructures, however, do not dictate routines or practices. Even though economic macrostructures, for example, are influential on most Western media, journalism as a field maintains a measure of autonomy, rooted in journalism's unique social capital built up over its history. Institutional characteristics and routines of news media provide gatekeepers with insulation from the power of outside influences.

The journalistic field is a unique social institution—more than the sum of its parts, the institution reflects the ways in which a whole range of micro, mezzo, and macro factors relate and interact with each other. Studying any one or two factors, as we have noted above, can provide an incomplete picture of the gatekeeping process. Benson and Neveu argue, based on Bourdieu's field theory, that "the 'field' opens up a new unit of analysis for media research: the entire universe of journalists and media organizations acting and reacting in relation to one another" (2005, p. 11). The concern echoes the ecological perspective of Lewin. The presence of each factor and each actor in the field shapes the influence of other factors and the behaviors of other actors. For example, the role of television news organizations shapes the role of newspaper organizations. The routines of gatekeepers are exploited by public relations practitioners. Ideology and cultural values limit options for gatekeeper behavior.

Although the term *unit of analysis* is not synonymous with level of analysis; nevertheless, Benson and Neveu (2005) raise a serious possibility for gatekeeping scholarship by pointing researchers to a new "field" of study. They propose that journalistic fields vary across social systems, which points gatekeeping research in the direction of cross-cultural studies. However, in at least one instance Benson and Neveu may overstate what field theory means for empirical gatekeeping research. "Influences emerging from the semiautonomous journalistic field—a mezzo level organizational, professional and ideological space—represent an additional variable not previously considered" (Benson & Neveu, 2005, p. 17). This is not so much a new, unexplored variable as it is a call for exploring how various (previously explored) variables interact with each other. Thus, we have not included this "variable" in the previous chapters in the section on levels of analysis. It rightly belongs here, where we consider how the variety of factors work together to shape and select the news. Benson and Neveu also argue that research on specific, independent factors that affect gatekeeping is of limited value. "Precisely because these effects are not independent, but act in relation to one another, the need for a more 'ample' theoretical model remains" (Benson & Neveu, 2005, p. 18). Again, the model is sound, as long as we explore how the factors cataloged in the model interact with each other.

Perhaps the biggest difference between Lewin's and Bourdieu's field theories is Bourdieu's attention to the role of history in understanding the gatekeeping process. History makes a difference on two levels. On one level, gatekeeping scholarship produces a body of work that creates a picture of how news turns out the way it does. We should not forget, however, that it is a moving picture. Historical changes in technologies, policies, or practices can precipitate changes in how items and information are selected and shaped into news. For example, the introduction of online news has presented new dynamics for gatekeeping. According to Singer: "Unlike the print newspaper, the Web is not a finite, concrete media form; instead, its form is simultaneously fluid and global and supremely individualistic" (2001, p. 78). What do these changes mean for gatekeeping? Do the "gates come down," as one book chapter title puts it (Gillmor, 2004)? Conclusions are mixed. Williams and Carpini (2004) conclude that organizational influences on gatekeeping are being rewritten. However, a number of studies (Arant & Anderson, 2001; Cassidy, 2006; Singer, 1997, 2005) see continuity between older and newer media. They conclude that routines established in print media maintain a grip on the online news media.

Technological changes did not start with the internet of course. Previous research (Abbott & Brassfield, 1989; Berkowitz, 1990b) explored how gatekeeping changed or remained the same with the arrival of television news. The research found changes in how gatekeeping occurred in these different organizational settings. However, explicit comparisons of print and electronic settings found similarity in the gatekeeping process (Abbott & Brassfield, 1989). The continuity between older and newer forms of media might lead us to conclude that history, in the end, is not important. The opposite is true. The studies suggest that, even in the face of technological and institutional changes, the tug of older, established routines shapes the newer environment. This historical continuity also underscores the relative autonomy of the journalistic field—journalism can withstand some exogenous forces.

On another level, Bourdieu's field theory suggests that history should reshape how we theorize about gatekeeping. Keeping abreast of historical changes has typically relied on well-used theoretical concepts applied in new historical settings. Thus, for example, the concept of *news subsidy* articulated by Gandy (1982) and others (e.g., VanSlyke Turk, 1986a) has been used to study new forms of subsidy, such as the video news release (e.g., Cameron & Blount, 1996; Machill, Beiler, & Schmutz, 2006). This sort of historical updating, however, does not change how we theorize about gatekeeping. What Bourdieu has in mind is the way that history can tilt the playing field, creating powerful actors or compelling routines. As Bourdieu puts it, gatekeeping is shaped by "the possibilities bequeathed by previous struggles, a space which tends to give direction to the search for solutions and, consequently, influences the present and future of production" (quoted in Benson & Neveu, 2005, p. 95).

One example of this is the historical emergence of various journalistic role conceptions. For a variety of reasons the disseminator role conception has emerged as the heart and soul of American journalism in the 20th and early 21st centuries (Schudson, 1978). We can think of the disseminator role as one value of the variable *journalistic role conception*. But role conceptions are not simply up to the individual gatekeeper to select—the disseminator role is a value that has been selected by historical processes. Efforts to change that role conception would be met with resistance from audiences who have come to expect it as the essence of American journalism. This is what new institutionalism (see, for example, P. A. Hall & Taylor, 1996; Pierson, 2004) has called *path dependence*—once a decision is made, exit costs emerge from a variety of sources, making change difficult. It should be noted that the disseminator role serves the interests of organizations (Berkowitz, 1987; Sigal, 1973) and the interests of powerful elites (Bagdikian, 2004). However, the disseminator role is not simply a creation of elites or organizations; it is a historical creation that has been reinforced by path dependent processes. Interestingly, the online media may represent a constitutive moment; i.e., the internet may be developing its own historical arc that grants it the opportunities to more fully embrace an interpretative role conception.

History does not change the gatekeeping model that is based on the five levels of analysis. It does affect how we think about the journalistic field, or, in other words, how we see the interaction of factors in the model. Gatekeepers are not always overrun by political elites or economic imperatives, because history has created a journalistic field that has its own rules and routines.

9 Gatekeeping Channels

People sometimes use gatekeeping as a metaphor to describe how "news" is discovered and selected by the media, but this is an inaccurate conceptualization—information becomes news only when published or transmitted by a news medium, whereas the source of information begins with *events*. People perceive events as more or less newsworthy, which causes them to select and pass along information about them. This is as true for sources as for journalists. For Gatekeeping Theory, the *event* is "ground zero"—the point at which the entire process begins. This is not to deny the *influence* of history on gatekeeping; rather we recognize that the *process* of gatekeeping begins every time an event occurs. This is, of course, hyperbole in the sense that events never have an *equal* chance of getting past the first gate. For example, our routine medical check-ups never make it into the major news media, unless we hold important social positions, such as president of a country. Still, the medical check-up is an event, and it is information about the event that enters or bounces off of gates. The history of our check-ups (for example, whether we were previously diagnosed with a cancer) definitely influences the whole process of selection, shaping, repetition, and timing.

THREE CHANNELS

Gatekeeping Theory has traditionally given journalists and their news media the primary responsibility for making the decisions that send information about world events to the audience each day; however, journalists would not know about most events without the existence of sources. Journalists have direct experience with only a handful of the events that might become news, and so most information about events flows from people who participate in the event, those who see it, and those who are knowledgeable about it. For example, when an airplane crashes, information comes from survivors of the crash, airport personnel and other observers, experts from government agencies, retired air personnel, air safety groups, and the companies that built parts of the plane.

Thus sources and the mass media can be thought of as two channels through which information flows about events around the world. Channels are composed of sections, with a gate in front of each section that controls entry into the next, and conceptualizing the flow of information through channels helps simplify and clarify our understanding of how information about events gets to the audience. The disadvantage of this simplification, however, is that channels seem fixed in time order—a bit of information must flow through section 1, then section 2—and there is no way for information to pass back and forth between seemingly impenetrable channel walls.

Lewin's diagram (Figure 1.1) shows two channels through which food reaches the table and therefore makes it seem as if these are the only channels through which food can travel. If creating this figure today, however, we would have to add channels for delivering food to the home, picking up take-out food on the way home, and ordering food shipped via the internet. When we apply Lewin's model to news, we also see that the channels are not limited to two and that the exact nature of channels varies by type and location of event and by time and space. Thus the channels are not fixed or impenetrable, but instead are fluid, and information flows between them on its way to the audience.

Once an event occurs (or once the media are informed that it will occur), some people participate in it, some observe it, and those who have a stake in it (such as government and private organizations, individuals, and interest groups) discuss it with journalists and others. In this source channel, people must either observe an event or have information relevant to it. Therefore important sections in the source channel include sources' skills in observation, their short- and long-term memory, and their decisions about what kind of information to give to journalists. Sources sometimes seek out journalists to get their interpretation of the event in the news, and journalists also may interview them to get information about the event.

The media channel carries journalists' (and other media employees' and policies') gatekeeping activities. Activities in the media channel usually begin after the event occurs and after information begins to flow to various sources, but journalists sometimes observe an event first hand. Most of the time, however, they rely on news releases, routine functions of government, and each other to learn what is happening in the world. Once journalists learn of an event, they may ignore it (and end the media part of the gatekeeping process) or seek more information from organizations and individuals. Once an event passes this first gate, journalists make decisions about how to prepare the message, such as which styles to apply or formats to use. Gates in the media channel include selection decisions, assessments of how important various pieces of information are, shaping of the news items, deciding how long the coverage will be, the graphic presentation, and position within the news medium. When reporters and editors first learn about the event, the substance or nature of the event is the strongest predictor of its newsworthiness. The more deviant and socially significant an event is, the more newsworthy journalists and editors think it is, and the more likely they are to open gates that will allow the event to become news

(Shoemaker & Cohen, 2006). Some of these messages are rejected or changed by editors, and so only a small number of processed messages make their way to the audience. This has been the traditional end of the gatekeeping process.

We propose, however, that at least one more channel should be included in the gatekeeping process—information about events that flows from audience members. Whereas journalists primarily get information directly from sources, the audience has traditionally received most of its information from journalists. Since Lewin's gatekeeping model was introduced, the emphasis of studies has been on selection, shaping, timing, and specifics of media content, whether on the internet, in newspapers, or on television and radio news. This model does not include an active role for the audience, except that it is assumed that the audience receives and consumes the content. Westley and Maclean's model (Figure 1.3) opens the possibility that the audience has a weak active role, sending feedback—primarily in the form of letters or telegrams at that time—but there is an assumption that the audience has little or no direct influence on content. Shoemaker's model (Figure 8.1) adds to this the possibility that audiences have indirect influence on content through advertisers, but even here there is no easy way for advertisers to know which content units audiences are interacting with, or what they are reading, viewing, or listening. Surveys, focus groups, diaries, and other methodologies provide data of questionable reliability and validity.

Since the mid-1990s many news media (newspapers first, then television and radio) have developed internet companion organizations. They (and the internet in general) have grown progressively stronger, until in 2008 online news media offered to their audiences streaming videos of speeches made by U.S. presidential candidates, accompanied by the automatically scrolling text, on the day the speeches were given and for weeks afterward. Not long after Senator Barack Obama spoke to the Democratic Party's nominating convention, the streaming video and text also appeared on the "most emailed" list of *nytimes.com*, indicating that many viewers and readers of the speech emailed its web link to other people.

Journalists select and present news items that they think are most important. In contrast, online media's routine use of lists that automatically reflect the popularity of content items tells readers and staff members in both the editorial and marketing sides what is most relevant to the lives of readers and, by extension, to their family and friends. *Most-emailed lists* reflect the combined judgments about what is important to journalists and to audience members.

Of course, the idea of a reader passing a newspaper story along to someone else is not new. People have often torn articles from newspapers and given them to family and friends, but this process was usually limited to handing or mailing one copy of a news item to one other person. Enthusiastic readers photocopied articles and sent news items to several people, but this involved more work on their part. In contrast, emailing an article to many other people takes little effort—no physical activity beyond a few taps on the computer's keyboard. This makes it possible for readers to send many news items to many other people, creating more pass-along readership, since those who receive an emailed news item may also send it to others. This results in exponentially increasing readership of the most popular items across time.

Figure 9.1 shows that information can flow through three channels—from the occurrence of events via both media and non-media sources to the news "table" for consumption and distribution by audience members. In the audience channel, we see that the internet now allows anyone to become a gatekeeper by passing along news items and commenting on them in many web sites, such as *digg.com*, *reddit.com*, *YouTube*, and *Facebook*. When readers browse through news items on the *New York Times* web site, they may come across something that is personally relevant or relevant to someone close—a friend, a family member, or a colleague. It is at this point that the journalists' perceptions of the newsworthiness of an event interact with the reader's perceptions of its personal relevance to increase the odds that the reader will click on an email link that sends the news item to someone else. Therefore, we must conceptualize readers as having their own gate, and they send news items to others in the audience when the interaction between newsworthiness and personal relevance is strong enough. The *New York Times* web site gives readers the opportunity to write a personal message to send along with the emailed news item, thus framing the original story with an opinion or comment, possibly to point out why it is important for the receiver. Just as journalists write in certain styles to engage the reader, audience members can pass along stories with a personal message to "engage the receiver."

READER ENGAGEMENT

Hook the reader from the start. Capture your reader's attention. These are fundamental guidelines for news writing (Brooks, Kennedy, Moen, & Ranly, 1996; Cappon, 2000; Sumner & Miller, 2005; Zinsser, 2001). News-writing books teach future journalists how to engage the reader by using techniques such as beginning with anecdotes or vivid scenes (Brooks et al., 1996; Cappon, 2000; Sumner & Miller, 2005). In fact, these techniques are often discussed in narrative journalism, which presents an alternative to the inverted pyramid. In narrative journalism, journalists can use "scenes, anecdotes and dialogue in chronology to build to a climax," whereas journalists array facts from most to least important in the inverted pyramid (Brooks et al., 1996, p. 375). Narrative journalism refers to writing with set scenes, characters, actions that unfold over time, the interpretable voice of a teller, some sense of relationship to the reader, and leading the reader toward a point (Kramer, 2008). First- or second-person reference (such as "I" and "You") is also used to involve the reader by encouraging the reader to identify with the person in the story (Rossiter, 1981).

Anecdotes are "stories embedded in stories" to inform and entertain (Brooks et al., 1996, p. 379). The beginning of the news story is the "bait" for the reader, and so journalists ask for and often use anecdotes there to grab the attention of

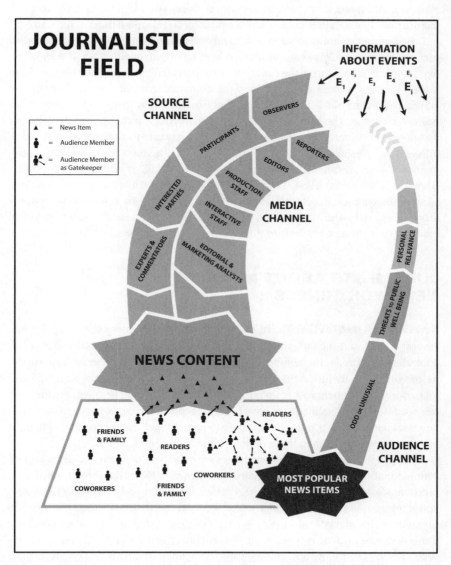

Figure 9.1 Source, media, and audience channels in the gatekeeping process.

the reader. An anecdotal lead (or lede) starts with a story about a person or an event (C. Rich, 2003). *Vivid scenes* are used "to make readers see, smell, feel, taste, and hear" (Brooks et al., 1996, p. 376). The Associated Press guidebook on news writing (Cappon, 2000) recommends that journalists write "visually" by giving the reader a picture based on details and specifics, what Rich (2003) calls a descriptive lead.

Studies in the areas of advertising and social psychology show that the use of *personal voice* (I and You) can stimulate reader involvement (Rossiter, 1981). Directive language is used to make messages look personally relevant to the reader, to make the event written about apply to the audience's present interest, needs, and activities (Greenwald & Leavitt, 1984; Petty & Cacioppo, 1984). The concept has been explored in the areas of advertising, marketing, and social and consumer psychology in discussions of how the perceived personal relevance of a message influences a person's evaluation of and reaction to the message or his/her consequent behavior (Baumgartner, Sujan, & Bettman, 1992; Christensen & Olson, 2002; Greenwald & Leavitt, 1984; Petty & Cacioppo, 1984). Thus the use of first- and second-person voice in news stories increases the odds that a news item will appear more relevant to the reader. This type of personal reference is often found in editorials or columns, but feature stories also use this linguistic style.

JUDGMENTS ABOUT AN EVENT'S NEWSWORTHINESS

News items on the *New York Times* "most-emailed" list have made their way through several source and media gates before finally appearing on the rank-ordered list. Journalists' and audience members' cognitive assessment of the event's newsworthiness is one of many forces that affect whether an event passes through media and audience gates (Shoemaker & Cohen, 2006). Therefore, in general we assume that items on the "most-emailed" list have been judged by readers as having a degree of newsworthiness higher than items failing to appear, and that items ranked highest are more newsworthy than those at the bottom.

Early research defined newsworthiness with a variety of factors, such as simplification, identification, and sensationalism (Ostgaard, 1965); significance, normality, prominence, and visuality (Buckalew, 1969a); novelty or oddity; conflict or controversy; interest; importance, impact, or consequence; sensationalism; timeliness; and proximity (Shoemaker et al., 1987). A later study suggested ten overall news values: the power elite, celebrity, entertainment, surprise, bad news, good news, magnitude, relevance, follow-up, and newspaper agenda (Harcup & O'Neill, 2006). However, we discuss here more recent notions of deviance and social significance, which help generalize two important aspects of newsworthiness overall (Shoemaker, 1991, 2006; Shoemaker et al., 1987).

Deviance. When an event strays from normal social values and beliefs, it can be said to be deviant in relation to those norms. As in previous studies, *deviance* is defined as a construct with three dimensions, normative, social change, and statistical deviance (Shoemaker et al., 1987; Shoemaker et al., 1991). *Normative* deviance is the extent to which social norms and laws have been broken. *Social change* deviance is the extent to which there is an apparent threat to the status quo of society, such as a large public protest. *Statistical* deviance is simply the extent to which an event is out of the ordinary or unusual. We assume that many events covered by the media exhibit statistical deviance to some degree. In a recent study of online news, Lee (2008) found that deviance was not only a significant predictor of newsworthiness, but also validated Shoemaker's (1996) proposition that people survey their environments for—and actively seek out—deviant news events.

Social significance. While newsworthy events often display a level of deviance, many also have a degree of importance to a society or culture. *Social significance* is defined as a construct with four dimensions, political, economic, cultural, and public significance (Shoemaker & Cohen, 2006). A *politically* significant event has the capacity to affect the political system at the international, national, or local levels, such as elections, government activities, and the passing or breaking of laws. An *economically* significant event has the capacity to affect business and commerce processes at the international, national, or local levels, such as unemployment, imports and exports, currency rates, and budgets. A *culturally* significant event has the capacity to affect social systems and institutions, such as religion, ethnicity, and language. A *publicly* significant event has the capacity to affect the well-being of citizens, such as issues of health, the environment, and natural disasters.

PREDICTING WHAT READERS SEND TO ONE ANOTHER

A study by Shoemaker, Seo and Johnson (2008) analyzed the characteristics of the news items on the most-emailed list. News item was the unit of analysis, consisting of both news articles and blog posts, as both appear on the *New York Times* most-emailed list. At any moment, 25 news items can appear. The scholars designed a custom collection script to take a snapshot of the most-emailed list once a day for a month.

The study found that most-emailed news items cover events that are odd or unusual (but not to the point of breaking laws or norms); that affect the public welfare, such as health or safety issues; and that include the use of journalistic conventions that can increase the odds that readers are personally engaged in the news items. The scholars found that journalistic and audience selection conventions differ. While journalists typically pass along events that are odd or unusual, break laws, or threaten the stability of the status quo, or that have political, economic, cultural, or public significance (Shoemaker & Cohen, 2006), but these event characteristics are not all important when readers act as gatekeepers. The odd and unusual event plays a huge role when readers decide to send news items around their email gates—a more important role than journalists use in selecting events. Whereas many news items are about breaking norms and laws (generally referred to as "bad news"), readers select articles about *keeping* laws and norms. News items that have political, economic, and cultural significance are not often selected by readers, but they do often select items about threats to the public's well-being.

This shows us that readers use different criteria for gatekeeping decisions than those used by journalists. Although one or two of the usual newsworthiness criteria are important to readers, Shoemaker, Seo and Johnson (2008) also show that readers prefer news writing practices that draw the reader into the story—something that journalism students learn and that apparently readers appreciate.

Therefore, the publication of information by the mass media is not the end of the gatekeeping process. Once journalists select events for coverage based on their judgment of its newsworthiness, readers take over. In this third gatekeeping channel, readers use criteria such as which stories are important for their family members, friends, and other acquaintances. After reading an online news item, one reader can decide to email it or move on to the next story. Often readers check out the "most-emailed" list and use it as a way to find interesting articles. Of course, new articles are added to the list each day, indicating that many readers also search out news items that they want to read and possibly to send on. The study shows that news items selected for emailing are likely to be written in a way that increases the odds that the news items are personally relevant to a wide audience.

The gatekeeping process in Figure 9.1 is considerably more complex than Lewin's original diagram, not just because more than two channels are presented, but also because the model shows that information flows back and forth among the channels. The relative influence of the source channel is largest early in the process, and then the media channel manipulates and produces the raw information about events into one or another form of news.

The most-emailed, most-blogged, and most-read article lists are used by many media, around the world, to provide information about the popularity of news items to their readers. The audience channel thus conveys to people in many countries what is of most interest to audiences in their own and in other countries. In addition, these popularity lists give some articles longer lives, both because it may take a long time for somebody to read the recommended article and because some articles stay on the list for many days after their ephemeral online news sites drop them from the front news page.

The result is that we now know much more about what the public reads than we did before online technology. Examining the public's use of online news has become increasingly important—the number of readers who go online to keep themselves updated with world events has surged over the last decade. The percentage of people who said they go online for news at least three times a week was a mere 2 percent in 1996, but that number jumped to 23 percent in only four years. In 2006 it was well over 30 percent (Pew Research Center for the People and the Press, 2006). Moreover, the increased consumption of news online has important implications for how the public is informed of news events (Althaus & Tewksbury, 2002; Heeter, Brown, Soffin, Stanley, & Salwen, 1989). Scholars have argued that online news media allow readers to have greater control over news exposure and to focus on issues they feel more relevant to themselves (Althaus & Tewksbury, 2002; Dozier & Rice, 1984; Heeter et al., 1989; F. Williams, Phillips, & Lum, 1985). But perhaps the most significant impact of the audience channel is that it requires the revision of the original gatekeeping model and updates a theory begun in the 1940s for the early 21st century.

10 Gatekeeping in the 21st Century

Gatekeeping Theory's central constructs—gates and gatekeepers, forces around the gates, channels through which items flow and sections that organize the channels—are as useful now as when Kurt Lewin developed his model (Figure 1.1) in the mid-20th century. What other theories used to study the mass media can claim an ancestry of such duration and with as many published works?

STUDYING ONLINE MEDIA

Although some have predicted that the idea of gatekeeping is now dead, a concept made moribund by the internet, the previous chapter shows that these constructs, and the overall theory, are useful in analyzing mass communication of the 21st century. The challenge is for scholars to think creatively about applying the theory to a changing world and to adapt research methodology that keeps pace. It makes little sense to study a changing media landscape with methods developed to study printed newspapers in the pre-computer era. New software is necessary to capture information about ephemeral, always changing internet sites, and we also need advances in ways to analyze the content.

For example, on the Friday before Barack Obama was inaugurated as President of the United States, the *nytimes.com* home page offered readers a chance to express their hopes for the Obama presidency in an interactive feature ("I hope so too," January 16, 2009). Floating and randomly moving in and out, back and forth, in a white space were blue words and phrases representing the hopes of 200 people the newspaper interviewed in person about issues such as border security, abortion, the environment, the US global image, government under God, and universal health care, among others. The reader clicked on an issue and listened to the interviewees' short messages ("I hope that …"). At any time readers could register their hopes by clicking "I hope so too," changing that issue's color to green. After readers considered the issues, they could compare their hopes with those of others who interacted with the feature, and they could see the number of people who selected each issue.

As a result of their interactions with this feature, the issue priorities of *New York Times* online readers were communicated to editors and other readers, as well as to politicians and other news sources. We can think of the issues/hopes as items that traveled first through the source channel (the 200 people interviewed); second, to the media channel (where the information was produced as an interactive feature); third, through the reader channel ("I hope so too"), and fourth, back to the media channel (the number of people who hoped for each issue). This is not a linear process, however; in fact the interactivity of the feature was designed to make the reading and voting/hoping process circular. Readers manipulated the issue items, sending information back through the media, source and reader channels—a loop repeating over and again, constrained only by the newspaper editors' decisions about the feature's newsworthiness and when to remove it from their package of Obama inauguration coverage.

In this example, two variables represent forces around the gates: First is the number of interviewees who named each issue, ranging from one to six. Second is the number of readers who voted for each issue, numbering in the thousands. We can hypothesize that the number of interviewees who name an issue is positively related to the number of readers who select it. We can also hypothesize that the number of readers interacting with the feature is positively related to how many days or hours this feature remains part of the site's Obama inauguration coverage.

But studying the movement of these issue items through source, media, and reader channels is a challenge for today's standard content analysis research methods. Although individuals have written software for specific studies, as in the preceding chapter's study, social science methodologies are not prepared to analyze online media. New or modified methods are needed if online media are to be studied and if Gatekeeping Theory is to advance.

The unique character of online content—continuous change—is a challenge for researchers. Scholars who want a snapshot of media content at one point in time are faced with a difficult decision: There are many points of time in a day, for example, 1,440 minutes, and which time point should be captured for study? In addition, if scholars want to generalize their results across a country or countries, they have an additional problem: Although *time* is a continuous variable, people experience time as categorized by the government into zones. These time zones correlate with changes in source and reader availability. If an online snapshot is captured such that New Yorkers see it at 6:00 p.m., it is 3:00 p.m. in California—prime time on the east coast but afternoon on the west. If the object is to study prime time online media, how do we define *prime time*?

Online content changes in real time. This allows people around the world to experience events such as the Obama inauguration as they happen. But scholars must consider the fact that real time interacts with the position of the sun in the readers' part of the world, influencing whether they are eating, sleeping, or working. Thus people across the world have different experiences with online media. Midnight in

China is noon in the United States. At which point in time is the measurement of source and reader characteristics to be correlated with the snapshot of online media content?

We need better ways of studying change, which is the most interesting and challenging aspect of online media—they instantly change as the news environment changes. But studying such change over time is complicated; continuous variables change continuously across time. Auto correlation and multi-collinearity are only two of the potential problems associated with analyzing data collected over time. Advances in time series analysis will make it easier to test theories such as gatekeeping, which is intended to describe, explain and predict a dynamic system.

Gatekeeping Theory is disarming to the casual reader, with its charming, yet irascible Mr. Gates making in or out decisions for news items presented to one newspaper. Lewin's genius was explaining a complex idea clearly, his metaphor of gates and channels being easily understood. Although his theoretical model was intended to study changes in the selection and distribution of food items in a social system, it was most often used to study the selection of news items, yet rarely as a dynamic process. Scholars studying 21st century mass media must return to Lewin's original application of the theory—studying social change. Methods and statistics that analyze static variables, in which there is change across cases at only one time point, must be remodeled to also study change across time. Scholars must push their analytical tools to study the dynamic processes of both traditional and online media in an increasingly fast paced world.

MORE CHALLENGES

Here we list other directions for future gatekeeping research, some of which were suggested by Shoemaker in 1991. This may imply that few theoretical advances have been achieved in the interval, but in reality much progress has been made, just not in ways anticipated in 1991. First, we must continue to explore how environmental changes shape gatekeeping. Studies that make ahistorical pronouncements look myopic a decade or less later. Herman and Chomsky's (1988) propaganda model predicts journalism's acquiescence to the demands of corporate America in static terms, but now we see that their model has had trouble explaining the news media's coverage of corporate scandals, such as with Enron and WorldCom. True, the topic of corporate corruption did eventually recede and media watchdogs did not exactly delve into all the related structural problems of the scandal, and many media were no doubt able to frame the stories as good businesses gone bad (Doyle, 2006). However, there continue to be serious stories that are contrary to the interests of the corporate world, for example the favorable news stories, commentaries, and editorials regarding online music and video file swapping. This practice challenges capitalistic assumptions (in the concrete if not the abstract), and something is going on that the Herman and Chomsky model does not fully predict or explain. As Swidler (1986) and Gans (1979a) have reminded us, even ideologies can change over time and under some circumstances. The body of knowledge that Gatekeeping Theory produces must keep pace.

Second, if we are to study gatekeeping at the social system level, more research must span social systems, because they may produce different types of media content. Some comparative studies have already shown promise. Ferree, Gamson, Gerhards, and Rucht (2002) have examined the selection and construction of news related to abortion in the United States and Germany. Their comparison examines variables at the social system, social institution, organizational, and routines levels, and crafts an explanation for the differences in news about abortion. Indeed, if we are to study journalistic fields in the way that Benson and Neveu (2005) have suggested, by necessity we will be required to engage in this kind of cross-cultural research. And while we should look for differences across systems, we also should explore similarities. Shoemaker and Cohen (2006) have examined similarities in how news is defined in ten countries—similarities that come in part from human evolutionary biology (see also Shoemaker, 1996).

Third, the move to more cross-cultural studies can be complicated by another phenomenon facing gatekeeping—globalization. Globalization presents a methodological problem for comparative studies since cases (social systems) are not necessarily distinct. Nevertheless, globalization, a kind of Wallerstein (1974) "world system" mentioned previously, presents several new realities for gatekeepers: Not only is CNN present around the globe, but so are other news organizations. Thus, organizational routines from one social system are being exported to other social systems where different political, economic, and extra-media influences operate. The story of this clash has yet to be fully told. Similarly, globalization has created interconnected news organizations that span national boundaries. Cohen, Levey, Roeh, and Gurevitch (1996) study how Eurovision News Exchange decides what is news. The video exchange service operates across borders through the cooperation of television organizations. This global institution has developed decision making that must accommodate gatekeepers from a number of countries. How this sort of interconnection rewrites routines in the face of social institution and social system influences deserves further scholarly attention. And finally, as the United States and other countries push for the expansion of the marketplace in countries around the world, media systems that were sheltered from a full range of marketplace forces have to cope with new influences. For example, indigenous journalistic routines face new pressures from audiences and economic elites. However, globalization is seldom the leveling influence its detractors claim, since social systems typically refract international pressures through their own values and institutions (Kitschelt, Lange, Marks, & Stephens, 1999). What is best or efficient in one social system may not be in another. In fact, there is no guarantee that a particular efficient practice will even be selected. Kitschelt and his colleagues (1999) conclude from this that the most likely changes will occur in countries with the least embedded institutions, with systems least tied to core national values, and with those least tied to powerful actors.

Thus the more flexible the system, the greater the globalization; the more embedded the system, the more likely only path dependent developments occur.

Fourth, more gatekeeping studies should specify news content as the dependent variable. This seems like an obvious point, yet many studies only describe the gatekeeping process or make only impressionistic observations about media content. These descriptive studies do make a valuable contribution to gatekeeping. For example, Heider's (2000) study of race in the newsroom offers valuable insights into the news making process, but it relies on community activists' accounts of media content. We need more studies, such as the one by Ferree and colleagues (2002), that identify how gatekeeping affects specific content. Thus, gatekeeping studies should include content analysis whenever possible, such as the study by Shoemaker and colleagues (2001) that examined news coverage of congressional legislation. This leads to greater precision in theorizing about the impact of gatekeeping on content.

Fifth, more studies need to span multiple levels of analysis. This can be done to weight the relative force of various factors, such as Shoemaker and colleagues' study at the individual and routine levels. Analysis across multiple levels can also be done to explore interaction effects, such as we described in a previous chapter. This, in effect, is the kind of field research that Benson and Neveu (2005) advocate and that Ferree and colleagues (2002) have accomplished. Many plausible interaction effects still need to be explored.

Sixth, the sociological turn in gatekeeping studies has left Mr. Gates as a minor character in the selection of news. Little room seems to be left for the agency of individual actors. How much autonomy and power do individual gatekeepers have to impose their own agendas on media content? What conditions are conducive to the exercise of personal judgment over more structural constraints? Given that human beings have creative capacity and a reflexive knowledge of the world outside, we should not give up entirely on the agency of individual gatekeepers. Anthony Giddens' (1979) structuration theory has acknowledged that formidable forces shape human action, but also that these structural forces are not inviolable—human beings are not without agency. Revolutions do happen. Structuration theory holds out the possibility of reclaiming power for Mr. Gates, and it bears elaboration when thinking about gatekeeping.

Seventh, newer statistical procedures are available to study gatekeeping as a "field." Procedures, such as hierarchical linear modeling, allow the scholar to assess quantitative data from more than one level of analysis. The major advantage of this is the extra precision gained by using data on lower levels as they were gathered instead of averaging or otherwise combining them in the data set from the highest level of analysis.

Eighth, this book has paid attention to the forces at the gate at each level of analysis. However, studies should do more with the gates themselves and the forces surrounding them. Does the number of items in front of or behind a gate affect the polarity and strength of the force exerted? Must forces always change polarity?

Is movement through a gate always unidirectional or could some items move "backward"? What would cause them to do so? Are some gates "lower" than others?

Ninth, more can be done with characteristics of the messages. Nisbett and Ross (1980) suggest that vivid messages are more likely than pallid messages to pass through a gate, but this idea is underexplored in gatekeeping research. We need to progress beyond the categorization of messages (such as human interest, economy, international issues) to develop a number of continuous dimensions on which messages can be measured. This will add much to our ability to predict whether and in what form a message passes through a gate.

Tenth, we should compare the gatekeeping activities of various types of communication organizations, such as the internet and online media, television networks and local stations, newspapers, radio stations, advertising agencies, public relations agencies, and magazines. Some of this has been done; for example, Abbott and Brassfield (1989) compared decision making at local television stations and at newspapers. More questions need attention. How do communication routines differ? How do the differing goals of these organizations affect inputs and outputs not just in terms of selection but also in terms of how the messages are shaped?

AND FINALLY

At least one more thing needs to be done with Gatekeeping Theory. When journalism was initially taught in American universities in the 20th century, most studies could be described as *applied* research, studies of interest to working journalists. By many accounts, one of the achievements of journalism scholarship at mid-century was its ability to move beyond applied to theoretical research (Rogers, 1994). Gatekeeping scholarship was at the forefront of that move (Reese & Ballinger, 2001).

It is ironic, then, that those in public relations and political communication have used gatekeeping research as a kind of applied science. The more we know about gatekeeping, the clearer the roadmap for those who try to influence the process of news selection and construction. It is perhaps doubly ironic that news and other media professions have largely ignored gatekeeping research, opening themselves up to manipulation by influences outside of the media. It is our hope that media professionals pay attention to gatekeeping scholarship. If audiences are dissatisfied with the kind of news they get from the mass media (Geary, 2005; Littlewood, 1998), then journalists need to pay closer attention to why the news takes its present form. News can be better than it is, however we define "better." But making the news better is not accomplished by force of will—it is a project that is built on understanding the forces that shape the news. The usefulness of Gatekeeping Theory in the 21st century depends largely on the creativity of scholars and their willingness to learn procedures that analyze dynamic systems.

About the Authors

Pamela J. Shoemaker, Ph.D. (Wisconsin-Madison, 1982), is the John Ben Snow Professor in the S.I. Newhouse School of Public Communications at the Syracuse University, Syracuse, New York, USA. She was previously director of the School of Journalism at Ohio State University and earlier was on the faculty of the Department of Journalism at the University of Texas at Austin.

She holds the M.S. in Communications and the B.S.J. in Journalism from the Scripps School of Journalism at Ohio University (1972) and was named the L.J. Hortin Distinguished Alumna in 2006.

Her books include *News Around the World: Practitioners, Content and the Public* (with Akiba Cohen, 2006); *How to Build Social Science Theories* (with James Tankard and Dominic Lasorsa, 2004); *Mediating the Message: Theories of Influences on Mass Media Content* (with Steve Reese, 1991, 1996); *Gatekeeping* (1991); and the *Journalism Monograph: Building a Theory of News Content* (1987).

Shoemaker has been co-editor (with Michael Roloff) of the top-ranked Sage journal *Communication Research* since 1997. Earlier she was associate editor of *Journalism and Mass Communication Quarterly* and has served on the editorial boards of many journals. Shoemaker has served as President of the Association for Education in Journalism and Mass Communication and received the 2007 Distinguished Educator Award for Excellence in Teaching and the Kreighbaum Under-40 Award for Achievement in Research, Teaching, and Public Service. She has also been the chair of the Mass Communication Division of the International Communication Association, and was chair of the Consortium of Communication Associations. She is a member of the American Association for Public Opinion Research, the International Association for Mass Communication Research, and the National Communication Association.

Tim P. Vos, Ph.D. (Syracuse University, 2005), is an assistant professor of journalism studies in the School of Journalism at the University of Missouri-Columbia, USA. He holds an M.A. in Journalism and Mass Communication from the University of Iowa (1995) and a B.A. in Philosophy and Political Studies from Dordt College (1984). He previously served on the faculty at Seton Hall University. He is author of book chapters on gatekeeping and media history, and of conference papers on media sociology, media policy, political communication, and media history. He has won the Leslie J. Moeller Award, Kappa Tau Alpha research award, and top three faculty paper award from the Association for Education in Journalism and Mass Communication. His dissertation at the S.I. Newhouse School of Public Communications at Syracuse University won the All-University Doctoral Prize. He was a member of the editorial board of the *Journal of Communication Inquiry*. He is a member of the Association for Education in Journalism and Mass Communication, International Communication Association, Broadcast Education Association, American Journalism Historians Association, and the American Political Science Association.

References

Abbott, E. A., & Brassfield, L. T. (1989). Comparing decisions on releases by TV and newspaper gatekeepers. *Journalism Quarterly, 66*(4), 853–856.

Adams, J. S. (1980). Interorganizational processes and organizational boundary spanning activities. In B. M. Staw & L. L. Cummings (Eds.), *Research in organizational behavior* (Vol. 2, pp. 321–355). Greenwich, CT: JAI.

Adams, R. C., & Fish, M. J. (1987). TV news directors' perceptions of station management style. *Journalism Quarterly, 64*(1), 154–162, 276.

Adams, W. C. (1982). *Television coverage of international affairs*. Norwood, NJ: Ablex Pub. Co.

Aday, S., Livingston, S., & Hebert, M. (2005). Embedding the truth: A cross-cultural analysis of objectivity and television coverage of the Iraq war. *Harvard International Journal of Press/Politics, 10*(1), 3–21.

Akhavan-Majid, R., & Boudreau, T. (1995). Chain ownership, organizational size, and editorial role perception. *Journalism & Mass Communication Quarterly, 72*(4), 863–873.

Alexander, A. (2004). *Media economics: Theory and practice* (3rd ed.). Mahwah, NJ: Lawrence Erlbaum.

Alexander, J. C. (1981). The mass news media in systemic, historical, and comparative perspective. In E. Katz & T. Szecsko (Eds.), *Mass media and social change* (pp. 17–51). Beverly Hills, CA: Sage.

Allen, C. (2005). Discovering 'Joe Six Pack' content in television news: The hidden history of audience research, news consultants, and the Warner class model. *Journal of Broadcasting & Electronic Media, 49*(4), 363–382.

Allen, C. (2007). News directors and consultants: RTNDA's endorsement of TV journalism's 'greatest tool'. *Journal of Broadcasting & Electronic Media, 51*(3), 424–437.

Althaus, S. L. (2003). When news norms collide, follow the lead: New evidence for press independence. *Political Communication, 20*(4), 381–414.

Althaus, S. L., & Tewksbury, D. (2002). Agenda setting and the 'new' news. *Communication Research, 29*(2), 180–207.

Altschull, H. J. (1984). *Agents of power*. New York: Longman.

An, S., & Bergen, L. A. (2007). Advertiser pressure on daily newspapers. *Journal of Advertising, 36*(2), 111–121.

An, S., & Jin, H. S. (2004). Interlocking of newspaper companies with financial institutions and leading advertisers. *Journalism & Mass Communication Quarterly, 81*(3), 578–600.

Andersen, R., & Strate, L. (2000). *Critical studies in media commercialism*. New York: Oxford University Press.

Anderson, D. A. (1987). How managing editors view and deal with newspaper ethical issues. *Journalism Quarterly, 64*(2/3), 341–345.

Anderson, D. A., & Leigh, F. A. (1992). How newspaper editors and broadcast news directors view media ethics. *Newspaper Research Journal, 13*(1/2), 112–122.

Ankney, R. N., & Curtin, P. A. (2002). Delineating (and delimiting) the boundary spanning role of the medical public information officer. *Public Relations Review, 28*(3), 229–241.

Arant, M. D., & Anderson, J. Q. (2001). Newspaper online editors support traditional standards. *Newspaper Research Journal, 22*(4), 57–69.

Arant, M. D., & Meyer, P. (1998). Public journalism and traditional journalism: A shift in values? *Journal of Mass Media Ethics, 13*(4), 205–218.

Armstrong, C. L., & Nelson, M. R. (2005). How newspaper sources trigger gender stereotypes. *Journalism & Mass Communication Quarterly, 82*(4), 820–837.

Attaway-Fink, B. (2004). Market-driven journalism: Creating special sections to meet reader interests. *Journal of Communication Management, 9*(2), 145–154.

Atton, C., & Wickenden, E. (2005). Sourcing routines and representation in alternative journalism: A case study approach. *Journalism Studies, 6*(3), 347–359.

Aufderheide, P. (1999). *Communications policy and the public interest: The telecommunications act of 1996*. New York: Guilford Press.

Badaracco, C. (2005). *Quoting God: How media shape ideas about religion and culture*. Waco, TX: Baylor University Press.

Badii, N., & Ward, W. J. (1980). The nature of news in four dimensions. *Journalism Quarterly, 57*(2), 243–248.

Bagdikian, B. H. (1983). *The media monopoly*. Boston: Beacon Press.

Bagdikian, B. H. (2004). *The new media monopoly*. Boston: Beacon Press.

Baker, C. E. (2002). *Media, markets, and democracy*. New York: Cambridge University Press.

Baker, C. E. (2007). *Media concentration and democracy: Why ownership matters*. New York: Cambridge University Press.

Baldasty, G. J. (1992). *The commercialization of news in the nineteenth century*. Madison: University of Wisconsin Press.

Bales, R. F., Strodtbeck, F. L., Mills, T. M., & Roseborough, M. E. (1951). Channels of communication in small groups. *American Sociological Review, 16*, 461–467.

Bantz, C. R. (1990a). Organizational communication, media industries, and mass communication. In J. Anderson (Ed.), *Communication Yearbook* (Vol. 13, pp. 502–510). Newbury Park, CA: Sage.

Bantz, C. R. (1990b). Organizing and enactment: Karl Weick and the production of news. In C. Corman, S. Banks, C. R. Bantz & M. Mayer (Eds.), *Foundations of organizational communication: A reader* (pp. 133–141). New York: Longman.

Bantz, C. R., McCorkle, S., & Baade, R. C. (1981). The news factory. In G. C. Wilhoit & H. deBock (Eds.), *Mass communication review yearbook* (Vol. 2, pp. 366–389). Beverly Hills, CA: Sage.

Barendt, E. M. (1997). *Libel and the media: The chilling effect.* New York: Oxford University Press.

Barthes, R. (1972). *Mythologies.* New York: Hill and Wang.

Bass, A. Z. (1969). Refining the 'gatekeeper' concept: A UN radio case study. *Journalism Quarterly, 46,* 69–72.

Baumgartner, H., Sujan, M., & Bettman, J. R. (1992). Autobiographical memories, affect, and consumer information processing. *Journal of Consumer Psychology, 1*(1), 53–82.

Bavelas, A. (1948). A mathematical model for group structures. *Applied Anthropology, 7,* 16–30.

Baysha, O., & Hallahan, K. (2004). Media framing of the Ukrainian political crisis, 2000–2001. *Journalism Studies, 5*(2), 233–246.

Beam, R. A. (1998). What it means to be a market-oriented newspaper. *Newspaper Research Journal, 19*(3), 2–20.

Beam, R. A. (2002). Size of corporate parent drives market orientation. *Newspaper Research Journal, 23*(2/3), 46–63.

Beam, R. A. (2003). Content differences between daily newspapers with strong and weak market orientations. *Journalism & Mass Communication Quarterly, 80*(2), 368–390.

Becker, S. (1984). Marxist approaches to media studies: The British experience. *Critical Studies in Mass Communication, 1*(1), 66–80.

Benjamin, L. M. (2001). *Freedom of the air and the public interest: First Amendment rights in broadcasting to 1935.* Carbondale: Southern Illinois University Press.

Bennett, W. L. (1988). *News: The politics of illusion* (2nd ed.). New York: Longman.

Bennett, W. L. (1994). The media and the foreign policy process. In D. Deese (Ed.), *The new politics of American foreign policy.* New York: St. Martin's Press.

Bennett, W. L. (1996). *News: The politics of illusion* (3rd ed.). White Plains, NY: Longman.

Bennett, W. L. (2005). Beyond pseudoevents: Election news as reality TV. *American Behavioral Scientist, 49*(3), 364–378.

Benson, R., & Neveu, E. (2005). *Bourdieu and the journalistic field.* Malden, MA: Polity.

Bergen, L. A., & Weaver, D. (1988). Job satisfaction of daily newspaper journalists and organizational size. *Newspaper Research Journal, 9*(2), 1–13.

Berkowitz, D. (1987). TV news sources and news channels: A study in agenda-building. *Journalism Quarterly, 64*(2), 508–513.

Berkowitz, D. (1990a). Information subsidy and agenda-building in local television news. *Journalism Quarterly, 67*(4), 723–731.

Berkowitz, D. (1990b). Refining the gatekeeping metaphor for local television news. *Journal of Broadcasting & Electronic Media, 34*(1), 55–68.

Berkowitz, D. (1992). Routine newswork and the what-a-story: A case study of organizational adaptation. *Journal of Broadcasting & Electronic Media, 36*(1), 45–60.

Berkowitz, D. (1993). Work roles and news selection in local TV: Examining the business-journalism dialectic. *Journal of Broadcasting & Electronic Media, 37*(1), 67–83.

Berkowitz, D., Allen, C., & Beeson, D. (1996). Exploring newsroom views about consultants in local TV: The effects of work roles and socialization. *Journal of Broadcasting & Electronic Media, 40*(4), 447–459.

Bernabe-Riefkohl, A. (2000). Government advertising placement and the First Amendment: Freedom of the press should outweigh the rights of the government as contractor. *Communications & the Law, 22*(1), 1–22.

Bicket, D., & Wall, M. (2007). Circling the wagons: Containing the Downing Street memo story's impact in America. *Journal of Communication Inquiry, 31*(3), 206–221.

Bissell, K. L. (2000). A return to 'Mr. Gates': Photography and objectivity. *Newspaper Research Journal, 21*(3), 81–93.

Blankenburg, W. B. (1995). Hard times and the news hole. *Journalism & Mass Communication Quarterly, 72*(3), 634–641.

Boczkowski, P. J. (2004). The processes of adopting multimedia and interactivity in three online newsrooms. *Journal of Communication, 54*(2), 197–213.

Boddewyn, J. J. (1991). Controlling sex and decency in advertising around the world. *Journal of Advertising, 20*(4), 25–35.

Boehlert, E. (2006). *Lapdogs: How the press rolled over for Bush*. New York: Free Press.

Boorstin, D. J. (1971). From news-gathering to news-making: A flood of pseudo-events. In W. Schramm & D. F. Roberts (Eds.), *The process and effects of mass communication* (pp. 116–150). Urbana: University of Illinois Press.

Boorstin, D. J. (1987). *The image: A guide to pseudo-events in America* (25th anniversary ed.). New York: Atheneum.

Bourdieu, P. (1977). *Outline of a theory of practice*. New York: Cambridge University Press.

Bourdieu, P. (1998). *Practical reason: On the theory of action*. Stanford, CA: Stanford University Press.

Bourdieu, P., & Johnson, R. (1993). *The field of cultural production: Essays on art and literature*. New York: Columbia University Press.

Boyd-Barrett, O. (1995). Early theories in media research. In O. Boyd-Barrett & C. Newbold (Eds.), *Approaches to media: A reader* (pp. 68–76). New York: St. Martin's Press.

Boyle, T. P. (2001). Intermedia agenda setting in the 1996 presidential election. *Journalism & Mass Communication Quarterly, 78*(1), 26–44.

Breed, W. (1955). Social control in the newsroom: A functional analysis. *Social Forces, 33*(4), 326–335.

Bridges, J. A., Litman, B. R., & Bridges, L. W. (2002). Rosse's model revisited: Moving to concentric circles to explain newspaper competition. *Journal of Media Economics, 15*(1), 3–19.

Brooks, B. S., Kennedy, G., Moen, D. R., & Ranly, D. (1996). *News reporting and writing* (5th ed.). New York: St. Martin's Press.

Brown, R. M. (1979). The gatekeeper reassessed: A return to Lewin. *Journalism Quarterly, 56*(3), 595–601, 679.

Bruns, A. (2005). *Gatewatching: Collaborative online news production*. New York: Peter Lang.

Bruns, A. (2007). Produsage: Towards a broader framework for user-led content creation. In *Proceedings of Creativity and Cognition 6*, (99–105). Washington, D.C. Retrieved February 26, 2008 from http://eprints.qut.edu.au

Bryski, B. G. (1998). Accuracy in media. In M. A. Blanchard (Ed.), *History of the Mass Media in the United States: An Encyclopedia* (pp. 3–4). Chicago: Fitzroy Dearborn.

Buckalew, J. K. (1969a). News elements and selection by television news editors. *Journal of Broadcasting, 14*, 47–53.

Buckalew, J. K. (1969b). A Q-analysis of television news editors' decisions. *Journalism Quarterly, 46*(1), 135–137.

Burch, E. A., & Harry, J. C. (2004). Counter-hegemony and environmental justice in California newspapers: Source use patterns in stories about pesticides and farm workers. *Journalism & Mass Communication Quarterly, 81*(3), 559–577.

Cameron, G. T., & Blount, D. (1996). VNRs and air checks: A content analysis of the use of video news releases in television newscasts. *Journalism & Mass Communication Quarterly, 73*(4), 890–904.

Cameron, G. T., & Haley, E. (1992). Feature advertising: Policies and attitudes in print media. *Journal of Advertising, 21*(3), 47–55.

Campbell, C. P. (1995). *Race, myth and the news*. Thousand Oaks, CA: Sage Publications.

Campbell, R. (1991). *60 minutes and the news: A mythology for Middle America*. Urbana: University of Illinois Press.

Cantor, M. G. (1980). *Prime-time television: Content and control*. Beverly Hills, CA: Sage.

Cantor, M. G., & Pingree, S. (1983). *The soap opera*. Beverly Hills, CA: Sage.

Cappon, R. J. (2000). *The Associated Press guide to news writing* (3rd ed.). Forest City, CA: IDG Books Worldwide.

Carey, J. W. (1988). *Media, myths, and narratives: Television and the press*. Newbury Park, CA: Sage Publications.

Carlston, D. E., & Skowronski, J. J. (2005). Linking versus thinking: Evidence for the different associative and attributional bases of spontaneous trait transference and spontaneous trait inference. *Journal of Personality and Social Psychology, 89*(6), 884–898.

Carlston, D. E., & Smith, E. R. (1996). Principles of mental representation. In E. T. Higgins & A. W. Kruglanski (Eds.), *Social psychology: Handbook of basic principles* (pp. 184–210). New York: Guilford Press.

Carr, D. (1986). *Time, narrative, and history*. Bloomington: Indiana University Press.

Carter, T. B. (1998). Electronic gatekeepers: Locking out the marketplace of ideas. *Communication Law & Policy, 3*(3), 389–408.

Carter, T. B., Franklin, M. A., & Wright, J. B. (2003). *The First Amendment and the fifth estate: Regulation of electronic mass media* (6th ed.). New York: Foundation Press.

Carter, T. B., Franklin, M. A., & Wright, J. B. (2005). *The First Amendment and the fourth estate: The law of mass media* (9th ed.). New York: Foundation Press.

Cassidy, W. P. (2006). Gatekeeping similar for online, print journalists. *Newspaper Research Journal, 27*(2), 6–23.

Cervone, D., & Mischel, W. (2002). *Advances in personality science*. New York: Guilford Press.

Chaffee, S. H. (1975). The diffusion of political information. In S. H. Chaffee (Ed.), *Political communication: Issues and strategies for research* (pp. 85–128). Beverly Hills, CA: Sage.

Chang, T.-K., Wang, J., & Chen, C.-H. (1998). The social construction of international imagery in the post-Cold War era: A comparative analysis of U.S. and Chinese national TV news. *Journal of Broadcasting and Electronic Media, 42*(3), 277–297.

Chang, T. K., & Lee, J. W. (1992). Factors affecting gatekeepers' selection of foreign news: A nationwide survey of newspaper editors. *Journalism Quarterly, 69*, 554–561.

Chibnall, S. (1975). The crime reporter: A study in the production of commercial knowledge. *Sociology, 9*(1), 49–66.

Chibnall, S. (1977). *Law-and-order news: An analysis of crime reporting in the British press*. London: Tavistock.

Chibnall, S. (1981). The production of knowledge by crime reporters. In S. C. J. Young (Ed.), *The manufacture of news: Deviance, social problems and the mass media* (pp. 75–97). Beverly Hills, CA: Sage.

Chomsky, D. (2006). 'An interested reader': Measuring ownership control at the New York Times. *Critical Studies in Media Communication, 23*(1), 1–18.

Chomsky, N. (2006). *Failed states: The abuse of power and the assault on democracy*. New York: Metropolitan Books/Henry Holt.

Christ, P. (2005). Internet technologies and trends transforming public relations. *Journal of Website Promotion, 1*(4), 1–14.

Christensen, G. L., & Olson, J. C. (2002). Mapping consumers' mental models with ZMET. *Psychology and Marketing, 19*(6), 477–502.

Clayman, S. E., & Reisner, A. E. (1998). Gatekeeping in action: Editorial conferences and assessments of newsworthiness. *American Sociological Review, 63*(2), 178–200.

Cohen, A. (1974). *Two-dimensional man: An essay on the anthropology of power and symbolism in complex society*. Berkeley: University of California Press.

Cohen, A., Levey, M., Roeh, I., & Gurevitch, M. (1996). *Global newsrooms, local audiences: A study of the Eurovision News Exchange*. London: John Libbey.

Cohen, B. C. (1963). *The press and foreign policy*. Westport, CT: Greenwood.

Cohen, E. D. (2005). *News incorporated: Corporate media ownership and its threat to democracy*. Amherst, NY: Prometheus Books.

Cohen, J., & Solomon, N. (1995). *Through the media looking glass: Decoding bias and blather in the news*. Monroe, ME: Common Courage Press.

Comrie, M. (1999). *The commercial imperative: Key changes in TVNZ's news during deregulation*. Auckland, New Zealand: University of Auckland.

Condit, C. M. (1994). Hegemony in a mass-mediated society: Concordance about reproductive technologies. *Critical Studies in Mass Communication, 11*(3), 205–231.

Cook, T. E. (1998). *Governing with the news: The news media as a political institution*. Chicago: University of Chicago Press.

Corner, J., Schlesinger, P., & Silverstone, R. (1998). *International media research: A critical survey*. New York: Routledge.

Craft, S., & Wanta, W. (2004). Women in the newsroom: Influences of female editors and reporters on the news agenda. *Journalism & Mass Communication Quarterly, 81*(1), 124–139.

Craig, D. A. (2007). The case: In-text ads: Pushing the lines between advertising and journalism. *Journal of Mass Media Ethics, 22*(4), 348–349.

Cranberg, G., Bezanson, R. P., & Soloski, J. (2001). *Taking stock: Journalism and the publicly traded newspaper company*. Ames, IA: Iowa State University Press.

Creeber, G. (2004). 'Hideously white'. *Television & New Media, 5*(1), 27–39.

Croteau, D., & Hoynes, W. (2006). *The business of media: Corporate media and the public interest* (2nd ed.). Thousand Oaks, CA: Pine Forge Press.

Crouse, T. (1972). *The boys on the bus: Riding with the campaign press corps*. New York: Random House.

Culbertson, H. (1983). Three perspectives on American journalism. *Journalism Monographs (83)*, 1–33.

Cunningham, A., & Haley, E. (2000). A look inside the world of advertising-free publishing: A case study of *Ms.* magazine. *Journal of Current Issues and Research in Advertising, 22*(2), 17–30.

Curtin, P. A. (1999). Reevaluating public relations information subsidies: Market-driven journalism and agenda-building theory and practice. *Journal of Public Relations Research, 11*(1), 53–90.

Cutlip, S. M. (1954). Content and flow of AP news: From trunk to TTS to reader. *Journalism Quarterly, 31*, 434–446.

Danielian, L. H., & Reese, S. D. (1989). A closer look at intermedia influences on agenda setting: The cocaine issue of 1986. In P. J. Shoemaker (Ed.), *Communication campaigns about drugs: Government, media, and the public* (pp. 47–66). Hillsdale, NJ: Lawrence Erlbaum.

de Almeida, A. T., & Bohoris, G. A. (1995). Decision theory in maintenance decision making. *Journal of Maintenance Engineering, 1*(1), 39–45.

Deacon, D., & Golding, P. (1994). *Taxation and representation: The media, political communication and the poll tax.* London: J. Libby.

Demers, D. P. (1994). Effect of organizational size on job satisfaction of top editors at U.S. dailies. *Journalism Quarterly, 71*(4), 914–925.

Demers, D. P. (1995). Autonomy, satisfaction high among corporate news staffs. *Newspaper Research Journal, 16*(2), 91–111.

Demers, D. P. (1996). *The menace of the corporate newspaper: Fact or fiction?* Ames: Iowa State University Press.

Dixon, T. L., & Linz, D. (2002). Television news, prejudicial pretrial publicity, and the depiction of race. *Journal of Broadcasting & Electronic Media, 46*(1), 112–136.

Donohue, G. A., Olien, C. N., & Tichenor, P. J. (1985). Reporting conflict by pluralism, newspaper type and ownership. *Journalism Quarterly, 62*(3), 489–507.

Donohue, G. A., Olien, C. N., & Tichenor, P. J. (1989). Structure and constraints on community newspaper gatekeepers. *Journalism Quarterly, 66*(4), 807–845.

Donohue, G. A., Tichenor, P. J., & Olien, C. N. (1972). Gatekeeping: Mass media systems and information control. In F. G. Kline & P. J. Tichenor (Eds.), *Current perspectives in mass communication research* (pp. 41–70). Beverly Hills, CA: Sage.

Donohew, L. (1967). Newspaper gatekeepers and forces in the news channel. *Public Opinion Quarterly, 31*(1), 61–68.

Doyle, G. (2006). Financial news journalism: A post-Enron analysis of approaches towards economic and financial news production in the UK. *Journalism, 7*(4), 433–452.

Dozier, D. M., & Rice, R. E. (1984). Rival theories of electronic news reading. In R. E. Rice (Ed.), *The new media: Communication, research, and technology* (pp. 103–127). Beverly Hills, CA: Sage Publications.

Dunwoody, S. (1978). Science writers at work. In *Research Report No. 7*. Bloomington: Center for New Communications, Indiana University.

Duran, J. (2001). *Worlds of knowing: Global feminist epistemologies.* New York: Routledge.

Dyer, C., & Nayman, O. (1977). Under the capitol dome: Relationships between legislators and reporters. *Journalism Quarterly, 54*(3), 443–453.

Eberhard, W. B. (1982). 'News value' treatments are far from consistent among newswriting texts. *Journalism Educator, 37*(1), 9–11, 50.

Edge, M. (2003). The good, the bad, and the ugly: Financial markets and the demise of Canada's Southam Newspapers. *JMM: The International Journal of Media Management, 5*(4), 227–236.

Ehrlich, M. C. (1995). The ethical dilemma of television news sweeps. *Journal of Mass Media Ethics, 10*(1), 37–47.

Eisinger, R. M., Veenstra, L. R., & Koehn, J. P. (2007). What media bias? Conservative and liberal labeling in major U.S. newspapers. *Harvard International Journal of Press/Politics, 12*(1), 17–36.

Emery, W. B. (1969). *National and international systems of broadcasting: Their history, operation, and control.* East Lansing: Michigan State University Press.

Entman, R. M. (2003). *Projections of power: Framing news, public opinion, and U.S. foreign policy.* Chicago: University of Chicago Press.

Entman, R. M. (2007). Framing bias: Media in the distribution of power. *Journal of Communication, 57*(1), 163–173.

Entman, R. M., & Rojecki, A. (2000). *The black image in the white mind: Media and race in America.* Chicago: University of Chicago Press.

Epstein, E. J. (1973). *News from nowhere: Television and the news.* New York: Random House.

Ericson, R. V., Baranek, P. M., & Chan, J. B. L. (1987). *Visualizing deviance: A study of news organization.* Toronto; Buffalo: University of Toronto Press.

Ericson, R. V., Baranek, P. M., & Chan, J. B. L. (1991). *Representing order: Crime, law, and justice in the news media.* Milton Keynes: Open University Press.

Esser, F. (1998). Editorial structures and work principles in British and German newsrooms. *European Journal of Communication, 13*(3), 375–405.

Ettema, J. S. (1988). *The craft of the investigative journalist.* Evanston, IL: Northwestern University.

Evensen, B. J. (1997). *The responsible reporter* (2nd ed.). Northport, AL: Vision Press.

Fahmy, S. (2005). U.S. photojournalists' and photoeditors' attitudes and perceptions: Visual coverage of 9/11 and the Afghan War. *Visual Communication Quarterly, 12*(3/4), 146–163.

Falk, E., Grizard, E., & McDonald, G. (2006). Legislative issue advertising in the 108th Congress: Pluralism or peril. *Harvard International Journal of Press/Politics, 11*(4), 148–164.

Fallows, J. M. (1996). *Breaking the news: How the media undermine American democracy* (1st ed.). New York: Pantheon Books.

Fargo, A. L. (2006). Analyzing federal shield law proposals: What Congress can learn from the states. *Communication Law & Policy, 11*(1), 35–82.

Ferguson, R. (1998). *Representing race: Ideology, identity, and the media.* New York: Arnold.

Ferree, M. M., Gamson, W. A., Gerhards, J., & Rucht, D. (2002). *Shaping abortion discourse: Democracy and the public sphere in Germany and the United States.* New York: Cambridge University Press.

Festinger, L. (1957). *A theory of cognitive dissonance.* Evanston, IL: Row.

Fico, F., & Freedman, E. (2001). Setting the news story agenda: Candidates and commentators in news coverage of a governor's race. *Journalism & Mass Communication Quarterly, 78*(3), 437–449.

Fink, C. C. (1989, March). How newspapers should handle upscale/downscale conundrum. *Presstime,* 40–41.

Fishbein, M., & Ajzen, I. (1981). Acceptance, yielding and impact: Cognitive processes in persuasion. In R. E. Petty, T. M. Ostrom & T. C. Brock (Eds.), *Cognitive responses in persuasion* (pp. 339–359). Hillsdale, NJ: Lawrence Erlbaum.

Flegel, R. C., & Chaffee, S. H. (1971). Influences of editors, readers, and personal opinions on reporters. *Journalism Quarterly, 48*, 645–651.

Foerstel, H. N. (1998). *Banned in the media: A reference guide to censorship in the press, motion pictures, broadcasting, and the Internet.* Westport, CT: Greenwood Press.

Frank, R. (2003). When bad things happen in good places: Pastoralism in big-city newspaper coverage of small-town violence. *Rural Sociology, 68*(2), 207–230.

Galtung, J., & Ruge, M. H. (1965). The structure of foreign news. *Journal of Peace Research, 2*(1), 64–90.

Gandy, O. H., Jr. (1982). *Beyond agenda setting: Information subsidies and public policy.* Norwood, NJ: Ablex.

Gans, H. J. (1979a). *Deciding what's news.* New York: Pantheon.

Gans, H. J. (1979b). The messages behind the news. *Columbia Journalism Review, 17*(1), 40–45.

Gaziano, C. (1989). Chain newspaper homogeneity and presidential endorsements, 1972–1988. *Journalism Quarterly, 66*(4), 836–845.

Gaziano, C., & Coulson, D. C. (1988). Effects of newsroom management styles on journalists: A case study. *Journalism Quarterly, 65*(4), 869–880.

Geary, D. L. (2005). The decline of media credibility and its impact on public relations. *Public Relations Quarterly, 50*(3), 8–12.

Geertz, C. (1973). *The interpretation of cultures: Selected essays.* New York: Basic Books.

Gentzkow, M., & Shapiro, J. M. (2006). What drives media slant? Evidence from U.S. daily newspapers [Electronic Version]. *Social Science Research Network* from www.nber.org/papers/w12707.pdf.

Giddens, A. (1979). *Central problems in social theory: Action, structure, and contradiction in social analysis.* Berkeley: University of California Press.

Gieber, W. (1956). Across the desk: A study of 16 telegraph editors. *Journalism Quarterly, 33*(4), 423–432.

Gieber, W. (1960). How the 'gatekeepers' view local civil liberties news. *Journalism Quarterly, 37*(1), 199–205.

Gieber, W. (1963). 'I' am the news. In W. A. Danielson (Ed.), *Paul J. Deutschmann memorial papers in mass communications research* (pp. 9–17). Cincinnati, OH: Scipps-Howard Research.

Gieber, W. (1964). News is what newspapermen make it. In L. A. Dexter & D. M. White (Eds.), *People, society and mass communication.* New York: Free Press.

Gieber, W., & Johnson, W. (1961). The city hall 'beat': A study of reporter and source roles. *Journalism Quarterly, 38*(2), 289–297.

Gilligan, C. (1993). *In a different voice: Psychological theory and women's development.* Cambridge, MA: Harvard University Press.

Gillmor, D. (2004). *We the media: Grassroots journalism by the people, for the people.* Sebastopol, CA: O'Reilly.

Gitlin, T. (1980). *The whole world is watching.* Berkeley: University of California Press.

Glasser, T. L., Allen, D. S., & Blanks, S. E. (1989). The influence of chain ownership on news play: A case study. *Journalism Quarterly, 66*(3), 607–614.

Goldenberg, E. N. (1975). *Making the papers: The access of resource-poor groups to the metropolitan press.* Lexington, MA: Lexington Books.

Golding, P. (1981). The missing dimensions: News media and the management of social change. In E. Katz & T. Szecsko (Eds.), *Mass media and social change* (pp. 63–81). Beverly Hills, CA: Sage.

Gossage, H. L., Rotzoll, K. B., Graham, J., & Mussey, J. B. (1986). *Is there any hope for advertising?* Urbana: University of Illinois Press.

Grabe, M. E., Zhou, S., & Barnett, B. (1999). Sourcing and reporting in news magazine programs: 60 Minutes versus Hard Copy. *Journalism & Mass Communication Quarterly, 76*(2), 293–311.

Graber, D. A. (2006). *Mass media and American politics* (7th ed.). Washington, D.C.: CQ Press.

Gramsci, A., Hoare, Q., & Nowell-Smith, G. (1971). *Selections from the prison notebooks of Antonio Gramsci.* London: Lawrence & Wishart.

Greenberg, B. S., & Tannenbaum, P. H. (1962). Communicator performance under cognitive stress. *Journalism Quarterly, 39*(2), 169–178.

Greenwald, A. G., & Leavitt, C. (1984). Audience involvement in advertising: Four levels. *Journal of Consumer Research, 11*(1), 581–592.

Grey, D. L. (1966). Decision-making by a reporter under deadline pressure. *Journalism Quarterly, 43*(1), 419–428.

Gunter, B. (2003). *News and the net.* Mahwah, NJ: Lawrence Erlbaum.

Haber, R. N. (1992). Perception: A one-hundred year perspective. In S. Koch & D. E. Leary (Eds.), *A century of psychology as science* (pp. 250–279). Washington, D.C.: American Psychological Association.

Hachten, W. A., & Hachten, H. (1999). *The world news prism: Changing media of international communication* (5th ed.). Ames: Iowa State University Press.

Haigh, M. M., Pfau, M., Danesi, J., Tallmon, R., Bunko, T., Nyberg, S., et al. (2006). A comparison of embedded and nonembedded print coverage of the U.S. invasion and occupation of Iraq. *Press/Politics, 11*(2), 139–153.

Hall, P. A., & Taylor, R. C. R. (1996). Political science and the three new institutionalisms. *Political Studies, 44*(5), 936–957.

Hall, S. (1989). Ideology. In E. Barnouw (Ed.), *International encyclopedia of communication* (Vol. 2, pp. 307–311). New York: Oxford Press.

Hallin, D. C. (1989). *The uncensored war: The media and Vietnam.* Berkeley: University of California Press.

Hallin, D. C., & Mancini, P. (2004). *Comparing media systems: Three models of media and politics.* New York: Cambridge University Press.

Hallock, S. (2006). Metroplex newspapers offer limited editorial competition. *Newspaper Research Journal, 27*(3), 37–51.

Halloran, J. D., Elliott, P., & Murdock, G. (1970). *Demonstrations and communication: A case study.* Baltimore: Penguin.

Hansen, K. A., Neuzil, M., & Ward, J. (1998). Newsroom topic teams: Journalists' assessments of effects on news routines and newspaper quality. *Journalism & Mass Communication Quarterly, 75*(4), 803–821.

Hansen, K. A., Ward, J., Conners, J. L., & Neuzil, M. (1994). Local breaking news: Sources, technology, and news routines. *Journalism & Mass Communication Quarterly, 71*(3), 561–572.

Harcup, T., & O'Neill, D. (2006). What is news? Galtung and Ruge revisited. *Journalism Studies, 2*(2), 261–280.

Hardin, M. (2005). Stopped at the gate: Women's sports, 'reader interest', and decision making by editors. *Journalism & Mass Communication Quarterly, 82*(1), 62–78.

Harding, S. G. (2004). Introduction: Standpoint theory as a site of political, philosophic, and scientific debate. In S. G. Harding (Ed.), *The feminist standpoint theory reader: Intellectual and political controversies* (pp. 1–16). New York: Routledge.

Hardt, H. (1979). *Social theories of the press: Early German and American perspectives.* Beverly Hills, CA: Sage Publications.

Hargittai, E. (2004). The changing online landscape: From free-for-all to commercial gatekeeping. In P. Day & D. Schuler (Eds.), *Community practice in the network society: Local actions/global interaction.* New York: Routledge.

Harmon, M. D. (1989). Mr. Gates goes electronic: The what and why questions in local TV news. *Journalism Quarterly, 66*(4), 857–863.

Harrison, E. F. (1996). A process perspective on strategic decision making. *Management Decision, 34*(1), 46–53.

Hart, R. P. (1994). *Seducing America: How television charms the modern voter.* New York: Oxford University Press.

Hays, R. G., & Reisner, A. E. (1990). Feeling the heat from advertisers: Farm magazine writers and ethical pressures. *Journalism Quarterly, 67*(4), 936–942.

Head, S. W. (1985). *World broadcasting systems: A comparative analysis.* Belmont, CA: Wadsworth Publishing Company.

Heeter, C., Brown, N., Soffin, S., Stanley, C., & Salwen, M. B. (1989). Agenda setting by electronic text news. *Journalism Quarterly, 66*(1), 101–106.

Heider, D. (2000). *White news: Why local news programs don't cover people of color.* Mahwah, NJ: Lawrence Erlbaum Associates.

Henningham, J. (1997). The journalist's personality: An exploratory study. *Journalism & Mass Communication Quarterly, 74*(3), 615–624.

Herman, E. S., & Chomsky, N. (1988). *Manufacturing consent: The political economy of the mass media* (1st ed.). New York: Pantheon Books.

Herman, E. S., & McChesney, R. W. (1997). *The global media: The new missionaries of corporate capitalism.* London; Washington, D.C.: Cassell.

Hess, S. (1981). *The Washington reporters: Newswork.* Washington, D.C.: Brookings Institution.

Hewes, D. E., & Graham, M. L. (1989). Second-guessing theory: Review and extension. In J. A. Anderson (Ed.), *Communication Yearbook* (Vol. 12, pp. 213–248). Newbury Park, CA: Sage.

Hickey, J. R. (1966). The effects of information control on perceptions of centrality. Unpublished Dissertation, University of Wisconsin, Madison.

Hickey, J. R. (1968). The effects of information control on perceptions of centrality. *Journalism Quarterly, 45*, 49–54.

Hindman, D. B., Littlefield, R., Preston, A., & Neumann, D. (1999). Structural pluralism, ethnic pluralism, and community newspapers. *Journalism & Mass Communication Quarterly, 76*(2), 250–263.

Hirsch, P. M. (1970). *The structure of the popular music industry*. Ann Arbor: University of Michigan, Institute for Social Research.

Hirsch, P. M. (1977). Occupational, organizational and institutional models in mass media research: Toward an integrated framework. In P. M. Hirsch, P. V. Miller & F. G. Kline (Eds.), *Strategies for communication research*. Beverly Hills, CA: Sage.

Hirsch, P. M. (1981). Institutional functions of elite and mass media. In E. Katz & T. Szecsko (Eds.), *Mass media and social change* (pp. 187–200). Beverly Hills, CA: Sage.

Holland, J. L. (1997). *Making vocational choices: A theory of vocational personalities and work environments* (3rd ed.). Odessa, FL: Psychological Assessment Resources.

Holtz, S. (2002). *Public relations on the net: Winning strategies to inform and influence the media, the investment community, the government, the public, and more!* (2nd ed.). New York: American Management Association.

Homans, G. C. (1950). *The human group*. New York: Harcourt, Brace & World.

Horwitz, R. B. (1989). *The irony of regulatory reform: The deregulation of American telecommunications*. New York: Oxford University Press.

Hoskins, C., McFadyen, S., & Finn, A. (2004). *Media economics: Applying economics to new and traditional media*. Thousand Oaks, CA: Sage Publications.

Hough, G. A. (1995). *News writing* (5th ed.). Boston: Houghton Mifflin.

Howard, C., & Mathews, W. (2006). *On deadline: Managing media relations* (4th ed.). Long Grove, IL: Waveland Press.

Huaco, G. A. (1986). Ideology and general theory: The case of sociological functionalism. *Comparative Studies in Society and History, 28*(1), 34–54.

Huckins, K. (1999). Interest-group influence on the media agenda: A case study. *Journalism & Mass Communication Quarterly, 76*(1), 76–86.

Humphreys, P. (1996). *Mass media and media policy in Western Europe*. New York: Manchester University Press.

I hope so too (January 16, 2009). *Nytimes.com. http://www.nytimes.com/interactive/2009/01/15/us/politics/20090115_HOPE.html?scp=18&sq=i%20hope%20+%20obama&st=cse*

Itule, B. D., & Anderson, D. A. (2007). *News writing and reporting for today's media* (7th ed.). Boston: McGraw-Hill.

Jablin, F. M. (1982). Organizational communication: An assimilation approach. In M. E. Roloff & C. R. Berger (Eds.), *Social cognition and communication* (pp. 255–286). Beverly Hills, CA: Sage.

Jacobs, R. N. (1996). Producing the news, producing the crisis: Narrativity, television and news work. *Media, Culture, and Society, 18*(3), 373–397.

Janis, I. L. (1983). *Group think: Psychological studies of policy decisions and fiascoes.* Boston: Houghton Mifflin.

Johnsen, S. S. (2004). News technology: Deconstructing and reconstructing news. *NORDICOM Review, 25*(1/2), 237–257.

Johnstone, J., Slawski, E., & Bowman, W. (1972). The professional values of American newsmen. *Public Opinion Quarterly, 36*(4), 522–540.

Johnstone, J., Slawski, E., & Bowman, W. (1976). *The news people: A sociological portrait of American journalists and their work.* Urbana: University of Illinois Press.

Jones, R. L., Troldahl, V. C., & Hvistendahl, J. K. (1961). News selection patterns from a state TTS wire. *Journalism Quarterly, 38*, 303–312.

Judd, R. P. (1961). The newspaper reporter in a suburban city. *Journalism Quarterly, 38*, 35–42.

Kahneman, D., Slovic, P., & Tversky, A. (Eds.). (1982). *Judgment under uncertainty: Heuristics and biases.* Cambridge: Cambridge Univeristy Press.

Kaniss, P. C. (1991). *Making local news.* Chicago: University of Chicago Press.

Keith, S. (2005). Newpaper copy editors' perceptions of their ideal and real ethics roles. *Journalism & Mass Communication Quarterly, 82*(4), 930–951.

Kellner, D. (2004). The media and the crisis of democracy in the age of Bush-2. *Communication & Critical/Cultural Studies, 1*(1), 29–58.

Kellogg, R. T. (2007). *Fundamentals of cognitive psychology.* Thousand Oaks, CA: Sage.

Kessler, L. (1989). Women's magazines' coverage of smoking related health hazards. *Journalism Quarterly, 66*(2), 316–322, 445.

Kim, H. S. (2002). Gatekeeping international news: An attitudinal profile of U.S. television journalists. *Journal of Broadcasting & Electronic Media, 46*(3), 431–453.

Kitschelt, H., Lange, P., Marks, G., & Stephens, J. D. (Eds.). (1999). *Continuity and change in contemporary capitalism.* New York: Cambridge University Press.

Kline, K. E. (1994). A study of press attention to foreign investments in the United States. *Mass Communication Review, 21*(1/2), 126–139.

Koch, S., & Leary, D. E. (1992). *A century of psychology as science.* Washington, D.C.: American Psychological Association.

Koch, T. (1991). *Journalism for the 21st century: Online information, electronic databases, and the news.* New York: Praeger.

Kramer, M. (2008). What is narrative? Founding director's corner. Retrieved February 12, 2008, from http://www.nieman.harvard.edu/narrative/what_is.html

Krasnow, E. G., Longley, L. D., & Terry, H. A. (1982). *The politics of broadcast regulation* (3rd ed.). New York: St. Martin's Press.

Kuhn, R. (2002). The first Blair government and political journalism. In R. Kuhn & E. Neveu (Eds.), *Political journalism: New challenges, new practices* (pp. 47–68). New York: Routledge.

Kuhn, R., & Neveu, E. (2002). *Political journalism: New challenges, new practices.* New York: Routledge.

Kurpius, D. D. (2000). Public journalism and commercial local television news: In search of a model. *Journalism & Mass Communication Quarterly, 77*(2), 341–354.

Kuttner, R. (1997). *Everything for sale: The virtues and limits of markets*. New York: Alfred A. Knopf.

Lacher, K. T., & Rotfeld, H. J. (1994). Newspaper policies on the potential merging of advertising and news content. *Journal of Public Policy & Marketing, 13*(2), 281–289.

Lacy, S., Coulson, D. C., & Cho, H. (2002). Competition for readers among U.S. metropolitan daily, nonmetropolitan daily, and weekly newspapers. *Journal of Media Economics, 15*(1), 21–40.

Laitin, D. D. (1986). *Hegemony and culture: Politics and religious change among the Yoruba*. Chicago: University of Chicago Press.

Larson, S. G., & Bailey, M. (1998). ABC's 'Person of the Week': American values in television news. *Journalism & Mass Communication Quarterly, 75*(3), 487–499.

Lazare, D. (1989 May/June). Vanity fare. *Columbia Journalism Review, 28*(1), 6–7.

Lee, J.-H. (2008). Effects of news deviance and personal involvement on audience story selection: A web-tracking analysis. *Journalism & Mass Communication Quarterly, 85*(1), 41–60.

Lee, J., & Berkowitz, D. (2004). Third gatekeeping in Korea: The screening of first-edition newspapers by public relations practitioners. *Public Relations Review, 30*(3), 313–325.

Lerman, K. (2006). *Social networks and social information filtering on Digg*. Marina del Ray, CA: University of Southern California, Information Sciences Institute.

Lerman, K. (2007). *Social information processing in social news aggregation*. Marina del Ray, CA: University of Southern California, Information Sciences Institute.

Levine, M. (2008). *Guerrilla P.R. 2.0: How you can wage an effective publicity campaign without going broke*. New York: Collins.

Levinson, P. (2001). *Digital McLuhan: A guide to the information millennium*. New York: Routledge.

Lewin, K. (1933). Environmental forces in child behavior and development. In C. Murchison (Ed.), *Handbook of child psychology*. Worcester, MA: Clark University Press.

Lewin, K. (1947a). Frontiers in group dynamics II. Channels of group life: Social planning and action research. *Human Relations, 1*, 143–153.

Lewin, K. (1947b). Frontiers in group dynamics: Concept, method and reality in science; social equilibria and social change. *Human Relations, 1*, 5–40.

Lewin, K. (1951). *Field theory in social science: Selected theoretical papers*. New York: Harper.

Lewin, K., & Gold, M. (1999). *The complete social scientist: A Kurt Lewin reader* (1st ed.). Washington, D.C.: American Psychological Association.

Lewis, J. (1999). Reproducing political hegemony in the United States. *Critical Studies in Mass Communication, 16*(3), 251–268.

Liebler, C. M. (1993). News sources and the Civil Rights Act of 1990. *Howard Journal of Communications, 4*(3), 183–194.

Liebler, C. M., & Smith, S. J. (1997). Tracking gender differences: A comparative analysis of network correspondents and their sources. *Journal of Broadcasting & Electronic Media, 41*(1), 58–68.

Lippmann, W. (1922). *Public opinion*. New York: Harcourt Brace and Company.

Litman, B. R. (1980). Market share instability in local television news. *Journal of Broadcasting, 24*(3), 499–514.

Littlewood, T. B. (1998). *Calling elections: The history of horse-race journalism*. South Bend, IN: University of Notre Dame Press.

Livingston, S., & Bennett, W. L. (2003). Gatekeeping, indexing, and live-event news: Is technology altering the construction of news? *Political Communication, 20*(4), 363–380.

Lowrey, W. (2006). Mapping the journalism–blogging relationship. *Journalism, 7*(4), 477–500.

Lull, J. (1995). *Media, communication, culture: A global approach*. New York: Columbia University Press.

Luttbeg, N. R. (1983a). News consensus: Do U.S. newspapers mirror society's happenings? *Journalism Quarterly, 60*(3), 484–488, 578.

Luttbeg, N. R. (1983b). Proximity does not assure newsworthiness. *Journalism Quarterly, 60*, 731–732.

MacDougall, A. K. (1988). Boring from within the bourgeois press. Part one. *Monthly Review, 40*(7), 13–24.

Machill, M., Beiler, M., & Schmutz, J. (2006). The influence of video news releases on the topics reported in science journalism. *Journalism Studies, 7*(6), 869–888.

Mahner, M., & Bunge, M. (2001). Function and functionalism: A synthetic perspective. *Philosophy of Science, 68*(1), 75–94.

Malek, A. (1997). *News media and foreign relations: A multifaceted perspective*. Norwood, NJ: Ablex.

Marcellus, J. (2005). Gender and newsroom cultures: Identities at work. *Feminist media studies, 5*(3), 398–400.

Marrow, A. J. (1969). *The practical theorist: The life and work of Kurt Lewin*. New York: Basic Books.

Martin, C. R. (2004). *Framed!: Labor and the corporate media*. Ithaca, NY: ILR Press.

Martin, L. L., & Davies, B. (1998). Beyond hedonism and associationism: A configural view of the role of affect in evaluation, processing, and self-regulation. *Motivation and Emotion, 22*(1), 33–51.

Massey, B. L. (1998). Civic journalism and nonelite sourcing: Making routine news-work of community connectedness. *Journalism & Mass Communication Quarterly, 75*(2), 394–407.

McCabe, J., & Akass, K. (2007). *Quality TV: Contemporary American television and beyond*. New York: I. B. Tauris.

McCann, R. M., & Honeycutt, J. M. (2006). A cross-cultural analysis of imagined interactions. *Human Communication Research, 32*(3), 274–301.

McCargo, D. (2003). *Media and politics in Pacific Asia*. New York: Routledge-Curzon.

McChesney, R. W. (1993). *Telecommunications, mass media, and democracy: The battle for the control of U.S. broadcasting, 1928–1935*. New York: Oxford University Press.

McChesney, R. W. (1997). *Corporate media and the threat to democracy*. New York: Seven Stories Press.

McChesney, R. W. (2004). *The problem of the media: U.S. communication politics in the twenty-first century*. New York: Monthly Review Press.

McCombs, M. E. (1994). News influence on our pictures of the world. In J. Bryant & D. Zillmann (Eds.), *Media effects: Advances in theory and research* (pp. 1–16). Hillsdale, NJ: Lawrence Erlbaum Associates.

McCombs, M. E., & Shaw, D. L. (1976). Structuring the 'unseen environment'. *Journal of Communication, 26*(2), 18–22.

McGee, M. (2005). *Self-Help, Inc.: Makeover culture in American life*. New York: Oxford University Press.

McKenna, R. J., & Martin-Smith, B. (2005). Decision making as a simplification process: New conceptual perspectives. *Management Decision, 43*(6), 821–836.

McLeod, J. M., & Chaffee, S. H. (1973). Interpersonal approaches to communication research. *American Behavioral Scientist, 16*(4), 469–499.

McManus, J. H. (1994). *Market-driven journalism: Let the citizen beware?* Thousand Oaks, CA: Sage Publications.

McNelly, J. T. (1959). Intermediary communicators in the international flow of news. *Journalism Quarterly, 36*(1), 23–26.

McQuail, D., & Windahl, S. (1981). *Communication models for the study of mass communications*. New York: Longman.

Miller, A., Goldenberg, E., & Erbring, L. (1979). Typeset politics: Impact of newspapers on public confidence. *American Political Science Review, 73*, 67–83.

Miller, B. (2006). Issue advocacy and traditional news content: A study of the impact of marketplace advocacy on local television news media. Paper presented at the International Communication Association.

Mills, C. W. (2007). White ignorance. In S. Sullivan & N. Tuana (Eds.), *Race and epistemologies of ignorance* (pp. 13–38). Albany: State University of New York Press.

Milner, M. (2004). *Freaks, geeks, and cool kids: American teenagers, schools, and the culture of consumption*. New York: Routledge.

Molotch, H., & Lester, M. (1974). News as purposive behavior: On the strategic use of routine events, accidents, and scandals. *American Sociological Review, 39*(1), 101–112.

Mooney, C. (2004, March–April). The editorial pages and the case for war. *Columbia Journalism Review, 42*(6), 28–34.

Moran, K. C. (2006). Is changing the language enough? *Journalism, 7*(3), 389–405.

Morrison, K. (1995). *Marx, Durkheim, Weber: Formations of modern social thought*. Thousand Oaks, CA: Sage.

Napoli, P. M. (2003). *Audience economics: Media institutions and the audience marketplace*. New York: Columbia University Press.

Napoli, P. M., & Yan, M. Z. (2007). Media ownership regulations and local news programming on broadcast television: An empirical analysis. *Journal of Broadcasting & Electronic Media, 51*(1), 39–57.

Nerone, J. C. (1995). *Last rights: Revisiting four theories of the press.* Urbana: University of Illinois Press.

Newcomb, T. M. (1953). An approach to the study of communicative acts. *Psychological Review, 60*(6), 393–404.

Niblock, S., & Machin, D. (2007). News values for consumer groups: The case of Independent Radio News, London, UK. *Journalism, 8*(2), 184–204.

Nisbett, R., & Ross, L. (1980). *Human inference: Strategies and shortcomings of social judgment.* New York: Prentice-Hall.

Noelle-Neumann, E. (1980). Mass media and social change in developed societies. In G. C. Wilhoit & H. deBock (Eds.), *Mass communication review yearbook* (pp. 657–678). Beverly Hills, CA: Sage.

Norris, P., Curtice, J., Sanders, D., Scammell, M., & Semetko, H. A. (1999). *On message: Communicating the campaign.* Thousand Oaks, CA: Sage.

Olson, K. K. (2004). First Amendment values in fair use analysis. *Journalism & Communication Monographs, 5*(4), 159–202.

Ostergaard, B. S., & Euromedia Research Group. (1992). *The media in Western Europe: The Euromedia handbook.* Newbury Park, CA: Sage Publications.

Ostgaard, E. (1965). Factors influencing the flow of news. *Journal of Peace Research, 2*(1), 39–63.

Ottosen, R. (1992). Truth: The first victim of war? In H. Mowlana, G. Gerbner & H. I. Schiller (Eds.), *Triumph of the image: The media war in the Persian Gulf, a global perspective* (pp. 137–143). San Francisco: Westview Press.

Paglin, M. D., Hobson, J. R., & Rosenbloom, J. (1999). *The Communications Act: A legislative history of the major amendments, 1934–1996.* Silver Spring, MD: Pike & Fischer.

Palmer, D. C., & Donahue, J. W. (1992). Essentialism and selectionism in cognitive science and behavior analysis. *American Psychologist, 47*(11), 1344–1358.

Paterson, C. A. (2001). The transfer of frames in global television. In S. D. Reese, O. H. Gandy & A. E. Grant (Eds.), *Framing public life: Perspectives on media and our understanding of the social world* (pp. 337–353). Mahwah, NJ: Lawrence Erlbaum Associates.

Patterson, T. E. (1993). *Out of order.* New York: A. Knopf.

Paul, R., & Elder, L. (2002). *Critical thinking: Tools for taking charge of your professional and personal life.* Upper Saddle River, NJ: Financial Times/Prentice Hall.

Pavlik, J. (2000). The impact of technology on journalism. *Journalism Studies, 1*(2), 229–237.

Perlmutter, D. D. (1998). *Photojournalism and foreign policy: Icons of outrage in international crises.* Westport, CT: Praeger.

Petty, R. E., & Cacioppo, J. T. (1984). The effects of involvement on response to argument quality and quantity: Central and peripheral routes to persuasion. *Journal of Personality and Social Psychology, 46*(1), 69–81.

Pew Research Center for the People and the Press. (2006). Online papers modestly boost newspaper readership. Retrieved September 15, 2007, from http://people-press.org/reports/display.php3?PageID=1064

Pierson, P. (2004). *Politics in time: History, institutions, and social analysis*. Princeton, NJ: Princeton University Press.

Pollard, G. (1995). The influence of professionalism, perceptions of organizational structure, and social attributes. *Journalism & Mass Communication Quarterly, 72*(3), 682–697.

Pool, I. D. S., & Shulman, I. (1959). Newsmen's fantasies, audiences, and newswriting. *Public Opinion Quarterly, 23*, 145–158.

Powers, A. (1990). The changing market structure of local television news. *Journal of Media Economics, 3*(1), 37–55.

Pracene, U. C. (2005). *Journalists, shield laws, and the First Amendment: Is the fourth estate under attack?* New York: Novinka Books.

Price, C. J. (2003). Interfering owners or meddling advertisers: How network television news correspondents feel about ownership and advertiser influence on news stories. *Journal of Media Economics, 16*(3), 175–188.

Prisuta, R. H. (1979). Local television news as an oligopolistic industry: A pilot study. *Journal of Broadcasting, 23*(1), 61–68.

Proffitt, J. M. (2001). *Gatekeeping and the editorial cartoon: A case study of the 2000 presidential campaign cartoons*. Paper presented at the Association for Education in Journalism and Mass Communication.

Protess, D., Cook, F. L., Doppelt, J. C., Ettema, J. S., Gordon, M. T., Leff, D. R., et al. (1991). *The Journalism of outrage: Investigative reporting and agenda building in America*. New York: Guilford Press.

Puette, W. (1992). *Through jaundiced eyes: How the media view organized labor*. Ithaca, NY: ILR Press.

Quenk, N. L. (2000). *Essentials of Myers-Briggs type indicator assessment*. New York: Wiley.

Rada, J. A. (1996). Color blind-sided: Racial bias in network television's coverage of professional football games. *Howard Journal of Communications, 7*(3), 231–239.

Ramsey, S. (1999). A benchmark study of elaboration and sourcing in science stories for eight American newspapers. *Journalism & Mass Communication Quarterly, 76*(1), 87–98.

Ranney, A. (1983). *Channels of power: The impact of television on American politics*. New York: Basic Books.

Ravi, N. (2005). Looking beyond flawed journalism: How national interests, patriotism, and cultural values shaped the coverage of the Iraq War. *Harvard International Journal of Press/Politics, 10*(1), 45–62.

Reber, B. H., & Kim, J. K. (2006). How activists groups use websites in media relations: Evaluating online press rooms. *Journal of Public Relations Research, 18*(4), 313–333.

Reese, S. D. (1990). The news paradigm and the ideology of objectivity: A socialist at The Wall Street Journal. *Critical Studies in Mass Communication 7*(4), 390–409.

Reese, S. D., & Ballinger, J. (2001). The roots of a sociology of news: Remembering Mr. Gates and social control in the newsroom. *Journalism & Mass Communication Quarterly, 78*(4), 641–658.

Reese, S. D., & Danielian, L. H. (1989). Intermedia influence and the drug issue: Converging on cocaine. In P. J. Shoemaker (Ed.), *Communication campaigns about drugs: Government, media, public* (pp. 29–46). Hillsdale, NJ: Lawrence Erlbaum.

Reisner, A. E. (1992). The news conference: How daily newspaper editors construct the front page. *Journalism & Mass Communication Quarterly, 69*(2), 971–986.

Rich, A., & Weaver, R. K. (2000). Think tanks in the U.S. media. *Harvard International Journal of Press/Politics, 5*(4), 81–103.

Rich, C. (2003). *Writing and reporting news: A coaching method* (4th ed.). Belmont, CA: Wadsworth/Thomson Learning.

Richardson, J. E. (2001). British Muslims in the broadsheet press: A challenge to cultural hegemony? *Journalism Studies, 2*(2), 221–242.

Rivenburgh, N. K. (2000). Social identity theory and news portrayals of citizens involved in international affairs. *Media Psychology, 2*(4), 303–329.

Rivers, W. L. (1965). *The opinionmakers.* Boston: Beacon.

Roach, T. (1995). Competing news narratives, consensus, and world power. In Y. R. Kamalipour (Ed.), *The U.S. media and the Middle East: Image and perception* (pp. 25–34). Westport, CT: Greenwood Press.

Roberts, M., & McCombs, M. E. (1994). Agenda setting and political advertising: Origins of the news agenda. *Political Communication, 11*(3), 249–262.

Rodriguez, M. A., & Steinbock, D. J. (2006). *The anatomy of a large scale collective decision making system.* Los Alamos, NM: University of California, Santa Cruz, Los Alamos National Labratory.

Rogers, E. M. (1994). *A history of communication study: A biographical approach.* New York: The Free Press.

Rolland, A. (2006). Commercial news criteria and investigative journalism. *Journalism Studies, 7*(6), 940–963.

Rose, M. (1991). Activism in the 90s: Changing roles for public relations. *Public Relations Quarterly, 36*(3), 28–32.

Roshco, B. (1975). *Newsmaking.* Chicago: University of Chicago Press.

Rosse, J. N. (1980). The decline of direct newspaper competition. *Journal of Communication, 30*(1), 65–71.

Rossiter, J. R. (1981). Predicting starch scores. *Journal of Advertising Research, 21*(5), 9–11.

Rothenbuhler, E. W. (2005). The church of the cult of the individual. In E. W. Rothenbuhler & M. Coman (Eds.), *Media anthropology* (pp. 91–100). Thousand Oaks, CA: Sage.

Russell, A. (1995). MADD rates the states: A media advocacy event to advance the agenda against alcohol-impaired driving. *Public Health Reports, 110*, 240–245.

Russial, J. T. (1997). Topic-team performance: A content study. *Newspaper Research Journal, 18*(1–2), 126–144.

Sallot, L. M., & Johnson, E. A. (2006). Investigating relationships between journalists and public relations practitioners: Working together to set, frame and build the public agenda, 1991–2004. *Public Relations Review, 32*(2), 151–159.

Sallot, L. M., Steinfatt, T. M., & Salwen, M. B. (1998). Journalists' and public relations practitioners' news values: Perceptions and cross-perceptions. *Journalism & Mass Communication Quarterly, 75*(2), 366–377.

Salwen, M. B. (2005). Online news trends. In M. B. Salwen, B. Garrison & P. D. Driscoll (Eds.), *Online news and the public* (pp. 47–80). Mahwah, NJ: Lawrence Erlbaum.

Sanders, K., Bale, T., & Canel, M. J. (1999). Managing sleaze: Prime ministers and news management in conservative Great Britain and socialist Spain. *European Journal of Communication, 14*(4), 461–486.

Sasser, E. L., & Russell, J. T. (1972). The fallacy of news judgment. *Journalism Quarterly, 49*, 280–284.

Schierhorn, A. B., Endres, F. F., & Schierhorn, C. (2001). Newsroom teams enjoy rapid growth in the 1990s. *Newspaper Research Journal, 22*(3), 2–15.

Schiffer, A. J. (2006). Blogswarms and press norms: News coverage of the Downing Street memo controversy. *Journalism & Mass Communication Quarterly, 83*(3), 494–510.

Schlesinger, P. (1987). *Putting 'reality' together: BBC News*. New York: Methuen.

Schramm, W. (1980). The beginnings of communication study in the United States. *Communication, 9*(2), 1–6.

Schudson, M. (1978). *Discovering the news: A social history of American newspapers*. New York: Basic Books.

Schudson, M. (2001). The objectivity norm in American journalism. *Journalism, 2*(2), 149–170.

Schudson, M. (2003). *The sociology of news*. New York: Norton.

Scott, D. M. (2007). *The new rules of marketing and PR: How to use news releases, blogs, podcasts, viral marketing and online media to reach your buyers directly*. Hoboken, NJ: John Wiley & Sons.

Shin, J.-H., & Cameron, G. T. (2005). Different sides of the same coin: Mixed views of public relations practitioners and journalists for strategic conflict management. *Journalism & Mass Communication Quarterly, 82*(2), 318–338.

Shoemaker, P. J. (1984). Media coverage of deviant political groups. *Journalism Quarterly, 61*, 66–75, 82.

Shoemaker, P. J. (1991). *Gatekeeping*. Newbury Park, CA: Sage Publications.

Shoemaker, P. J. (1996). Hardwired for news: Using biological and cultural evolution to explain the surveillance function. *Journal of Communication, 46*(3), 32–47.

Shoemaker, P. J. (2006). News and newsworthiness: A commentary. *Communications: The European Journal of Communication Research, 31*(1), 105–111.

Shoemaker, P. J., Chang, T. K., & Brendlinger, N. (1987). Deviance as a predictor of newsworthiness: Coverage of international events in the U.S. media. In M. McLaughlin (Ed.), *Communication yearbook* (Vol. 10, pp. 348–365). Newbury Park, CA: Sage.

Shoemaker, P. J., & Cohen, A. A. (2006). *News around the world: Content, practitioners, and the public*. New York: Routledge.

Shoemaker, P. J., Danielian, L. H., & Brendlinger, N. (1991). Deviant acts, risky business and U.S. interests: The newsworthiness of world events. *Journalism & Mass Communication Quarterly, 68*(4), 781–795.

Shoemaker, P. J., Eichholz, M., Kim, E., & Wrigley, B. (2001). Individual and routine forces in gatekeeping. *Journalism & Mass Communication Quarterly, 78*(2), 233–246.

Shoemaker, P. J., & Mayfield, E. K. (1987). Building a theory of news content. *Journalism Monographs, 103*.

Shoemaker, P. J., & Reese, S. D. (1996). *Mediating the message: Theories of influences on mass media content* (2nd ed.). White Plains, NY: Longman.

Shoemaker, P. J., Seo, H., & Johnson, P. (2008). Audience gatekeeping: A study of the New York Times most-emailed items. Paper presented to Convergence and Society: The Participatory Web, University of South Carolina, South Carolina, October.

Shoemaker, P. J., Tankard, J. W., & Lasorsa, D. L. (2004). *How to build social science theories*. Thousand Oaks, CA: Sage.

Siebert, F. S. (1956). *Four theories of the press: The authoritarian, libertarian, social responsibility, and Soviet communist concepts of what the press should be and do*. Urbana: University of Illinois Press.

Siebert, F. S., Peterson, T., & Schramm, W. L. (1973). *Four theories of the press: The authoritarian, libertarian, social responsibility, and Soviet communist concepts of what the press should be and do*. Freeport, NY: Books for Libraries Press.

Sigal, L. V. (1973). *Reporters and officials: The organization and politics of newsmaking*. Lexington, MA: D. C. Heath.

Sinclair, U. (1906). *The jungle*. New York: Doubleday Page & company.

Sinclair, U. (1920). *The brass check: A study of American journalism*. Pasadena, CA: The author.

Singer, J. B. (1997). Still guarding the gate? The newspaper journalist's role in an on-line world. *Convergence: The Journal of Research into New Media Technologies, 3*(1), 72–89.

Singer, J. B. (1998). Online journalists: Foundations for research into their changing roles. *Journal of Computer Mediated Communication, 4*(1).

Singer, J. B. (2001). The metro wide web: Changes in newspapers' gatekeeping role online. *Journalism & Mass Communication Quarterly, 78*(1), 65–81.

Singer, J. B. (2005). The political j-blogger: 'Normalizing' a new media form to fit old norms and practices. *Journalism, 6*(2), 173–198.

Skewes, E. A. (2007). *Message control: How news is made on the presidential campaign trail*. Lanham, MD: Rowman & Littlefield Publishers.

Skolnick, J. H. (1968). Coercion to virtue: The enforcement of morals. *Southern California Law Review, 41*(3), 588–626.

Snider, P. B. (1967). 'Mr. Gates' revisited: A 1966 version of the 1949 case study. *Journalism Quarterly, 44*(3), 419–427.

Snodgrass, J. G., Levy-Berger, G., & Hayden, M. (1985). *Human experimental psychology*. New York: Oxford University Press.

Soley, L. C. (1992). *The news shapers: The sources who explain the news*. New York: Praeger.

Soley, L. C. (2002). *Censorship, Inc.: The corporate threat to free speech in the United States*. New York: Monthly Review Press.

Stark, K., & Soloski, J. (1977). Effect of reporter predisposition in covering controversial story. *Journalism Quarterly, 54*(1), 120–125.

Stegall, S. K., & Sanders, K. P. (1986). Coorientation of PR practitioners and news personnel in education news. *Journalism Quarterly, 63*(2), 341–393.

Stempel, G. H., III. (1959). Uniformity of wire content in six Michigan dailies. *Journalism Quarterly, 36*, 45–48, 120.

Stempel, G. H., III. (1962). Content patterns of small and metropolitan dailies. *Journalism Quarterly, 39*(1), 88–91.

Stempel, G. H., III. (1985). Gatekeeping: The mix of topics and the selection of stories. *Journalism Quarterly, 62*(4), 791–796, 815.

Stempel, G. H., III. (1989). Content analysis. In G. H. Sempel, III & B. H. Westley (Eds.), *Research methods in mass communication* (pp. 124–136). Englewood Cliffs, NJ: Prentice-Hall.

Sternberg, R. J. (1999). *The nature of cognition*. Cambridge, MA: MIT Press.

Stewart, P. L., & Cantor, M. G. (1982). Introduction. In P. L. Stewart & M. G. Cantor (Eds.), *Varieties of work*. Beverly Hills, CA: Sage.

Stinchcombe, A. L. (1987). *Constructing social theories*. Chicago: University of Chicago Press.

Streitmatter, R. (1997). *Mightier than the sword: How the news media have shaped American history*. Boulder, CO: Westview Press.

Strohm, S. M. (1999). The black press and the black community: The *Los Angeles Sentinel*'s coverage of the Watts riots. In M. S. Mander (Ed.), *Framing friction: Media and social conflict* (pp. 58–88). Urbana: University of Illinois Press.

Sturm, J. F. (2005). Time for change on media cross-ownership regulation. *Federal Communications Law Journal, 57*(2), 201–208.

Sumner, D. E., & Miller, H. G. (2005). *Feature and magazine writing: Action, angle, and anecdotes* (1st ed.). Ames, IA: Blackwell Publishing.

Sumpter, R. S. (2000). Daily newspaper editors' audience construction routines: A case study. *Critical Studies in Media Communication, 17*(3), 334–346.

Sun, T., Chang, T.-K., & Yu, G. (2001). Social structure, media system, and audiences in China: Testing the uses and dependency model. *Mass Communication & Society, 4*(2), 199–217.

Swidler, A. (1986). Culture in action: Symbols and strategies. *American Sociological Review, 51*(2), 273–286.

Tanesini, A. (1999). *An introduction to feminist epistemologies*. Malden, MA: Blackwell Publishers.

Tankard, J. W., Jr., Middleton, K., & Rimmer, T. (1979). Compliance with American Bar Association fair trial-free press guidelines. *Journalism Quarterly, 56*(3), 464–468.

Thomason, T., & LaRocque, P. (1995). Editors still reluctant to name rape victims. *Newspaper Research Journal, 16*(3), 42–51.

Thussu, D. K. (2002). Managing the media in an era of round-the-clock news: Notes from India's first tele-war. *Journalism Studies, 3*(2), 203–212.

Todd, R. (1983). New York Times advisories and national/international news selection. *Journalism Quarterly, 60*(4), 705–708, 676.

Traquina, N. (2004). Theory consolidation in the study of journalism: A comparative analysis of the news coverage of HIV/AIDS issue in four countries. *Journalism, 5*(1), 97–116.

Trayes, E. J. (1978). Managing editors and their newsrooms: A survey of 208 APME members. *Journalism Quarterly, 55*(4), 744–749, 898.

Tuchman, G. (1972). Objectivity as strategic ritual: An examination of newsmen's notions of objectivity. *American Journal of Sociology, 77*, 660–679.

Tuchman, G. (1978). *Making news: A study in the construction of reality*. New York: Free Press.

Tuchman, G. (1997). Making news by doing work: Routinizing the unexpected. In D. Berkowitz (Ed.), *Social Meanings of News* (pp. 173–192). Thousand Oaks, CA: Sage Publications.

Tuggle, C. A., & Huffman, S. (1999). Live news reporting: Professional judgment or technological pressure? A national survey of television news directors and senior reporters. *Journal of Broadcasting & Electronic Media, 43*(4), 492–505.

Tunstall, J. (1971). *Journalists at work*. London: Constable.

Turner, G. (2002). *British cultural studies: An introduction* (3rd ed.). New York: Routledge.

Turow, J. (1997). *Breaking up America: Advertisers and the new media world*. Chicago: University of Chicago Press.

Underwood, D. (1993). *When MBAs rule the newsroom: How the marketers and managers are reshaping today's media*. New York: Columbia University Press.

VanSlyke Turk, J. (1986a). Information subsidies and media content: A study of public relations influence on the news. *Journalism Monographs, 100*.

VanSlyke Turk, J. (1986b). Public relations' influence on the news. *Newspaper Research Journal, 7*(4), 15–27.

Vettehen, P. H., Nuijten, K., & Beentjes, J. W. J. (2005). News in an age of competition: The case of sensationalism in Dutch television news, 1995–2001. *Journal of Broadcasting & Electronic Media, 49*(3), 282–295.

Voakes, P. S. (1998). What were you thinking? A survey of journalists who were sued for invasion of privacy. *Journalism & Mass Communication Quarterly, 75*(2), 378–393.

Voakes, P. S. (1999). Civic duties: newspaper journalists' views on public journalism. *Journalism & Mass Communication Quarterly, 76*(4), 756–774.

Vos, T. P. (2005). Explaining media policy: American political broadcasting policy in comparative context. Unpublished Dissertation, Syracuse University, Syracuse, NY.

Wackman, D. B., Gillmor, D. M., Gaziano, C., & Dennis, E. E. (1975). Chain newspaper autonomy as reflected in presidential campaign endorsements. *Journalism Quarterly, 52*(3), 411–420.

Wallerstein, I. M. (1974). *The modern world-system*. New York: Academic Press.

Wang, X., Shoemaker, P. J., Han, G., & Storm, E. J. (2008). Images of nations in the eyes of American educational elites. *American Journal of Media Psychology, 1*(1/2), 36–60.

Warren, C. A., & Vavrus, M. D. (2002). *American cultural studies*. Urbana: University of Illinois Press.

Wasburn, P. C. (2002). *The social construction of international news: We're talking about them, they're talking about us*. Westport, CT: Praeger.

Weaver, D. H., Beam, R. A., Brownlee, B. J., Voakes, P. S., & Wilhoit, G. C. (2007). *The American journalist in the 21st century: U.S. news people at the dawn of a new millennium*. Mahwah, NJ: Lawrence Erlbaum Associates.

Weaver, D. H., & Wilhoit, G. C. (1986). *The American journalist: A portrait of U.S. news people and their work*. Bloomington: Indiana University Press.

Weaver, D. H., & Wilhoit, G. C. (1996). *The American journalist in the 1990s: U.S. news people at the end of an era*. Mahwah, NJ: Erlbaum.

Webb, E. J., & Salancik, J. R. (1965). Notes on the sociology of knowledge. *Journalism Quarterly, 42*, 595–596.

Weick, K. (1979). *The social psychology of organizing*. Reading, MA: Addison-Wesley.

Weill, S. (2001). Hazel and 'Hacksaw': Freedom summer coverage by the women of the Mississippi press. *Journalism Studies, 2*(4), 545–561.

Westley, B. H. (1953). *News editing*. Cambridge, MA: Houghton-Mifflin.

Westley, B. H., & MacLean, M. S., Jr. (1957). A conceptual model for communications research. *Journalism Quarterly, 34*, 31–38.

White, D. M. (1950). The 'gate keeper': A case study in the selection of news. *Journalism Quarterly, 27*, 383–390.

Whitney, D. C. (1981). Information overload in the newsroom. *Journalism Quarterly, 58*, 69–76, 161.

Whitney, D. C., & Becker, L. B. (1982). 'Keeping the gates' for gatekeepers: The effects of wire news. *Journalism Quarterly, 59*(1), 60–65.

Williams, B. A., & Carpini, M. X. D. (2004). Monica and Bill all the time and everywhere: The collapse of gatekeeping and agenda setting in the new media environment. *American Behavioral Scientist, 47*(9), 1208–1230.

Williams, F., Phillips, A. F., & Lum, P. (1985). Gratifications associated with new communication technologies. In K. E. Rosengren, L. A. Wenner & P. Palmgreen (Eds.), *Media gratifications research: Current perspectives* (pp. 241–252). Beverly Hills, CA: Sage Publications.

Williams, R. (1977). *Marxism and literature*. New York: Oxford University Press.

Wilson, L. J. (2004). *Strategic program planning for effective public relations campaigns* (4th ed.). Dubuque, IA: Kendall/Hunt.

Wolfsfeld, G. (1984). Collective political action and media strategy. *Journal of Conflict Resolution, 28*, 363–381.

Wood, D. J., & Gray, B. (1991). Toward a comprehensive theory of collaboration. *Journal of Applied Behavioral Science, 27*(2), 139–162.

Woodward, B., & Bernstein, C. (1974). *All the president's men*. New York: Simon & Schuster.

Wright, P., & Barbour, F. (1976). The relevance of decision process models in structuring persuasive messages. In M. Ray & S. Ward (Eds.), *Communicating with consumers* (pp. 57–70). Beverly Hills, CA: Sage.

Wu, F., & Huberman, B. A. (2007). *Novelty and collective action*. Palo Alto, CA: HP Labs, Information Dynamic Laboratory.

Yoon, Y. (2005). Legitimacy, public relations, and media access: Proposing and testing a media access model. *Communication Research, 32*(6), 762–793.

Young, S. (2006). Not biting the hand that feeds? *Journalism Studies, 7*(4), 554–574.

Zaller, J., & Chiu, D. (1996). Government's little helper: U.S. press coverage of foreign policy crises, 1945–1991. *Political Communication, 13*(4), 385–405.

Zinsser, W. K. (2001). *On writing well: The classic guide to writing nonfiction*. New York: Quill.

Zoch, L. M., & Turk, J. V. (1998). Women making news: Gender as a variable in source selection and use. *Journalism & Mass Communication Quarterly, 75*(4), 762–775.

Index